Why We Do What We Do

JAY NEMBHARD

Copyright © 2020 Jay Nembhard

All rights reserved.

ISBN: 9798686210332

DEDICATION

I dedicate this book to my father, Veron, for his constant encouragement since my teens and my late mother, Philomena, whose love for books was imparted into me.

CONTENTS

	Acknowledgments	i
1	World Evangelism	1
2	Evangelism	26
3	Church Discipline	52
4	Lay-Preaching and Church Planting	95
5	Male Leadership	116
6	Discipleship	150
7	The Altar Call	185
	About the Author	207

ACKNOWLEDGMENTS

This book was written after much procrastination. I would like to thank my wife, Cheryl, for her constant prodding to get this book finished after first starting in 2017. I want to thank Pastor Peter Ajala for planting the seed of writing a book, way back in 2002 when I sent him a study I did on the altar call. I want to also thank Pastor Kosi Amesu for his encouragement in getting me to write in the first place.

I want to thank Pastor Harold Warner for the time taken to read various chapters and giving great feedback. I would like to also thank everyone in the Fellowship who bought my book. The response was better than expected, not to mention the encouragement given.

Lastly, I want to thank David Drum for his encouragement and his invaluable help, well above the call of duty, in editing and putting this book together. Truly, a brother is born for adversity.

1 WORLD EVANGELISM

I don't think that it is a coincidence that on the first day I stepped into church, the 11th of July 1993, the very first sermon I heard was on world evangelism. I had never heard anything like this in the entire eight months of my salvation, and my soul was electrified.

The Potter's House Church was meeting at the end of a lonely street in Kennington, South London, in the Kurdish Cultural Centre, which I knew to be Islamic. On top of that, there were caretakers in the office at the front smoking like chimneys. "What kind of a church meets in a place like that?" I thought to myself as I hesitated out front listening to the faint singing of the praise and worship of the church coming from the room behind the office.

I contemplated going home but then thought, "Since I am already here, I might as well go in." I did feel apprehensive going in, but I did not need to worry because, in just a short space of time, three life-changing events happened to me at the same time. The first was that during the praise and worship, I felt the Spirit of God impress on me that this was the church for me. Bear in mind that I was going to a far more impressive looking church with highly educated and professional people who were members and here were a handful of people, mainly teenagers and young adults, meeting in an Islamic community center.

The second thing is that during the "meet and greet" I noticed that the young lady doing the overhead projector for the praise and worship was my ex-girlfriend who broke up with me less than eighteen months before. I knew then that it wasn't a coincidence and I am happy to report that we got married less than two years later.
The third thing was the preaching on the topic of world evangelism that was

so soul-stirring that I knew right then and there, I was called to preach. And as I went home, the first thing I did was to pray like I hadn't prayed in a long time and felt the call of God to go to Jamaica to preach the gospel.

Right from the very beginning, I was introduced to what the Christian Fellowship Ministries was all about – reaching the world for Jesus Christ. That sermon I heard was so hot it seared into my spirit like a branding iron, and I couldn't shake it and believe me, how I tried.

I remember getting off my kitchen floor, stunned at the revelation of God calling me back to Jamaica. You see, I was born in London, but my father had been recruited to work for a hospital in Montego Bay, Jamaica. The fact that my mother was a registered nurse, in their eyes, made it a twofer. This hospital, in its day, was the premier state-of-the-art hospital in the entire British West Indies where hospitals as far as the Bahamas, Barbados, and Trinidad would send their most acute patients. All through my childhood in Jamaica I felt like a fish out of water (something my sons also felt when we went back there as missionaries).

When I left at eighteen to go back to England, it was with the mindset that apart from the occasional visit to see the family, and I would have nothing to do with that country ever again. And so when I felt the call to go to Jamaica, I said to God, "I would rather go to Iran and preach to the Ayatollah than go to Jamaica." And I meant it!

But God wouldn't leave me alone, and so in October 1993, at my very first conference, I went with an open heart for God to convince me about Jamaica. It was either on Thursday or Friday morning, Pastor Alvin Smith preached on world evangelism. In his sermon, he said, "Some of you need to go back where you came from!" And I said to myself, "I wasn't even born there." As soon as I said that in my mind, Pastor Smith shouted back, "I don't care if you weren't born there. You need to go back." Talk about a spiritual slap in the face. I was stunned.

But even then, I had doubts and still needed convincing. I felt all the while the Spirit of God impressed upon me the story of Jonah, the disobedient prophet. I remember praying, "God, if You want me to go to Jamaica, let Pastor Warner's sermon speak to me." On that Friday night, Pastor Warner got up to preach and said, "Open your bibles to the book of Jonah." That was it. I was sold. Once again, the major theme of that conference was world evangelism.

What got me locked into our church there in South London wasn't the size of the church (My pastor Paul Stephens said once, "The entire church could fit inside an elevator"). It wasn't the grand building because there was nothing remarkable, and it wasn't even theirs. What got me locked in was the vision of our church to world evangelism. While the Baptist church I was going to was nice looking and professional, it was just a church doing ordinary church stuff. The Potter's House Church was a church with a global vision to reach the world for Jesus. That spoke volumes to me and made me bypass the insignificant details about size and building. From the very beginning, I learned to look past the superficial in regard to church and see the vision of reaching nations with the gospel of Christ.

I gave that brief testimony to let you know just how much world evangelism made itself real to a young convert. It wasn't something forced. It wasn't just something said now and again just to tick off the list of issues that a church has to talk about from time to time. It was very much intrinsic, like breathing or eating. World evangelism wasn't just something we did; world evangelism was what we were. It is what we still are. It is the heartbeat of our fellowship, and just like the organic heart, it plays a fundamental part in what we are. Just like the biological heart, the removal of it will result in death.

When Jesus said in Matthew 28:19, "Go therefore and make disciples of all the nations," it wasn't just something that the church in general does and therefore we are exempt from personal responsibility. Christians like to think they are a part of world evangelism because they have given a one-time offering to an overseas mission or hosted a visiting missionary from some faraway land who stopped by to raise money to fund his next trip. World evangelism is more than that. It is our mandate, our prime directive.

The Importance of World Evangelism

Many essential aspects of the Christian faith warrant our attention, but I would have to say that one that is of fundamental importance is world evangelism. The reason is simple. God the Father wants to have a relationship with as many people as possible. This is why He created the human race. It is incredible to think that the Creator of the universe would want to have a personal relationship with every man and woman. He created us in His image with the ability to think for ourselves, to be social creatures belonging to different social groups and each a unique individual in their own right. He created us in His image and with free will and the ability to choose for ourselves to have a relationship with Him or not.

King David hit the nail on the head when he said in Psalm 8:3-4, "When I consider Your heavens, the work of Your fingers, the moon, and the stars, which You have ordained, what is man that You are mindful of him, and the son of man that You visit him?" As we look around the known universe and consider the galaxies that stretch for many light-years with stars that make our Sun look like a pebble, and then consider just one human being on Planet Earth, you have to wonder just like David did. We, who are minute in the vast scheme of things, are the objects of God's desire. It is mind-blowing stuff. It is both humbling and dignifying at the same time.

We were so important to Him that He came as one of us. When, as a result of the demonic temptation, humanity chose the path of sin, he inadvertently chose separation from his Creator. The holiness of God hates sin, and sin is not merely just a mistake; it is the antithesis of who God is. God cannot abide in the presence of sin, and as a result of that, man separated from the Holy God who created him.

The creation of religion is simply man's best effort to bridge the gap that now exists between man and God. But religion was never God's solution, and the best that religion had to offer, Judaism, was simply a means to an end; the end is to restore the relationship that man had in the beginning with God. The apostle Paul points out in Galatians 4:4-6, "But when the fullness of the time had come, God sent forth His Son, born of a woman, born under the law, to redeem those who were under the law, that we might receive the adoption as sons. And because you are sons, God has sent forth the Spirit of His Son into your hearts, crying out, "Abba, Father!"

Without going into the depth about what adoption is, one thing we know for sure that it speaks of is relationship. Because of sin, we are separated from God, but due to Christ's birth, death, and resurrection, we have now united again with God. We have been adopted into His family, and we have the Spirit of Jesus living in us, testifying that God is our Father.

In the Bible, from the beginning, the middle, and to the very end, we see God's heart towards the world. When He made a covenant with Abraham, He includes in it the words recorded in Genesis 22:18, "In your Seed, all the nations of the earth shall be blessed…" Later in the book of Exodus, God informs Pharaoh of the reason for his existence. Exodus 9:16 says, "But indeed for this purpose I have raised you up, that I may show My power in you, and that My name may be declared in all the earth." Reaching the world with the knowledge of the one true God was never just a New Testament concept but a truth that He made known from the early days.

God wants to be known by all humanity, and He has called the Church to be His messenger to invite all of humanity to have a relationship with Him.

David says in Psalm 86:9-10, "All nations whom You have made shall come and worship before You, O Lord, and shall glorify Your name. For You are great, and do wondrous things; You alone are God." How shall the nations come unless someone goes and tells them about the invitation? Psalm 96:2-5 says, "Proclaim the good news of His salvation from day to day. Declare His glory among the nations, His wonders among all peoples. For the Lord is great and greatly to be praised; He is to be feared above all gods. For all the gods of the peoples are idols, but the Lord made the heavens."

This same theme we see repeated in Revelation 14:6, where it says, "Then I saw another angel flying in the midst of heaven, having the everlasting gospel to preach to those who dwell on the earth—to every nation, tribe, tongue, and people…"

There are many essential things we need to focus on as Christians, but this is one thing we must not neglect amidst the other important things we are dealing with. On the day Jesus ascended into heaven, one of the last words He spoke to His disciples about was reaching the world with the gospel. Acts 1:8-9 says, "…you shall be witnesses to Me in Jerusalem, and in all Judea and Samaria, and to the end of the earth." Now when He had spoken these things, while they watched, He was taken up, and a cloud received Him out of their sight."

Christ was never a Man to trifle with His words. Considering this to be true, we can safely say that He would have treated His last words to His disciples with critical importance. We have evidence from church history that they did indeed treat Jesus' last words with the seriousness they deserved. We know that these twelve men scattered throughout the known world at the time and, except for John, the brother of James, were all martyred for being witnesses of Jesus.

The apostle Paul, though not one of the Twelve, nevertheless took his calling as the apostle to the Gentiles seriously, and throughout the New Testament, we read of Paul being in Israel, Turkey, Italy, Greece, Cyprus, Malta, Lebanon, and Crete. Paul was a busy man traveling over land and sea to win converts to Christ.

If we consider that the first wave of Christian persecution took place in 64 AD by the mad emperor Nero, we have to realize that it took just over 30 years from the time of the resurrection of Christ for Christianity to become so noticeable that it was deemed a threat to the state.
The authorities may or may not have realized that the incredible spread of the church was due to the great Roman peace (Pax Romana) that was created

by the Empire subduing and incorporating neighboring regions. This peace allowed these early missionaries easy access into these conquered areas. What also helped was the fantastic road system the Empire created to quickly move their military (and goods) across the Empire should there be an uprising or an external threat along its borders. These roads were so expertly engineered that some have remained usable to this day.

When Paul spoke of "the fullness of time" in Galatians 4, he meant all the conditions met for the advent of Christ. One of those conditions was the Pax Romana, which made reaching the world far easier than at any time until that point. And the Church took full advantage of that, and within three centuries, Christianity made a massive impact on the Roman Empire. Christianity's influence on the Roman Empire demonstrated Christ's parable of leaven. In Matthew 13:33, Jesus said, "The kingdom of heaven is like leaven, which a woman took and hid in three measures of meal till it was all leavened." If the Twelve Disciples knew that in less than three hundred years, Christianity would have impacted the dreaded Roman Empire, I believe they would have been astounded.

The Collapse of True World Evangelism

1. The Merging of Church and State

Ironically, it was the success of evangelism that brought about the collapse of true missionary endeavors. From its ignoble start as the religion of slaves and women, true Christianity began to influence the upper classes slowly, and in 313AD, Constantine the Great legalized Christianity. Good news to be sure, but in 380AD Theodosius I went one step further and made it the official state religion. It was then that the church and state merged, and the politico-religious Roman Catholic Church formed. It was here that Christianity was defeated by victory as the faith took a downward turn.

At the time of the legalizing, Christians were approximately 10% of the Roman Empire. With Christianity now being in fashion, the Church no longer had to go looking for converts as "converts" came flocking in. As a result, personal one-to-one evangelism went out the door, and mission work became the exclusive work of the clergy. Thus, the evangelical zeal of the early Christians came to an end as nominal Christianity became the status quo.
What made matters worse is not only did Theodosius make Christianity the official state religion; he simultaneously made all other religions illegal. In doing so, he forced pagans to become Christians, which from a spiritual point

of view, is impossible as true faith can only be produced from free will, not coercion. In so doing, he initiated the foundation of intolerance in the Christian church.

Please forgive me for going off course for just a moment, and because it is only for a moment, what I am about to say is a very simplistic approach to a very complicated issue. There is an excellent Jamaican proverb that says, "It's not the same day that a leaf falls that it rots." Yes, Christianity did become the state church, but the corruption into what we know as the Roman Catholic Church did not happen overnight. Evangelism of some sort continued, but eventually, it became a perversion of what it once was. And what was once the work of everyday ordinary Christians, was now in the hands of priests and monks.

As the Western Church coalesced into what is now known as Roman Catholicism, priests and monks would roam the pagan lands of Europe looking for converts. Patrick of England became a missionary to the Irish. Columba of Ireland was sent to reach the people of Scotland. Augustine of Canterbury was sent to England by Pope Gregory I to "reestablish" Christianity. Boniface of England was sent into what would be today's Germany (this was he who chopped down the sacred oak of Thor).

The same thing occurred in the Eastern part of Europe in what is now known as the Orthodox Church. Since the church had merged with the state, it became a hybridized syncretistic politico-religious system. In simple terms, it was as much political as it was religious. Before I get into the evangelical works of the Orthodox Church, I must once again deviate.

There were some theological differences between the Catholics and the Orthodox, but the main reason was due to political and cultural differences. We must remember that the Roman Empire got so big that it eventually became two regions – the Eastern Empire and the Western Empire.

Since the church was state influenced, it is no surprise that the church split across political lines as well. When you consider that the liturgy of the Eastern Church based in Greek and the West in Latin, you can see the difference in culture also playing out. The Catholic and Orthodox churches were more or less one church until the Great Schism of 1054, where there was a formal split between the churches of the East and West of the Roman Empire. The division was only official in 1054, but in actuality, they had deviated from one another a few centuries before.

While the Catholics continued its main mission work to the west and north-west of Europe, the Orthodox Church reached out to the east. The brothers, Cyril and Methodius, from Greece, became known as the "Apostles to the Slavs," establishing Orthodox churches in Moravia (this was after the king had kicked out the Catholics). Russia was reached for the Orthodox Church by the end of the 10th century AD.

While there were individual missionaries who still reached out to pagan lands, in many cases, the Catholic Church used either the carrot or the stick instead of reaching the hearts of men.

With the use of the carrot, "conversion" to Christianity was a political move done to gain some sort of advantage in life. For example, in 911AD, King Charles III of France offered Viking leader Rollo, French coastal lands along the English Channel (Normandy), if he and his men would, in return, stop their invasion into France and convert to Christianity. This was by no means the only time a deal was struck to "convert" the pagans of Europe.

In other cases, the stick was used, primarily when those doing the "converting" were not the ones victimized. Conversion in these cases wasn't a result of conviction, but the threat of death and torture. Such as the "conversion" of Jews during the Spanish Inquisition and the Native Americans by the Conquistadors. In this, we see there was no difference between Islam and Catholicism, and I would dare to say that they are, in fact, sister religions as both are politico-religious systems. Evangelism continued, but eventually, it decayed into being a means of subjugating or enticing people and true evangelism as we know it fell into limbo.

2. The Rise of Islam

The other primary disaster to hit the church and her missionary endeavor was the rise of Islam. By the seventh century AD, the eastern Roman Empire (Byzantium) was no longer the military force it once was. Neither was Christianity. The state and church, more or less, created the conditions that precipitated the rise of Islam. Those conditions were like a field of dry wood during a scorching summer, and Islam spread like wildfire. Within ten years after the death of Muhammad in 632AD, three major cities within the Byzantium Empire fell – Damascus in 635AD, Jerusalem in 638AD, and Alexandria in 641AD.

The Byzantines and the Sasanians of Persia were so busy fighting one another that they paid little attention to a new force rising from Arabia. So underestimated were the Muslims that the Patriarch of Jerusalem, Sophronius, said just before the invasion that "If we repent of our sins we will laugh at the demise of our enemies the Saracens [Muslims] and in a short time see their destruction and complete ruin. For their bloody swords will pierce their own hearts, their bows will be splintered, their arrows will be left sticking in them, and they will open the way to Bethlehem for us."[1]

Not everyone felt about the Muslims like Sophronius, as many local Christians saw the collapse of the Empire as a sign of God's judgment on the Byzantine Orthodox Church and embraced the invaders, seeing the invasion not as a disaster but as an opportunity. Taxes were reduced, and Christians of splinter groups such as the Nestorians and Monophysites that were quite popular in the region were given religious freedom.

Without getting off-topic, what we can safely say is that Christianity was stopped dead in its tracks east and south of Greece with the coming of Islam as the new religion spread into South-East Europe, North Africa, and the Middle East. With that, all roads to Asia were cut off from Christianity, and whatever churches that formed in those regions wilted away and died.

The Rebooting of World Evangelism

On the 31st of October 1517, Martin Luther sent his now-famous 95 theses to the Archbishop of Mainz, thus triggering the start of the Reformation. To be fair, the rejection of Catholic ideas didn't start with Luther and can be seen in the centuries before with men like John Wycliffe and Jan Hus. Still, conditions were ripe (the creation of printing for one) for Luther's principles for reforming the church, and his teachings spread like wildfire throughout Europe.

It is only fair to say that with the rebirth of New Testament teachings that the church had to be pioneered all over again. Starting in Switzerland and Germany, Luther's teachings on salvation through faith spread to Austria, Scotland (through John Knox), France (the Huguenots), Netherlands, and so on. We may not recognize it, but the Reformation was the rebooting of world evangelism that organically took the gospel across many borders.

The Reformation began soon after the "discovery" of the New World by Christopher Columbus. It was at this time thousands of Europeans began to pour into the Americas, hoping to create a better life for themselves. Many of these Protestants, fleeing persecution by the Catholics, went to these new lands where they could be free to worship God in the way of the Scriptures.

---

[1] The Great Arab Conquests: How the Spread of Islam Changed the World We Live In, Hugh Kennedy,

As mass migration ensued, there was the need for preachers as well. You could technically call that world evangelism as clergymen from all denominations went to minister to those who had immigrated to the new lands.

Very soon, some preachers made it their mission to reach the indigenous populations of the land. Men like David Brainerd and Jonathan Edwards and denominations like the Moravians made it their mission to reach Native Americans with the gospel in North America. The Moravians were the very first protestant denomination to be involved in world evangelism starting around 1732. They were amongst the first to reach not only Native Americans but also plantation slaves with the gospel, much to the chagrin of their owners.

In a sense, up until this point, world evangelism was low key. It was done, but it not given the attention it deserved. But in 1793, nearly three hundred years after the start of the Reformation, a significant leap in world evangelism began. William Carey, a Baptist minister, decided to leave England and to preach the gospel in India. He was by no means the very first modern-day missionary to India having met Dutch Baptists already in India. Still, he was the one to have a serious impact, not only in India, having translated the Bible into various Indian languages, but also in England stirring people towards missions.

About eight years before going to India, while serving as a schoolmaster, he read Jonathan Edwards' biography on the life of David Brainerd. David's life, along with the life of the apostle Paul, so inspired Carey that he made up his mind to reach those who had never heard the gospel. (As a side note, David Brainerd died at 30 and with just a handful of converts and to the natural eyes looked like a failure, but he inspired not only Carey but also Jim Eliot and Adoniram Judson.) Carey's decision to leave everything behind and go to India revolutionized the Baptist church in England, and a year before leaving England, the Baptist Missionary Society (BMS) was formed.

Carey may have been the first to go with the aid of the BMS, but in the years to follow, missionaries were sent all over the world, following the lead of the Moravians. Over the next century, Moravians, Baptists, Methodists, and Anglicans (Episcopalians) gave themselves to reaching the world with the gospel of Jesus.

In 1906 a new impetus was given to boost world evangelism. It was the start of the Azusa Street revival in Los Angeles. Within a year of the revival's birth, Pentecostal missionaries were sent overseas. In 1908, one of the movement's leading players, John G. Lake, went to South Africa to preach the gospel. Thomas Barratt is recognized as being the first to spread the Pentecostal message throughout north-west Europe. The early Pentecostals recognized the empowerment of the Holy Spirit given so that the gospel could be preached throughout the world.

Let me just clarify that while the biblical idea of Pentecostalism spread throughout the Christian communities of the world, those who were empowered by the Spirit also reached out to the unsaved. It wasn't just a matter of converting Christians to their way of thinking. As important as that might have been, we have been empowered by God to reach the lost world. World evangelism is not an easy matter, and Satan has no desire to see us reach the nations with the gospel. Much of world evangelism is supernatural warfare. We do not wrestle against flesh and blood, and the weapons of our warfare are not natural.

We must consider what type of people constituted the early Pentecostal movement. Of course, you had influential leaders with great intellectual ability like William H. Durham, Charles Parham, John G. Lake, and so on. Still, much of the early Pentecostals were not the brightest, most gifted or well educated. Many came from the poorer classes and yet were touched with evangelical zeal to reach the world for Jesus. Case in point, the Apostolic Faith Mission Church on Azusa Street was no cathedral by any stretch of the imagination, as it was a former stable converted into a church.

Professor Wonsuk Ma of the Oral Roberts University said, "Early Pentecostals at the turn of the twentieth century were "poor" in many ways. Most participants of the Azusa Street revival came from the lower socio-economic bracket of society. Urban African-Americans and ethnic immigrants, with "sprinkles of whites," made up this controversial epicenter of one of the most significant revivals in modern church history. Practically marginalized by the society, and sometimes by established churches, they understood themselves to be eager recipients of the Messiah's message of hope, who came "to preach good news to the poor" under the anointing of the Holy Spirit."[2]

My point is not so much that these people were poor, but one would hardly think that poor people would have a world vision, and yet something happened to them that would cause people without education and no real connection to the outside world to have a heart for the nations.

---

[2] p41-42, Chapter 3: "When the poor are fired up", The Spirit in the World: Emerging Pentecostal Theologies in Global Contexts, William B Eerdmans Publishing Company, Grand Rapids, Michigan / Cambridge, UK.

Considering the Christian Fellowship Ministries, Pastor Wayman Mitchell would admit that our Fellowship as it is today was not an orchestrated plot. As that small church in Prescott, Arizona began to see fruitfulness, it never crossed his mind that a handful of people would eventually grow into a worldwide movement. And why would he? Pastor Mitchell did not come from a cosmopolitan city like New York City but the rural South West.

I have met people living in the Midlands of England who had never been overseas, not even to London, and had no intention to. I'm not saying that Pastor Mitchell was in that category, but in general, many people like to stay close to home, especially those from rural areas. Pastor Mitchell acknowledged himself that world evangelism wasn't on his mind until the late 1970s.

In his own words, he said, "When I went into Australia in 1977, God set me up. I had no understanding of what was happening. I was simply responding to an invitation to preach at a convention there. As I stepped off the plane, God struck me, as it were with a sledgehammer and made me know that he had placed me there by His sovereign moving to respond to that need. I had resources and understanding in my ministry that I could direct into that nation toward evangelism and ministry. Little did I understand what God was going to do there."

I would also add that little did he understand what God was going to do, not only there, but everywhere. In 1978 Pastor Mitchell fulfilled his obedience to the will of God, and the first missionary work was planted in Perth, Australia. Today the Christian Fellowship Ministries are in 120 countries across the world preaching the gospel of Jesus Christ. As Pastor Mitchell began planting churches overseas, other fellowship churches caught the vision and started doing the same.

I was both delighted and impressed when Pastor Fred Rubi showed me a website where Pastor Mitchell was listed as one of the top ten most famous missionaries in world history. Ultimately God will be the judge of that, but it was still an impressive thing to see recognition given by a secular newspaper.[3] What is particularly impressive is that world evangelism is not only the work of churches in the First World, but Third World nations like Namibia and Sierra Leone are sending workers overseas as well. It is truly a powerful thing to see that the countries where workers were sent to are now sending workers

---

[3] https://www.newsmax.com/fastfeatures/christian-history-famous-missionaries/2015/05/07/id/643345/

of their own. This truly demonstrates the power of the gospel to change and transform the lives of the people it touches. While secular aid to third world countries almost always results in those nations continually dependent on funding, the spiritual assistance of the gospel empowers people to rise up and help others. Men and women who once lived introverted lives, trying their best to look after themselves and their immediate families, are now touched with a divine vision to look to regions beyond their borders and help others just as they were helped.

The Resistance to World Evangelism

While I am pleased with the steady increase of men and women responding to the call of God to go overseas and preach the gospel of Christ, the sobering truth is that just like the days of the early church, that call is resisted. The inclination of our fellowship towards world evangelism isn't something that should be taken for granted.

One can be forgiven for believing that it is an automatic chain reaction that continues to move on under the steam of its own power when we see conference after conference couples rising up to meet the need of the gospel in the nations of the world. You can almost take it for granted that on every Thursday night of a conference there will be announcements made for new churches to be started in a new nation.

The sad truth is that the continuation of world evangelism is something that must be fought for. This is perhaps one arena in spiritual warfare where we can quickly lose ground if we are not careful. It is easy to lose vision. It is easy to lose couples willing to sacrifice it all for the sake of the gospel, considering the age of materialism we live in. It is easy to lose people who are willing to give towards reaching the world with the gospel. It is easy to lose sight of the nations that lie beyond our borders and seas.

In 2015, the International Mission Board (IMB) of the Southern Baptist Convention announced that because of overspending in world evangelism, they would have to cut back on their missionary activities. They announced that between 600 and 800 missionaries and staff positions would be axed for them to start restructuring. Six months later, the IMB announced that 983 missionaries chose to accept early retirement or resignation. This was far more than they had initially estimated.

In a report on the South Baptists in 2003 called "The State of Giving in the Southern Baptist Convention," it reads, "The disturbing, and potentially devastating factor is the declining percentage of contributions by Southern Baptist members and churches, even during times of economic growth...The alarming fact is not just that the 2.03% giving average falls miserably short of the tithe (10%), but that the percentage has dropped dramatically in the last thirty years. In a time when Southern Baptist members arguably were experiencing financial prosperity, they have been giving a shrinking percentage of their available income to the local church...This same trend is evident in the percentages the churches give to missions. The report by empty tomb, inc. further states contributions to the category of Benevolences (their term for any kind of missions outside the local congregation) have been declining proportionately faster than those to Congregational Finances between 1968 and 1998. Not only are American church members giving smaller percentages to their churches, their churches are giving smaller percentages to anything outside the congregation's needs."[4]

The Southern Baptists, like many other churches, have been hit with the double whammy of declining membership and revenue. From the report, it once again emphasizes the paradox of Christian prosperity and poverty of vision. It is a deadly reminder of the influence of affluence. The more materialistic Christians become, the less concerned they are for spiritual issues. In a time where we have more resources than any other period in world history, the heart for reaching the world is no longer a priority in the hearts of many.

No one realizes the power of gravity until he tries to come against it. I doubt anyone reading this book has recently thought about gravity, and yet for a rocket to reach outer space, it takes a tremendous amount of energy to achieve that feat.

Personally, it took a great effort to respond to the call to go overseas. I shared the initial stages of that at the introduction of this chapter. Eventually, years later, the Holy Spirit awakened that decision I made to go to Jamaica, and there was no hesitation on my part. When my wife, Cheryl, and I were announced on the Thursday night of our conference, I thought that was that. No big deal. Or so I thought.

Right then and there, I faced the full wrath of my mother, who ripped into me and accused me of being irresponsible as I was now bringing my family (her grandchildren) into a very volatile nation. My mother-in-law cut all ties with my wife and refused to speak to her (they have since made up). When we started to consider how we were going to get rid of all our stuff and

---

[4] http://www.baptist2baptist.net/b2barticle.asp?ID=293

possibly sell our home, I realized just how much we had accumulated all these years, and a part of me didn't want to give it up. Oh, we obeyed God and went, but it wasn't as easy as I thought it would be.

Money! It is such a necessary ingredient in reaching the world with the gospel. Without it, men and women find it difficult to answer the call. And yet, at the same time, it is such a hindrance in mission work. Firstly, the influence of money is such that it takes our eyes off the world's needs and focuses them on our wants. Where our eyes go, our wallets follow in suit. Secondly, it stops us from responding to the call of the gospel, which invariably means giving up our comforts to reach the world for Jesus. The more we have, the more of a gravitational pull it influences on us. The influence of materialism is that it impacts for the worse, both those sent and those doing the sending.

According to the International Bulletin of Missionary Research (Vol. 39, No.1), in a report written in 2015, the global personal income of all church members is US$42 trillion. Of that, only US$45 billion is given to global foreign missions.[5] Simply put, it means for every $1,000 a church member earns, $1.07 goes to world evangelism. This is a measly 0.107%. It goes to show the value the church community puts on reaching the world for Jesus.

According to a report by "The Traveling Team", (a Christian organization dedicated to inspiring university students across the United States to get involved in world missions), there is estimated to be around 6,909 languages worldwide, and 4,400 of those are without any type of Scripture available. While translation projects are underway for approximately 1,600 languages, there are 2,500 languages where translation hasn't even started.
This is amazing to me, considering that there are approximately 50 translations in the English language alone! Why would one language have so many translations where thousands don't even have one? The answer, when you boil it down to the bare nitty-gritty, is that there is more money to be made in translating the Bible into a language that people can afford to buy. This may seem a bit cynical, but I believe it is true. Therefore, when it comes to translating the Bible, the nations of the world are not a priority.

It is a travesty that those who have been entrusted with the most resources are the ones who are less likely to use it properly. It is an unfortunate paradox that does not seem to be changing any time soon. Materialism, it seems, has blinded us from seeing the plight of the world.

---

[5]https://static1.squarespace.com/static/4f661fde24ac1097e013deea/t/550f7d77e4b0907feba099b0/1427078519637/StatusGlobalChristianity2015_CSGC_IBMR.pdf

Let me also add that materialism has affected the Christian much more than by just merely keeping resources to ourselves. Materialism is living life in excess. We in the West live a life of luxury compared to any generation in world history. You have to consider that even people on the lower end of the financial spectrum have life more comfortable than the rich people in the days of Jesus.

We live in times of great peace (we do not live in cities with walls), freedom from tyrannical rulers and oppression, human rights, education, and the ability to jump from lower social classes to a higher one, opportunities not available to most in times gone by. We live in a time of great technological breakthrough with the ability to harness the power of oil, the atom, the sun, and the wind. We can fly from one side of the world to the other in mere hours rather than weeks or even months. What we can do in the 21st century is far greater than at any other time in the history of humanity.

As a result, people in the West are spoiled. We take things like a faucet or a flushing toilet in our homes for granted. Doesn't everyone have running water in their homes? Don't we take air conditioning or central heating as standard? Even amongst the very poorest in Jamaica, two things I have seen in every home are a smartphone and color television.

Solomon may have been rich, but he never wore Armani or Calvin Klein. No doubt, he may have had the best clothing in his time, but the technology today to create the best types of fabric is unprecedented. Solomon may have been rich, but he never had an iPhone or an Apple MacBook. Solomon may have been rich, but he never traveled first class (or economy for that matter). Solomon may have been rich, but he never had a fridge or ate Ben and Jerry's ice-cream. Solomon may have been rich, but he never had a hot shower. Solomon may have been rich, but he never went to Disneyworld. Solomon may have been rich, but he never had ice-cubes in his orange juice. Solomon may have been rich, but he never had a triple Mocha Frappuccino.

I have not mentioned anything outrageous in my examples. These are basic everyday things that ordinary Westerners experience. And the question to be asked is, having all of that, why would I be willing to give that up to go overseas to a third world nation? (I'll be honest, in the six years we were in Jamaica, I was longing for Starbucks, and the irony is that they opened their first branch two months after I left.)

Materialism has made us take comfort as the natural default setting for our lives. And who likes to be uncomfortable? One again, I will be candid. Back in 2007, Pastor Nigel Brown asked me to take over a church in Ndola,

Zambia. I told him I was open, and he paid for me to go, preach and have a look. When I got there, I saw roads so bad it made Jamaica look like the First World. I have to be shamefully honest and say I was looking for anything that was remotely western. I saw nothing. No McDonalds, no Burger King, no Pizza Hut. NOTHING!

The only thing they had that looked anything western was a South African fast-food outlet called "Hungry Lion". The town consisted of two roads intersecting. I'll be honest; I was not feeling it at all. But I was still open, and I understood that my subconscious propensity towards comfort could be a part of the problem. That week while I was there, a man in the village by the church had died of cerebral malaria. That made the alarms ring in my mind. What would happen to my kids if they came here? What would happen if they got malaria? What would they do? There was nothing for children to do in Ndola.

I went back to England, and I began to pray that if the problem was me and my carnality that God would change my heart towards Zambia. And he did. One morning as I prayed, I felt as if my "heart" snapped into place, and I was now willing to go. It was amazing. I know it was supernatural because I spoke to my pastor later that day, Pastor Peter Ajala, and he said that morning as he prayed for me, he felt it too. It was the confirmation I needed. I spoke to my wife, who is willing to go anywhere the Holy Spirit would lead. Then I went to Pastor Brown, and he went to talk to Pastor Vicary in Australia. A few days later, Pastor Brown got back to me and said Pastor Vicary had another couple lined up to go.

I was now off the hook. Although I did feel slightly disappointed, I have to admit there was a bit of relief. Looking back, I knew it was my Abraham-Isaac moment. It was a test of my obedience. I'm glad I passed, but it also made me realize the "forces" working inside of me, and one of those was the love of western life. I could understand the struggle men have to answer the call of God to go into the world to preach because life is so easy in the West. I am not saying I am on the Abraham level when it comes to obedience, but I do wonder how many men would have said "No!" at the get-go?

We have all sorts of reasons as to why we can't answer the call. "It's the children. They would struggle in a foreign country." "It would break my wife's poor mother's heart if she had to go." "My father is a widower and lives by himself." "It took me years to get my business off the ground, and it still needs a bit of work." "I don't know how my church would survive if I had to leave now." "I don't think I could work thru a different culture."

This is nothing new. Jesus said in Mark 10:29-30, "Assuredly, I say to you, there is no one who has left house or brothers or sisters or father or mother or wife or children or lands, for My sake and the gospel's, who shall not receive a hundredfold now in this time—houses and brothers and sisters and mothers and children and lands, with persecutions—and in the age to come, eternal life."

The more things we accumulate, the more difficult it is to break free from them. The more things we acquire in life, the higher the level of comfort we become accustomed to. There is nothing more uncomfortable than going into unfamiliar territories and different cultures and ways of doing things.

It was in October 2012, 14 months after relocating to Jamaica, when I felt I was losing my mind. Frustration was getting to me. Power cuts and water shortages, waiting in long lines, insane traffic, incompetence, and no regard for time drove me to the brink. I thought I knew Jamaica. My father is Jamaican. I grew up in Jamaica. But I realized the lens I knew Jamaica through was that of a sheltered child. It was as if all I knew was the top of the iceberg only to slowly realize that there was so much more under the surface. It was culture shock in all of its horrific glory. Culture shock is uncomfortable, and no one likes to be uncomfortable.

Let me also add, while we may accept the call to world evangelism and acknowledge that it may be uncomfortable, human nature being what it is, we will try our very best to make ourselves as comfortable as we can. When it comes to missions, much of world evangelism is reaching places where the gospel has already gone. It is a lot easier to sow in areas where the fallow ground has tilled by others who were there before.

I know I was called to go to Jamaica. As I said before, it was a place that I didn't initially want to go. I didn't choose it out of convenience. However, I had it more comfortable than others because Jamaica already had a Christian heritage that I used to my advantage. Firstly, there was the liberty to preach the gospel in a nation where people still had some reverence for God. Unlike Britain, I could freely set up on the streets and in communities with zero resistance. The schools welcomed me to do devotions with the children. Being a pastor was still a respectable position and would open doors for me. I had no language barriers whatsoever, not because of my knowledge of Jamaican creole, but because English was their first language. For all my culture shock, I had relative ease in ministering to the people.

Yet in the closest country to me, Cuba, a mere 90 miles away, a fellow missionary from Vologda, Russia was having a warm time in Havana. Here was a Slav in a Latino country, a Russian ministering to Spanish speaking people who unfortunately got arrested and put behind bars. What do you do when you are in prison in a foreign country, and there is no one you know who can help you?

What do you do when God calls you to reach a nation that doesn't speak your language, which has a different culture and has no concept of the gospel? My brother, who has lived in Japan for many years, once showed my sister-in-law the film, "The Passion of the Christ." It completely blew her mind because she had no reference points. How do you minister when there is no infrastructure already there?

A missionary society once asked David Livingstone, "Have you found a good road where you are? If so, we want to send other men to help you." His response was, "If you have men who will only come if they know there is a good road, I don't want them. I want men who will come if there is no road at all." It is no different today. We want convenience. We want infrastructure put in place, and then we may decide to play our part.

This is why reaching the unreached is not popular. I had previously mentioned that for every $1,000 earned by a Christian, just $1.07 goes towards missionary activities. Almost all of that $1.07 goes towards ministering to those already saved or heard the gospel in those foreign nations. According to the Traveling Team, "In 2001, only 1% of giving to "Missions" went to unreached - if that trend holds true today it would be $450 million. The estimated $450 million going toward UPG's [Unreached People Groups] is only .001% of the $42 trillion income of Christians. For every $100,000 that Christians make, they give $1 to the unreached."[6]

What does this say? It says we have no real heart to reach the unreached with the gospel. For every $1,000 we earn, we give 99¢ to ministering to those who have already heard the gospel and 1¢ to reaching those who have never heard about Jesus. Think about it! That penny lying under your sofa or lost in your attic is what we give to world evangelism.

Also, it is shocking to realize that we are 100 times more likely to use resources to support mission work in places that have already heard the gospel than areas that haven't. How is that possible? Well, we would first have to find someone to send and secondly, after that, support. Then we come to the chicken and egg question. Is it that we can't find anyone to send, and so there is no reason to support, or is it that we have no desire to support

---

[6] http://www.thetravelingteam.org/stats/

and hence no ability to send? It may be a bit of both, but whatever it is, the fact remains there is much of the world that is still not reached.

We often quote the apostle Paul on a myriad of topics and issues. Still, one thing I haven't heard many people preach or write about is his statement in Romans 15:20-21, "And so I have made it my aim to preach the gospel, not where Christ was named, lest I should build on another man's foundation, but as it is written: "To whom He was not announced, they shall see; and those who have not heard shall understand." Paul is a personal hero of mine for many reasons, and one of those is his seeming fearlessness in going to regions beyond where there was no gospel infrastructure built. These are just a handful of words, but they speak volumes, and they are words we can't just idly ignore just because they are trying.

Then there is the issue that goes beyond mere convenience and comfort. It is our unwillingness to put our lives on the line for the gospel's sake. We might find carrying our crosses inconvenient, but we much prefer carrying an uncomfortable cross than being crucified on one. I think in our day and age of luxury, the idea of carrying a cross may be seen as radical. Those who do are the supermen and superwomen of the faith. But to die for the gospel? That is just totally out of the question. That is completely unheard of. Who does that? Why would God allow that?

On November 17th, 2017, John Allen Chau, an American missionary, was killed on the island of North Sentinel Island in the Indian Ocean. His death created massive shockwaves the world over. Why is a Christian evangelizing to an endangered people? Why was this unnecessary death not avoided? What kind of brainwashed individual would knowingly risk his life going to an island where the natives are hostile to outsiders? He is supposed to be a Christian, so why is he breaking the law, knowing the tribesmen were legally declared a protected people group?

I understand that unsaved people without revelation would not get it. I have no problem with their ignorant comments. But so-called Christians who are governed by carnal thinking, that bothers me. The fact that he died, to them, means that it wasn't of God or he did what he did without being adequately trained.

That's the type of thinking that comes from those living in ease and have never gone through anything. There was a time in mission work where people died like flies. Anyone who has read accounts of missionaries in Africa will know that they died in droves, many even a few days after landing on Africa's shores. Africa was once called the missionary's graveyard. European missionaries had no immunity to the various tropical diseases that plagued the continent and would die within months, if not weeks, on arrival. And yet they kept on coming knowing the risks.

These weren't one-off John Allen Chauses, but a steady stream of Christian workers who gave their lives to preach the gospel, many never even getting a chance to reach one soul. Richmond College, a Methodist missionary training center in England, gave a record of the men sent to West Africa to preach the gospel. Almost half of them died within ten years of entering college, and nearly one in six died within four years. In the early 1850s, roughly half of them died within four years.

Dietrich Bonhoeffer found inspiration from these men and used their martyrdom to inspire pastors in Germany who were resisting the Nazi regime. He said, "I am not asking you to do or suffer anything new. This has always been the way of the witness. What, over there in Richmond College there are boards with the names of the Methodist missionaries who died on the field, and when one fell there was another to take his place."[7]

There was a time when reaching the unreached meant something to the church. Men were willing to die on a conveyor belt of martyrdom. Today we say they are irresponsible. Luxury and ease have so dulled our minds we can no longer see what normal Christianity is. I am not saying that we develop an eagerness to die for the gospel, but we should understand that dying to self has always been the bare essence of Christianity.

Where is the willingness to go? Many of these 19th-century missionaries went with the understanding that they may never return home alive. They recognized that they might not live long enough even to make any sort of an impact. Yet they were willing to go because they heard the voice of God and obeyed.

It's right here where we face the slippery slope of obedience and fruitfulness. At times the thought of fruitfulness can be dangled like a carrot on a stick. It is the idea that if I am fruitful there, then I will go. We want our lives to have meaning in the way we imagine meaning to be, and that is to be productive and have an impact. While I long for fruitfulness like any well-thinking individual, I can't help but think that God has never put fruitfulness on par with obedience. It has always been obedience first. If fruitfulness comes, well, that's a great blessing. If we are going to spend considerable resources in reaching the world, then I want more bang for my buck. The truth is that a

---

[7] https://www.methodist.org.uk/media/6406/nothing-more-than-the-dawn.pdf

lot of what we use to reach the world looks like throwing good money down the toilet. And yet, when we step into eternity and see what was accomplished, we will know that it was never a wasted investment in reaching the world for Christ.

John Allen Chau, like Jim Eliot before him, never even managed to get one word of the gospel out before he was brutally killed. But I believe he was obedient, and in our day of luxury, his death will have more impact on a complacent church than anything he could have imagined. I believe Chau's witness will challenge people to rise up and answer the call to reach the lost without trying to make any kind of deal with God.

Personal Responsibility

One of the things I have noticed about departmental group emails is how easy it is for them to be ignored because everyone in that department thinks someone else is going to do it. In the end, nobody does. It is very much the same thing with world evangelism. I am sure every genuine Christian believes that reaching the world for Jesus should be done and assumes that it is being done. The statistics that I gave previously must be a shock to readers because it shows that it is not, and the reason for that is because we have passed the responsibility to others. Surely God will raise up someone else to go. Surely God will challenge the right people to give. And in the end, hardly anyone responds.

Forgive me if I take a moment to vent my inner frustrations and vexations. I am not bitter, but it does grate my soul. It is something I have had to process over the years, and believe me, I have come to terms with it. But this inner irritation is people who love conferences to see who will be sent out. The drama, the expectation, the excitement, the intrigue, and the cheers as names after names are announced to cities and nations. And then they go back to their homes and forget about them.

Please forgive me if I display a bit of bitterness that I need to cleanse from my system. It amazes me to be at conference after conference and see people in their Jamaican T-shirts and flags and cheering when the pastors from Jamaica give their reports. But most of them never once came on an impact team or even sent a text of support saying, "We are thinking of you and praying for you." They will cheer for Jamaica but will never visit because it is too dangerous. They will cheer, but they can't afford it (though they go on holidays overseas). It amazes me also that pastors who were either of Jamaican parentage or birth who had never been to Jamaica to preach in the thirty-plus years there has been a Fellowship church in Jamaica. I often shook my head when I saw men of other nations visiting our churches there, and yet just a tiny fraction of pastors of Jamaican roots ever came out.

I'm sure Jamaicans do not have a monopoly on inconsiderateness. (I have used that word deliberately because 'consider' means "to think carefully about something" or "to look attentively at".) We, as a Fellowship, have often prided ourselves on the diversity of our churches. Yet I have to wonder just how many in our churches that have roots in other nations actively think about reaching them. We shouldn't assume that just because we have people of different backgrounds in our churches that there is automatically real thoughtfulness in reaching the nations for Jesus.

I guess, since I am revealing a bit of cynicism on my part, now that I have started let me continue. There are some songs we shouldn't sing unless we mean them. There are songs like "Here am I, send me to the nations", "Make us and break us and send us as bread to the nations," or "Bury my heart on the mission field, Lord". Really? Can people sing those songs IN CHURCH knowing that the vast majority, considering the statistics, don't mean it?

Isaiah 29:13 says, "Therefore the Lord said: "Inasmuch as these people draw near with their mouths and honor Me with their lips, but have removed their hearts far from Me…" We have often used those scriptures for religious people who live a life of sin and yet have no problem in coming to church and giving God praise. But how many of us can sing songs about world evangelism full well knowing that our hearts are far from God's heart, as His heart is towards reaching the world for the gospel?

I remember being at a conference a few years ago, sitting beside my "brother from another mother", Pastor Courtney Lowe, during a particular worship song. I said to him, "Courtney, I don't know if I can sing this song now. It demands too much from me." There are some songs that I will have to wrestle with God in prayer before I can sing. I'm sure the song "Bury my heart on the mission field" gets its inspiration from David Livingstone, whose heart was buried in Zambia (his body repatriated to England). That is not an easy song to sing and shouldn't be seen as such. Yet it is a challenge for us to recognize where our heart really is and prayerfully seek to bring it back in line with the will of God.

Let me say that I am not without sympathy or understanding in this matter. I understand in the West; it is a fast-paced, dog-eat-dog world. It is pretty much full speed ahead from the minute we wake up until we get to bed at night. We get up, get ready, have our devotions, go to work/school, hit the gym, eat something, catch up on a few things, go to church, go home, go to bed, and repeat. Life can be so fast that we have no time to think beyond our little world.

It's not that we purposely try to be inconsiderate; it's that there is so much to think about that many vital issues get crowded out of our minds and pushed way to the back. We always think we will get to it, and yet once it is out of our minds, it is out of our lives.

But I don't believe that it has to stay that way. While we can't stop the relentless pressure of life, we can put checks in place to prevent life from crushing world evangelism out of our system. The first thing we should do is keep world evangelism as a part of our prayer life. We can start by praying for people we know (even incidentally) that are involved in mission work overseas. I believe if we start there and then gradually add to our list, world evangelism can be something that is continuously in our thoughts.

The next thing we can do is we can start to give to world evangelism. I think one reason why we don't give with consideration (thinking) when it comes to world evangelism is just the sheer magnitude of the endeavor. It's like Andrew's words to Jesus in John 6:9, "There is a lad here who has five barley loaves and two small fish, but what are they among so many?" But considering that just over $1 out of every $1,000 earned goes towards world evangelism, giving a mere $20 is eighteen times more than most believers give. You have to start from somewhere, and sadly anything given to world evangelism is better than most. Don't wait until you strike it lucky before you give because the odds are you will never give.

As you pray for world evangelism every day and give to world evangelism every week or month, I believe that is a great place to start connecting your heart with God's heart for the nations. Perhaps you could gather a few of your friends for an occasional prayer meeting where you dedicate that meeting to pray for a few overseas churches. Maybe you could ask your pastor to plan in the not too distant future an overseas impact team. If we wait till we all get the money, we will be waiting a mighty long time, but I'm sure any church can plan to send a team in two years if people start saving today. Perhaps a few churches could work together to invite an overseas missionary to do a revival and stir the churches about world evangelism.

World evangelism is an issue of ginormous proportions that can easily intimidate us. But, as Bob Marley once said, "So if you are the big tree, we are the small ax ready to cut you down..." We may be a small fellowship of just 2,500 churches, and that's nothing to be ashamed of, but instead, let us rejoice in that because when we are weak, we are strong. We may be small, but we are making a lot more impact than some of the so-called megachurches. We may be a small fellowship, but we have a big vision. Little endeavors, done systematically and continuously, can overcome significant obstacles over time. Let's not worry about the enormity of the challenge of reaching this world for Jesus. Let us just take personal responsibility to do all that we can and leave the rest to the Master.

2 EVANGELISM

"I have but one candle of life to burn, and I would rather burn it out in a land filled with darkness than a land flooded with light." – John Keith-Falconer

A Gospel Fellowship

I went to my very first street outreach two Saturdays after first coming to church, and I was blown away at seeing young men and women preaching in the open streets. I was saved for about eight months at the time and had a bit of a self-righteous streak about me, as I was the only one I knew from my old church who actively gave himself to sharing the gospel with friends and strangers alike. I would even take tracts and hand them out to people on the street, and so I considered myself a bit of a fireball for the gospel.

But here I saw something I had never seen before. A radical, bold declaration of the gospel in the form of street preaching, and it disturbed my soul. Weeks before I had prayed that God would bring me to a church who believed what I believed and at that outreach, I was reminded of an old saying, "Be careful what you wish for because you may just get it."

I was asked several times if I wanted to get in on the act, and each time I would fearfully reject the offer. Finally, without my consent, Peter Ajala, then a disciple, pushed me out into the street, and I faced a choice. I could look stupid by doing nothing, or I could preach. I chose the latter, and for about a minute, I preached Jesus, and I was filled with the Holy Spirit as I felt the power of God flowing through my being, and I testified until my voice got hoarse.

It wasn't the most magnificent debut by far, but it triggered something in me that would continue for years to come – the passion for evangelism and preaching the gospel of Christ. Outreach would become a significant theme in my life. As young disciples of Jesus, we would preach up and down London, on the streets, in the buses, and even in elevators where we had a trapped audience for about sixty seconds who had no choice but to listen.

Four and a half years later I would be pioneering my first church in Manchester, England and what dawned on me in those early days was the fact that our church was the only one of two (the other being a fellowship church) who would preach in the streets of the city center. While pioneering my second church in Wolverhampton, while we did see churches come out now and again, we were the only ones who were consistently on the streets every week.

Even in Jamaica pioneering my third church, I found it surprising that in a country so religious, we are the only church in our town that was consistently evangelizing the gospel weekly.

Thus, the questions need to be asked: Why do we evangelize? Why do we consistently go on outreach when the majority (and I mean the majority) of the church world have no desire to reach out to the lost? Why do we make ourselves look like the black sheep of the church world by going out with our bullhorns and PA systems and making ourselves look like weirdos?

Think about it. There are so many churches that have grown and prospered without being on the streets. Many megachurches across the world have not even so much as made a systematic effort to reach the unsaved. While pioneering in Mandeville, Jamaica, there was another church-plant from Canada. In five years, without flyers or even a sign, they grew into a self-supporting church of about 150 people, many from the middle classes. That is an incredible achievement in Jamaica. Why should they go out into the communities with a PA system and preach the gospel when they see real growth?

[Please note: Evangelism is a broad field and therefore done in many ways, but for the sake of this book, when I speak of evangelism, I take it to mean any structured church activity we use to reach the unsaved with the gospel. This usually means our Saturday or mid-week outreaches organized by the church where in general, we hit our town centers or communities as a group in the hope of communicating Christ to those lost in sin.]

The Downside to Outreaching

If we are honest, these are some of the questions we ask ourselves from time to time, especially when we have given our best effort hitting the streets with thousands of flyers with help from an invasion team or with a handful of faithful disciples from our church. We then top it up with an evening concert only to see a dismal three people pray the sinners' prayer, and only one show up the following Sunday morning if any. It is always disappointing to put so much effort into something and not see much to show for it. Yet the church down the road has its parking lot filled, and apart from the annual children's Christmas play, they have never done a single event to win people to Christ.

Sometimes outreaching seems like self-abuse as we languish in the cold to the point where we can't even feel our feet anymore or hold on to a flyer because our hands are so numb. Our ears feel like they are on fire, our eyes are dryer than the Sahara Desert, and our noses run like a faucet. All that time, we look longingly at Starbucks, imagining ourselves drinking a cup of hot coffee.

Some summers are so scorching hot that we feel like bacon sizzling in a frying pan. In Jamaica, there were times it felt as if my brain was being oven-roasted, as I talked to people in the sun. I go home only to observe in the mirror that I look like a broiled lobster having forgotten yet again to apply sunscreen.

Added to all that is the constant rejection of the people we have gone out into the street to evangelize. It can be soul-destroying to have so many people pass us by pretending that we don't even exist. But even worse are those who do take the time to verbally abuse, calling us all manners of names under the sun, crushing up and throwing back the flyers in our faces. What can we say but, "God bless you" in return? To the unsaved or the carnal Christian, we must be crazy to put ourselves through all that.

So why? Why go through all that hassle when there is a much easier way to see progress? Why chose to make ourselves the red-headed step-child of the church world? Why in the world would our fellowship make it such an essential and intrinsic part of our core? Why is evangelism reiterated from our pulpits even though there seems to be a more practical way of doing things? Doesn't Pastor Mitchell know that we are in the 21st century? Doesn't he know that there is the Internet and the various social media that it carries that can do the work at the click of a button?

Let me just say that there is a place for technology, and we have seen many visitors come to church as a result of a website or a Facebook page. We ought not to be Christian Wahhabis. Technology is not of the devil, and it can be a great tool when it comes to church building, and I believe that we ought to embrace whatever there is out there to make reaching out to people more productive.

Like it or not, we are now in the Internet Age, and we just have to get used to it; otherwise, we will be relics. Many of us who got saved in the seventies to the nineties can remember those times when we had smug, self-righteous attitudes, sneering at the old traditional churches and their anachronistic ways of doing things. I can remember feeling embarrassed watching the performance of a Salvation Army's brass band, with the young adults my age looking at them with incredulousness. Yes, revolutionary in the 1890s, but in the 1990s, it was archaic. We have to be very careful that we do not become the very thing at which we once shook our heads.

Social media is a useful tool in getting the gospel out. It is impressive as to how far an audience and how wide a scope we can get our message to the masses. This is especially true due to the new generation of Millennials and Generation Z that are now our teenagers and young adults in society today. You can't separate them from their cell phones, tablets, or laptops and so you have to work with what you have because culture will not bend to our will. You can try your best, but you will only end up frustrating yourself and becoming detached from the society that God has called us to reach.

The Reason for Personal Evangelism

But in saying that, there is no substitute for traditional evangelism. Human beings are still human beings, whether we live in Sumer back in 2500 BC or Tokyo in 2019 AD. There is something special about human contact, about communicating with people eyeball to eyeball that technology can never replace. God has engineered us to be social creatures, and, regardless of technology, we are all hardwired to interact with one another on a social level.

I'm all for using the tool of social media to reach out to society. I think YouTube, Instagram, Twitter, and other platforms are essential in letting people know of our events, however they must be a means to an end and not the end in itself. They should be how we ultimately get in human contact with the people out there.

God's plan has always been human interaction. God uses human personality to impress His truths upon others. It is a fantastic mystery that God would use me, just as I am, to reach others. This is why I am against using other people's sermons verbatim. Yes, get inspired by the ideas of other men, but put your personality into the sermon because that is what God uses effectively. And it's great having sermons online, but there is something about human contact that the Internet can never duplicate.

The Motive for Evangelism

So…why is evangelism still crucial in the 21st century? There are several reasons that I will categorize into different groups for clarity and understanding. But the first reason is the most obvious, and that is because evangelism is God's means of reaching the world's lost.

It may come to a shock to you, but reaching the lost is God's priority, not Him building a church. Establishing a church is technically the by-product of evangelism, i.e., reaching the lost.

Let me explain further. I do understand that being sent out as a pastor, and with money invested in our ministry, we feel the responsibility of seeing a church established. No one knew that more than I, being a missionary overseas with the sacrificial offerings of saints in the mother church in my ministry. But we can be so focused on seeing a church grow that we no longer see the real reason behind evangelism.

People are more than attendance numbers or padded wallets sent by God to support a ministry. People are souls for whom Christ died. They are the lost in need of direction from the Good Shepherd, Jesus Christ. Every day as we drive or walk through our streets, we see people on their way to hell unless the gospel of Christ saves them. There are people in our cities who are seriously contemplating suicide; there are people bound by alcohol, drugs, and pornography. Young men and women are being molested by the very people who should be caring for them, not hurting them. Some people have no idea of where to go or who to turn to in life.

The gospel is God's means of reaching such people. Jesus, in Luke 4:18-19, said, "The Spirit of the LORD is upon Me, because He has anointed Me to preach the gospel to the poor; He has sent Me to heal the brokenhearted, to proclaim liberty to the captives and recovery of sight to the blind, to set at liberty those who are oppressed; to proclaim the acceptable year of the LORD." God cares more about evangelism than He does in stroking a pastor's ego by bringing in an extra ten people to the next Sunday service.

We need reminding of that sometimes. I know I do. There are times when I am so fixated with numbers that I forget that the church is built by individuals, each with their own unique story of how they came and why they are still there. We can lose sight of the individual when we make the size of the church our primary focus. From time to time, I am brought back to reality when an individual shares the story of how God brought him or her into the church. When you see just where these people are coming from and how God sent you to reach out to them, you see that the church is far more than only numbers, nickels, and noise.

True and False Motives in Evangelism

Therefore, we have to be very careful as to our motives. It is possible to be doing all the right things for all the wrong reasons. It is possible to start out doing the right thing with the right motive but, over time, subtly see the purpose slowly change. But because we are still doing the right thing, we fail to realize that the reason has gone wrong.

Years ago, a relative of my wife suddenly fell sick and was taken to the hospital. His situation was critical, and so my wife rang up a fellowship pastor in that city to go to the hospital and pray for him. This was a pastor I had known for many years (He has since left the Fellowship). Sadly, he never did go, and my wife's relative died a few days later. His excuse was that he was too busy and didn't have the time. Now I know in some cases that can be the situation, but I knew this pastor. Here was a man who was very good at building his congregation, but it dawned on me that visiting a sick old man in the hospital did not bring any benefits to him. He was about to check out from this plane of existence, and so he wouldn't be able to come to church, tithe, or be a part of his ministry.

Before anyone says I may be too harsh on this pastor, I have to say that when I thought about this, I did not condemn him for being uncaring. If anything, it made me search my heart and consider if I would have done the same. It made me evaluate my motives as to why I evangelize. Do I go on outreach to build my ministry or to see people get saved? It was then that it dawned on me that my motive for doing what I do could change without me even realizing simply because I am still doing the right thing. As a result, it is something I ask myself year after year. It is so easy to lose sight of the genuine motives of evangelism, while still evangelizing.
So while I recognize my responsibility to build a church, I am acutely aware of what comes first, and that is to share the love of Jesus with a lost and dying world. Most of the people I witness to will never come to my church, but what I have done is to share Christ and allow them to turn from their sinful

ways. The apostle Paul puts it aptly in 1 Corinthians 9:16 when he said, "…woe is me if I do not preach the gospel."

From time to time, I will meet people who will tell me that I once shared Christ with them on outreach, or they once came to church or a gospel concert, and now they are Christians. While part of me would love them to be a part of my congregation, there are people saved today in another church due to my faithfulness in sharing the gospel. Only eternity will reveal just how much impact we have had on those cold or hot days witnessing on the streets.

At the risk of sounding defeatist, I would say that the primary purpose of outreaching is simply to be obedient to the Great Commission. Mark 16:15 says, "Go into all the world and preach the gospel to every creature." Our task has never been about a large church, but to tell every lost soul that we come into contact with about the saving power of Christ through His gospel. As Mother Theresa once said, "God has not called me to be successful; He has called me to be faithful."

It may be ego-shattering to some to hear that, but these questions must be asked. Why are you involved in evangelism? Is it to let others know about Christ, or is it to build up your ministry? There is nothing wrong with a large church, but God's primary focus has always been reaching as many people as He can with His gospel.

The Church: The By-Product of Evangelism

This doesn't mean that the church is an afterthought. The church is on God's top priority list. The apostle Paul said in Ephesians 5:25 that, "…Christ also loved the church and gave Himself for her…" He also added in Acts 20:28, "…the church of God which He purchased with His blood." Christ died for the church, and so the church is not some stray dog that God looks after out of pity.

The Church is God's means by which He reaches the world. She is His light in a darkened world. She is His voice in a world crying out for direction and help. God will always bless evangelism so that His work, the church, will continue to grow and to thrive in the earth.

Years ago, while I was still a disciple in the South London church, I remember being on outreach in Leicester Square, Central London, and meeting an American evangelist who had a crowd around him as he preached the gospel. This man was as on fire as they come, and we bumped into him a few times on outreach, and on every single occasion, he had a massive crowd hanging unto every word he said.

I can remember one particular time he made a complaint to Pastor Carnegie that he had so many converts that he couldn't pass on to other churches that he had no choice but to have church services in his living room. He was having fifty people in these services. He said to Pastor Carnegie, "I'm not a pastor, I'm an evangelist. I can't keep having services at my house."

That always stayed with me because here was a man who was a human outreaching machine, and as a result, he couldn't help but build a church whether he liked it or not because the by-product of evangelism is the creation of a church.

The Discouraging Work of Evangelism

But Rome was not built in a day, and herein lies the problem we have with evangelism. When it comes to almost any other endeavor, we usually see the equivalent amount of success seen in the amount of effort we put in. If we study hard, we often get good grades. If we work hard, we usually get the benefits. Yet when it comes to evangelism, at times, it seems to be hit and miss.

The New Testament makes it clear again and again that evangelism is like sowing seed. Matthew 13:24 says, "The kingdom of heaven is like a man who sowed good seed in his field…" We all know that in farming, you never reap in the same season that you sowed and that different seeds bear fruit at different times. It would be ridiculous for the farmer to plant today and get up the next morning, expecting to receive a harvest. It would also be silly for him to expect to reap bananas in the same season he sowed peppers.

In pioneering a church, we are starting from scratch. It is possible to reap where others have previously sowed, but many times we are laying a foundation from the beginning. All a farmer can do is plant as many seeds as he can and leave the rest to nature. All the preacher can do is evangelize to as many as he can and leave the rest to God. We in ourselves cannot save a single soul, but we can tell them about the good news of the gospel.

Not only is the pioneer pastor to sow seed, but he must also sow in faith, believing that God will use his words to impact the hearts of those who hear him. Too many times, a discouraged and disillusioned pastor will go on outreach merely handing out flyers. There is no faith to believe that God could move on that very outreach and touch a key convert who would bring thirty people to his church in a matter of days. The book of Hebrews points out that without faith, it is impossible to please God, and so merely going through the motions of an 'outreach' is not going to result in people getting saved.

The Building-Up of the Saints

The truth is, the church down the road may have hundreds more in attendance than you without outreaching, but there are vital things not taken into consideration.

We can't make the mistake of measuring effectiveness simply by the traditional outward trappings of success. There are things that evangelism does for the spiritual growth of a Christian that could never come from any other source. And so while people may not get saved in masses, personal involvement in evangelism creates depth on the inside. In other words, the benefits of evangelism aren't just for those who need to receive the gospel, but also for the one giving the gospel. While the results of sharing the gospel may appear to be hit and miss, there is always something done in the heart of the saint.

1. Evangelism creates bold Christians

The first thing evangelism does for the Christian is it causes them to deal with the issue of shame. Mark 8:38 says, "For whoever is ashamed of Me and My words in this adulterous and sinful generation, of him the Son of Man also will be ashamed when He comes in the glory of His Father with the holy angels." One real aversion many Christians have towards evangelism (hence the reason why most Christians will never find themselves on the streets of their local town) is they do not want anyone they know to see them.

Rare is the individual who, at the very beginning of their salvation, is not inwardly a bit ashamed of the gospel. "What if my old friends see me with these Christians?" "Will they call me names?" "Will they disapprove?" Many churchgoers like to be undercover Christians or, at the very least, be hidden by the four walls of the church where no one on the outside can see.
Evangelism causes us to face ourselves, to face those issues under the surface of shame and fear, and seek God for boldness to be the men and women He has called us to be.

Acts 4:29-31 says, "Now, Lord, look on their threats, and grant to Your servants that with all boldness they may speak Your word, by stretching out

Your hand to heal, and that signs and wonders may be done through the name of Your holy Servant Jesus. And when they had prayed, the place where they were assembled together was shaken; and they were all filled with the Holy Spirit, and they spoke the word of God with boldness."

2. Evangelism helps in the production of godly Christians

Secondly, evangelism creates Christians who take their faith seriously. Another reason why some saints have a problem with evangelism is that it would expose their Christianity to the world. They would prefer that it would remain a secret, not because of shame but because once exposed, they will have to live the life that they proclaim.

Once you let the world know that you are a Christian, many will watch what you do, what you say, who you associate with, and where you go. You no longer have the freedom to be anonymous, and you can no longer get away with things that sinners get away with. So evangelism makes us accountable to the gospel we publicly declare. There is nothing worse than to be called a hypocrite, especially because that is what we once called Christians before salvation, and now the shoe is on the other foot.

In Jamaica, I was keenly aware of this. Many addressed me as "Pastor" who I had never seen in my life. But they saw me preach on the streets of Mandeville and knew who I was even if I wasn't aware of their existence. As a result, I tried to be my best even though there were so many things in a third world country that made me want to get bent out of shape. In a nation that is cynical and mistrustful of pastors, it behooved me to conduct myself in such a way that it didn't reproach the gospel I preached.

3. Evangelism creates socially developed Christians

Thirdly, evangelism also teaches the saints people skills. I find it amazing how I can just approach a total stranger and strike up a conversation without any fear or trepidation. I have learned that through evangelism. Whereas I was once a shy and introverted guy before salvation, I have the boldness to talk to anyone I want to without fear. You also learn patience in talking with people, as on outreach, you face many times ignorant, angry, or obnoxious people who stretch your patience thin. What do you do when someone tells you to go to hell or crushes up your leaflet and throws it in your face? You know that they are only doing that because you are a Christian, as they wouldn't have dared do that if you were passing out fliers to a hip-hop concert. You learn to develop a thick skin and not let people's words offend you.

You also learn to articulate things in the right way. The art of evangelism is getting people to listen to what you have to say. If you present yourself as a know-it-all, obnoxious, or as a goofball, then people will switch off and you would have wasted your time. Saying stuff like, "You are going to burn in hell, you stinking sinner" is not the right way to win friends and influence people.

Effective evangelism is learning to read people and their temperament and act accordingly. Some are as prickly as a cactus and you have to approach with tact. There are the easy-going, the self-righteous, the academic, the agnostic, the atheist, and a plethora of different intellectual and personality types that you have to learn to steer through.

But let me just add another thought before we move on. Evangelism helps to build social skills only when your motive for evangelism is winning people to Christ. You desire to be as effective as you can, and you realize that how you approach people goes a long way in reaching them for Jesus.

But there are some whose only purpose of evangelizing comes from a perverted form of self-righteousness. What I mean is, they are only on outreach to revel in the fact that they are right and the sinner is wrong. They have no burden for the lost, and as long as they win the argument with the sinner to prove that he is a sinner, they are satisfied. They are indifferent to the fact that they have offended people and actually take great pride because it must mean they are presenting the gospel correctly.

I recall, on more than one occasion, hearing disciples preaching on the streets. While what they say is technically correct, their preaching grates my spirit because all I hear are words of condemnation and judgment with no promise of the hope of salvation. They have no interest in being productive, and so evangelism plays no part in developing their social skills.

Perhaps you have heard the old story of a Christian woman who finally succeeded in bringing her unsaved husband to church one Sunday morning after many years. But at that service, the pastor preached on hell, and the husband left fuming, vowing never to return. It took over ten years later for the husband to revisit the church, and during that time, a new pastor was in charge. Co-incidentally that pastor preached on hell too, and the wife, remembering that was the same topic preached ten years before, was bracing herself for her husband's backlash but was shocked when he answered the altar call to get saved.

While she was delighted in her husband's new-found salvation, she was also quite puzzled at the two completely different reactions on what was the same topic. When she asked, his response was, "When the first pastor preached on hell, it was as if he wanted me to go there, but when the second pastor preached on hell, it was as if he would do anything to keep me from going."

If evangelism is going to help the Christian, it is because the Christian has a heart for souls.

4. Evangelism creates Christians with convictions

Fourthly, evangelism helps Christians to understand why they believe what they believe. I have met many Christians who have been unable to articulate what they believe to an unbeliever. They have no concept of things that I would consider Christianity 101, and it gives the impression to the unbeliever that the Christian is shallow, superficial, and lacks substance. It also makes the sinner believe that he is smarter than he is because his questions have resulted in silence.

1 Peter 3:15 says, "…always be ready to give a defense to everyone who asks you a reason for the hope that is in you…" Being ready to give a defense often comes by trial and error. As a new convert on outreach, you face a question to which you have no answer. Many times, non-Christians will ask you questions you would have never thought up on your own. As a result, you go home, and you read, and you ask questions until finally, you get an appropriate solution.

Questions like that will come again, and so the next time someone comes with the same problem, you have the answer for them. There are times when a new convert will call me alongside to help answer a question an unsaved person has asked. As I give a clear and precise answer, the new convert invariably marvels at my depth and insight, not realizing that I have heard that question many times throughout the years. A Christian who has never been on outreach will never be exposed to that type of querying and, as a result, will never know the answers to critical questions.

5. Evangelism leads to more evangelism

I read somewhere that only 3% of Christians ever reach another person for Christ. That means 97% of Christians never win a soul for Jesus. This simply means that most Christians never evangelize. While there are many reasons, I do believe an important aspect is a fact that many churches do not have an outreach program. An organized outreach is an excellent foundation in helping Christians to overcome their fear of evangelism and to train them to reach the lost.

As a result, organized outreach creates a platform that leads to other types of evangelism. Once the disciple knows how to "sail" on the high seas of evangelism, he or she should be able to navigate into different zones. Once I got the hang of evangelizing on a Saturday afternoon with my brothers and sisters in Christ, I soon began to do my own evangelism, such as knocking on doors or preaching on the busses.

Back at the mother church in London, as disciples, the regular Saturday outreach was just one of the many different outreaches we had. Most were organized with no input from the pastor. Had there been no regular outreach, I can almost guarantee, as I have seen this from experience, that there would be no other outreach as well.

6. Evangelism leads to growth and personal edification

I can't tell the number of times that I have gone on outreach, not wanting to go because I was down in the dumps for whatever reason, only to have gone out and come back home stirred, excited, and full of victory. My circumstances had not changed one iota, but there was something about witnessing, in particular, a good witness, which got me buzzing again. Not only did the Spirit of God move through me as I witnessed and re-energized my soul, but it also put my life in perspective after talking to someone whose life had been devastated by sin. After hearing the horror stories of living in the world, my problems shrank in comparison.

Right here, I would speak about the benefits of an impact team. When we talk about invasion or impact teams, we mean a group from our church going into another city to help, usually, a pioneer work. On paper, it looks like a larger church going to help a smaller church and so the benefit seems to be only in one direction.

But going on teams does so much for the church that sends, as well as the one that receives. For one, new converts who may feel a sense of shame and fear in evangelizing in their towns and cities are a lot more confident in starting in a new city where no one knows them. Once they brave the great unknown, going unto the streets of their city isn't as nerve-racking as it was previously.

Secondly, it is incredible how much you can learn from another church from how they do things. I'm not the greatest when it comes to innovation and ideas for evangelism, but when I see a good idea, I take it. It is the idea of cross-pollination that the apostle Paul refers to in Romans 1: 11-12, "For I long to see you, that I may impart to you some spiritual gift, so that you may be established— that is, that I may be encouraged together with you by the mutual faith both of you and me."

Evangelism, both locally and outside our cities, keeps us from becoming incestuous. A long-standing joke made about rural people is how they end up marrying their cousins. There is truth in that joke because, in old times, rural people were more or less cut off from the outside world, and therefore the only people available were their cousins. This had devastating effects on the gene pool. We see the same with the Amish and other similar groups that cut themselves off from the rest of the society.

When we lose the vision for evangelism, churches end up becoming incestuous. There are many churches, more than can be counted, that are closed off organizations because there is no evangelism. Not only are they cut off from a new source of converts, but they also are cut off from ideas and strategies created when we get into contact with likeminded people.

When I was between pastorates, as I was preparing to go to Jamaica, I was an evangelist for around six months. On one overseas trip, I really didn't want to go. There were too many holdups hindering me from going to Jamaica, and I was not in the mood. But this revival was booked months in advance and so out of duty I went. When I checked into my hotel, I was invited by the pastor to attend the concert before the revival. I didn't want to go because I didn't want to be there in the first place, but I had no real excuse not to go, and so I went. I have to say that I am glad I did go because I learned so much from that experience, and it was then that Romans 1:11-12 made sense to me.

The Aversion to Evangelism

Therefore, it is through evangelism that you grow in ways that you couldn't otherwise. With that being true, it means that there are many Christians who are underdeveloped in their spiritual lives in which evangelism could have made a difference. Whether it is through the fear of shame, the fear of accountability, or the fear of the unknown, many saints miss a vital aspect to Christian maturity and depth.

What is interesting is if you should challenge them in this area, they will use spirituality to justify their submission to fear. I have heard on more than one occasion of individuals when asked about personal evangelism respond by saying, "I haven't got the gift of evangelism." As they see individuals on the street boldly declaring the gospel or confidently sharing their faith with people, they wrongfully conclude that it is a 'gift.' They create an accommodating theology.

"Look at them. They are so courageous and articulate in sharing their faith. I could never do what they do. It is a gift from the Lord. We all have different gifts. Some people can sing, others can play an instrument or perform on stage, and some people can evangelize the gospel."

The last thing they want to hear is that there are no 'gifts' when it comes to evangelism and that everyone has been given the mandate by God to declare their faith to a lost and dying world. Everything that looks easy has often been the result of sheer, old fashioned hard work and dedication, and evangelism is no different.

Let me just say that an organized church outreach should not be the end-all and be-all of evangelism for the individual Christian. There needs to be a balance because church outreach can be elevated to a point where it becomes the only time Christians share the gospel. As a result, we develop a kind of "clocking in and clocking out" mentality with outreach where we gather together on a Friday night, Saturday morning, or whenever and hit the streets of our local community. Evangelism should be more than that, and usually, it should be where we have our most significant influence, that is, the relationships we have built up over the years – school, work, home, and neighborhood.

The truth is most people come to a relationship with Christ through people they know as opposed to random strangers on the street. I can think of one convert in my first church in Manchester who reached his best friend, and those two reached out to their friends and family members and, in the end, around thirty-nine people becoming a part of that church. The same happened in Jamaica, where one young lady who got saved brought a truckload of friends and family to church (I remember picking her up and her crew a few Sunday mornings for church and having a car with a dozen people where it should only seat seven).

That being said, without a properly organized church outreach, just how many people will continue to be faithful in evangelism? There is no zeal like that of a new convert, and it is usually through new converts that most of our other converts come from as they reach out to their various relational connections. But what happens when those connections are exhausted?

The truth is, evangelism dries up the longer people remain Christians. The very word 'gospel' means 'good news,' and good news is contagious. But, as John MacArthur said, "The young believer soon discovers not everyone thinks the gospel is such good news...Eventually, as the disciple becomes more and more familiar with the gospel, that profound initial sense of wonder and amazement fades somewhat. The gospel is still good news, of course, but we begin to think of it as old news, and that sense of urgency is lost."[8]

If you get rid of the local organized outreach, entropy envelops the church. I have seen churches that were blazing hot in the beginnings cool to a Siberian atmosphere later on. Give a church a few years to freewheel under its own steam, and you will end up with a dead church. That excitement and passion that was there in the early days, if we are not careful, can fizzle out into staleness and stagnation. Granted, most people do not visit the local church due to organized church outreaches. At the same time, they are vital in keeping the vision alive, continuing the theme of soul-winning and reaching new people who will reach new people.

A Passion for the Gospel

Back in 1848, in what would be modern-day Sacramento, California, James Marshall, the construction superintendent on a sawmill owned by John A. Sutter, while inspecting the flow of water on the mill, observed something shiny at the bottom of a ditch. On closer scrutiny, it turned out to be a small gold nugget. Further examination revealed several nuggets, and he duly reported his findings to his boss, John Sutter.

Sutter was worried that the laborers on the mill would stop working to search for gold and so he tried to make a deal. If they continued working for him, they could search for gold on his property in their spare time, but they were not to tell anyone about the discovery.
In the book, "The World Rushed In" by J.S. Holliday, the author writes, "Such startling news could not be contained. Stutter himself talked of it, and in a letter, he boasted: "I have made a discovery of a gold mine which, according to the experiments we have made, is extremely rich.""[9] Against his own advice, Sutter couldn't help but share the good news of the discovery of gold to the outside world, and that was the start of the great California Gold Rush of 1849 and the legendary forty-niners.

---

[8] p viii, Evangelism: How to Share the Gospel Faithfully, John F. MacArthur, Thomas Nelson, 2011
[9] p33, The World Rushed in: The California Gold Rush Experience, 2002, University of Oklahoma Press

Sutter, because he couldn't contain himself, lost out on gold prospecting, as in a few months, the whole world turned up at his doorsteps, but how can you blame him? How can you keep good news a secret? That is unless you don't see good news as good news. Perhaps the reason why some Christians fail to evangelize the gospel is that they don't see it as good news.

But how can this be? The reason the gospel is called the good news is that humanity was lost in sin and destined for a devil's hell for all eternity. But God in His grace sent His only Son to die in our place, the righteous for the unrighteous, the innocent on behalf of the guilty. Thus, we who were sure to be lost for all eternity would receive the Lord's forgiveness, adoption into the family of God, and inheritance in His heavenly kingdom.

This is truly good news, but for some, the significance of the gospel has not profoundly resonated with us. The full importance of where we were spiritually and what Christ did for us on the Cross of Calvary has not hit us. If it did, evangelism would be not only natural but spontaneous as well. How can we touch others with the gospel if the gospel hasn't touched us in the first place?

While I do understand that the fear of shame and accountability may seek to hold us back from evangelizing, the excitement and revelation of the good news of the gospel should be more than enough to break any shackle or limitation that fear may have over us. May God help us not to be so familiar with the gospel message that it loses meaning for us over the years as that will no doubt affect our passion for the gospel of Jesus and our commitment to evangelism.

I find it amazing that the innate passion for evangelism is the catalyst to an area of spiritual growth that could never be manufactured otherwise. The excitement created in receiving the good news gives us the heart to reach the lost. It results in us overcoming our fears, taking our faith seriously, cultivating our people skills, and developing our convictions. It is like downloading one small program on the computer, and on opening, it releases a whole series of applications.

Evangelism and the Church

While we can see the profit in evangelism for the sinner and the saint, there is another by-product of evangelism that we need to look at. Evangelism means challenging the kingdom of darkness. It means establishing spiritual dominion. While to the carnal unsaved eyes, street preaching may not seem like much, in the unseen spiritual realm, things are happening. Evangelism, primarily street preaching, is the public confrontation of supernatural darkness and represents spiritual pushback.

Jesus instructed His disciples in Matthew 10:7-8, "And as you go, preach, saying, "The kingdom of heaven is at hand." Heal the sick, cleanse the lepers, raise the dead, cast out demons." What we can understand about evangelism is we are establishing God's dominion, His kingdom on the earth, and if there is nothing else accomplished, at least we know that is done. Interestingly, everything else achieved supernaturally comes after the preaching because it is the preaching that establishes supernatural dominion.

By giving up on street evangelism, the church world has given up ground to Satan. Ground given up is not easy to get back. You either use it or lose it. Establishing and maintaining a presence on the street of one's local town or city is vital in spiritual warfare. It is hard to get established and easy to lose.

A good example is a church with a presence on the streets, but due to a change of pastors or direction, they stop outreaching. When they do restart, they face opposition from city officials, despite the fact they had been on the street previously for years.

Once you have established dominion and gained favor with the city, do not give up that ground whatever you do. At the very least, people know who you are, and while thousands may not be getting saved on the street, you are highlighting your church amidst the tens or even hundreds that may be in your city.

There is a possible favor that can result from establishing your presence in the city. It amazes me how many know the church and me and yet, have never been to one of our services. As a result of that, doors have been made open for me. There may be Christians from other denominations that pass by your outreaches. While they may not do what you do, they are impressed by your bold declaration of the gospel, and should the opportunity arise, they will help you advance the cause of the gospel in your city. They (or even the unsaved) could be in critical positions of local government or businesses, and because they know who you are, what you do and what you stand for will be more than willing to open doors for you.

Possible Pitfalls to Avoid

Let me just point this out. I have seen outstanding street evangelists who have been very effective in sharing the gospel and winning people to Christ. There have been occasions where people were offended, not because of the man but of the message. I can live with that.

But I have also observed through the years three types of problem street evangelists. The first is the Lone Ranger Christian types who belong to no particular church and who believe that most churches are apostate. They think they are the last bastion of true Christianity and will have nothing to do with the established religious churches that they look on with extreme suspicion. There is something about isolation that makes people kooky, and these individuals are incredibly kooky with no accountability to anyone but "Jesus". But because of their kookiness, they do not draw much attention to themselves and are easily ignored and so, again, do relatively little damage.

The second is the exhibitionists who will make a spectacle of themselves to procure a crowd, and once they have the attention of the masses will then street preach. I have seen some of these men operate, and it is quite useful. God did tell Ezekiel the prophet to be a spectacle by lying on his side for three hundred and ninety days (Ezekiel 4:9). If you are an itinerant evangelist going from town to town, I can suppose that much harm won't be done, but if it is a church, one has to be very careful. I'm not saying that we can't, from time to time, do things that draw a crowd to preach the gospel, but if we do that, we have to do it with great tact and choose wisely the "spectacle" we are going to be.

Then there is third, the obnoxious street preacher. While we can get away with number two, we must be cautious to avoid number three. I have seen street preachers go out of their way to be as obnoxious as they can, drawing the ire of the crowd, not realizing they are of no effect in reaching people for Christ. If anything, they do the exact opposite.
Sadly, I have seen men in our Fellowship do the same thing having a "them and us" mentality and believing that the only way to be effective is by offending everyone that they can. They rail at the homosexual, they rail at the fornicator, they rail at the drinker, and while I know we need to preach on sin, there is no balance in what was said and all they have accomplished is to make themselves abhorrent in the eyes of the unsaved and the church world.

Just as you can make your church attract favor, you can also draw disfavor. By obnoxious street preaching, you can marginalize yourself in a matter of months and make yourself "persona non grata." The amazing thing is that you won't even see that you are the source of all your problems, but you will blame Satan, the religious establishment, and the unsaved. You won't learn from your mistakes, but rather be even more obnoxious as you push back against the "persecution" you are facing. It is possible to be banging your head against a wall and yet never stopping to consider "why?"

Arrogance has no small part to play in us being obnoxious, as we ride into town on our white horse with both guns blazing declaring how we are a part of the "Fellowship" and how we are going to clean up this two-bit town filled with religious demons. My advice is not to have zeal without knowledge. Don't believe that you can go full bore on obnoxiousness, and somehow it is going to add up to incredible favor and that magically things are just going to work out.

You have to consider why we do what we do, and while we must all evangelize regardless of where we are, we must also be mindful of our surroundings. It is easy to have hard, confrontational, in-your-face preaching in cities like London and the like, but in a small town of 5,000 people, the reaction may be completely different.

In an area like Brixton, South London you will have thousands passing through every day. There are a range of different people and groups doing their own thing – the Socialist workers, the Nation of Islam, Muslims, gay rights activists, Mormons, Black Israelites, etc. Having an outreach amid other people doing their thing can be done quite easily (albeit with slight distractions of debating with the abovementioned). But in a little town with a few thousand, that same type of outreach is going to bring about a different reaction.

A pastor coming from a big city to pioneer in a little town must be wise in terms of the dynamics of that town. It can't be a matter of "this is how we do it in my home church, and so, therefore, I am going to follow the pattern," but rather understanding that while evangelism is in the DNA of our fellowship, how we express ourselves in evangelism may change. What I mean is while we will always follow the pattern of evangelism, how we evangelize may change.

It is easy to do what you know to do, and while that can be great, it can also be a sign that you aren't thinking as to why you do what you do. You must understand why we do what we do. People hurt themselves by not thinking things through, and pioneer churches hurt themselves by not understanding why they do things.

I have seen pioneer churches sing long, elaborate songs as a part of their praise and worship. There aren't more than ten people in the building, but they are singing the songs that their home church sings. But the home church has a full band with good singers! The pioneer church has a pastor who sings off-key and a wife who can barely play the keyboard. There is no need for that. What happened to the good old choruses like "Alive, Alive" and "What a mighty God we serve? Simple songs so that new people can catch on, and when you finally get somewhere, introduce those elaborate songs.

I know it may seem that I am digressing, but my point is that people don't think as to why things are done the way they are. Why do we do what we do? We do what we do to get people saved, to establish dominion, and to train disciples. It isn't outreaching for outreaching sake. It isn't so that you don't feel guilty on a Saturday afternoon. It isn't so that you can feel connected to the Fellowship by repeating the same activity.

Consider our churches in nations like China, where Christians are not free to outreach on the streets publicly. It doesn't mean because they can't street preach they can't evangelize. It means they have got to find another way to share the gospel. China has the fastest-growing Christian population in the world, and yet they do not have the right to assemble as Christians or the right to free speech as we have. They do not have advertised mass rallies, pass out fliers for gospel concerts, or street preaching and yet there is revival and spiritual dominion.

In summary, the whole purpose of evangelism is to share the gospel and to be as effective as we can in doing it. Is the gospel being spread? Are people getting saved? Are disciples being raised up? Are we establishing spiritual dominion in our city? Does the devil know we are there? Are we considering new methods of reaching people with the gospel? Are we using multiple methods in propagating the gospel?
As long as we know why we are doing what we are doing and are doing it, we can be effective in reaching our communities and, ultimately, the world for Jesus Christ.

Steps to Evangelism

Sometimes we begin to think to ourselves that a perfect witness is one who has no fear or who has all the right words to say. I can assure you that it is not valid. If you believe that lie, Satan will succeed in keeping you from sharing the gospel to those who desperately need it and who God has brought your way.

1. Facing Fear

For one, fear will always raise its ugly head when you witness. Why would Satan give you an open platform for you to take away his captives? I can assure you that more significant individuals than you and I have felt this fear on them. Take the great apostle Paul who said in 1 Corinthians 2:3-5, "I was with you in weakness, in fear, and in much trembling. And my speech and my preaching were not with persuasive words of human wisdom, but in demonstration of the Spirit and of power, that your faith should not be in the wisdom of men but in the power of God."

If you have been in church for a while, outside of the name of Jesus, the second most frequent person you will hear mentioned is Paul. You can be forgiven, therefore, to think of Paul as this super-apostle, the spiritual Green Lantern – the Man without Fear. But Paul admits the contrary and that he had fears, but somehow, through that, God gave him the power to preach and to declare the gospel in a very effective way.

Again I will mention that American evangelist in London, who to me, was the best example I had ever seen when it came to street preaching. I heard this man take on people on the street and silence them in a way I have only read Jesus do. It was amazing. With great wisdom and courage, he took on all comers, and his answers refuted with cutting effectiveness every one of their criticisms about Christianity.

I can remember asking him how he was so courageous in street preaching, and he told me that he gets nervous every single time he does it. That admission blew my mind because he seemed so authoritative and so in control.

It was Mike Tyson's old trainer, the legendary Cus D'Amato, who said, "I tell my kids, what is the difference between a hero and a coward? What is the difference between being yellow and being brave? No difference. Only what you do. They both feel the same. They both fear dying and getting hurt. The man who is yellow refuses to face up to what he's got to face. The hero is more disciplined, and he fights those feelings off and he does what he has to do. But they both feel the same, the hero and the coward. People who watch you judge you on what you do, not how you feel."[10]

So true, because as I watched Dirk Wood preach in Leicester Square before hundreds, all I saw was a man who was bold in faith for his God. We all have

---

[10] p97, In this corner, Peter Heller, 1989

fear, but what we need is to face that fear, confront that fear and ask God for the boldness of the Holy Spirit to overcome that fear that we may be used of God. The great side benefit of that is to see just how effective we can be, and that the victories gained are not of us but the God who works in and through us.

2. Overcoming inarticulateness

Another manifestation of fear is our fear of speaking. Many times we know what it is we believe, and we see the reality of Christ in our lives, but we don't know how best to articulate it. This is especially true for me as a new believer, where I didn't know anything. I remember saying in a group discussion at a Bible study that Jesus wept at the tomb of John the Baptist!

We know what has happened to us, but what do we say? We are afraid of saying things the wrong way, saying things that aren't true, or saying things we aren't sure of. We are scared of babbling on incoherently, not making any sense whatsoever. We so overanalyze what we are to say that we end up saying nothing. It is the classic paralysis of analysis.

But it is incredible what our God can do in weakness. I can recall Pastor Carnegie mentioning in a sermon when he was pioneering in Kingston, Jamaica, they had an outreach and the microphone was given to a brother who was terrified. All he could shout was "Jesus" repeatedly and in so doing, cars began to stop, and people began to turn their heads, and everyone paid attention to what was going on.

As a new convert, at a time when I didn't know much about the Bible or the God who saved me, I had many powerful witnesses. I got saved in a hostel for teenagers and young adults, and within a few weeks, I had about six guys my age converted, and we would have church in one of our rooms. Some of the most powerful times in my spiritual life happened in that hostel.

There have been times when I have looked back to then and where I was present and concluded that although I was now a pastor and a man who knew his Bible, there was a lot more going on for me then. I knew where I had to get back to. But I digress. The main point is that not being a Biblical scholar doesn't disqualify you from being a witness. Acts 4:13 says, "Now when they saw the boldness of Peter and John, and perceived that they were uneducated and untrained men, they marveled. And they realized that they had been with Jesus." All you need is your testimony of what Christ has done in your life, and God will do the rest.

3. Lean upon your church

Fear can make evangelism a lonely experience. I can recall pioneering my first church and having to go out into the neighborhood knocking on doors and telling them about Jesus. I couldn't count the number of times I had the door slammed in my face. My wife was heavily pregnant, and I was 200 miles away from home. It was just me, myself, and I.

Now and again, my good friend, Courtney Lowe, would come and help me out. It would be like old times when we used to go outreaching together on a Thursday evening in Brixton, South London. Those were good times, and we had some interesting times on outreach, to say the least. There is nothing like having someone with you when you evangelize. It is good to have someone there who you can lean on, and they, in turn, can lean on you.

It's no coincidence that when Christ sent people out to evangelize, He did send them out two by two. Mark 6:7 says, "And He [Jesus] called the twelve to Himself, and began to send them out two by two, and gave them power over unclean spirits." There is no problem going out on your own to tell people about Jesus. We see this with Philip the Evangelist in Acts 8, but it never hurts, from a morale point of view (as well as security) to have someone with you.

The truth is that many times if left to our own to evangelize, we would hesitate. Having someone with us gives us more of an incentive, and the more, the merrier. It is a great comfort to have your church with you in numbers as you are on the street, declaring the good news. I can tell you that from personal experience having been on my own the first eight months of my salvation trying to tell people about Jesus. It was a very lonely experience. When I came to the South London church, it felt so good to know that there were people who had my back when I was sharing the gospel.

4. Asking the Holy Spirit for help

Outreaching without the Holy Spirit is merely canvassing for a religious organization. Psalm 127:1 says, "Unless the Lord builds the house, they labor in vain who build it; unless the Lord guards the city, the watchman stays awake in vain." We can have the world of confidence, have the gift of the gab, and have the nicest flyer design in the history of fliers, the best PA system of all time, and yet without the Holy Spirit's help, evangelism is merely campaigning for church attendance.

It amazes me at the flippant attitudes of some of our church people who turn up late for an outreach, grab a bunch of flyers and start to hand them out in a scattershot manner. They may win the award for handing out the most flyers in the shortest time, but that isn't evangelism. They haven't taken the time to pray, get the mind of God, and allow God in their witness.

I'm not going to get religious about it and say that there should be a prayer meeting before every outreach, but prayer is essential. We should pray for God's help, boldness, and Him leading us in a way that would make the outreach effective. While everyone needs to hear the gospel, I am sure that there are people in the city who God would want us to speak to. Perhaps they could be people He is already dealing with, and we are the final link in the chain leading them to Christ.

Then there is the issue of demonic hindrances as you can bet your last dollar that Satan isn't happy seeing us on the street telling people how to escape his clutches. Prayer makes all the difference in the supernatural realm as it combats the satanic agenda that would seek to make our evangelism ineffective. We do not battle against flesh and blood, and so evangelism has got to be seen as the spiritual work it really is.

The apostle Paul said in Ephesians 2:2, "In which you once walked according to the course of this world, according to the prince of the power of the air, the spirit who now works in the sons of disobedience..." He points out that there are demons at work in those who are not saved, and we must be mindful that functioning in the natural will not accomplish a spiritual task. In 2 Corinthians 4:4, the apostle Paul also says, "...whose minds the god of this age has blinded, who do not believe, lest the light of the gospel of the glory of Christ, who is the image of God, should shine on them."

Eloquence and Bible knowledge are not enough to convert the soul, and we must seek the help of the Holy Spirit in the awesome task of reaching the lost. And when I mean 'awesome', I am not merely saying 'amazing' but the sheer magnitude of the task of seeing true conversion. It is like staying at the base of Mount Everest, looking way up, and trying to grasp the enormousness of the mission to reach the top. This work is something that can only be done by the power of the Holy Spirit, and so prayer is not only important, it is fundamentally important.

Conclusion

I know that there is much more that could be said about evangelism. I have only scratched the surface, but hopefully, you will realize just how important this is to us as a church and why it is essential to be a good witness for Christ and have an effective outreach strategy in place within the local church.

3 CHURCH DISCIPLINE

Life Before the Establishment of Modern Human Rights

One of the most remarkable achievements made in modern times is the universal establishment of human rights. This is something that many are ignorant of and take for granted, but there was a time when most of us did not have rights.

There was a time in the not too distant past when most people in society were treated just a bit better than animals. All they had to look forward to in life was a brutal and oppressive existence from the day they were born until they took their last breath. As the great reggae singer Freddie McGregor once said, *"To be poor is a crime,"* and it wasn't too great either for ethnic minorities, most women, and children.

There was a time not long ago where it was legal to own another human being and to treat them like dirt. I have read many accounts of West Indian and American slavery, and it seems that some farm animals had a life far better than that of slaves. It is horrifying to see how brutal one human being could be towards another. How horrific it must have felt to be dragged from one's home and shackled into the bottom of a ship, confined to space of 6ft x 1½ft unable to move, and to wallow in one's own excrement for weeks until dragged off and hauled to a plantation.

Slavery, it is said, made monsters out of everyone – slave-masters, slaves, and freedmen. As Haiti's struggle for independence broke out in 1791, tensions between the three ethnic groups [whites, blacks, and mulattoes (mixed race)] in Haiti got increasingly worse.

In the book "Christophe: King of Haiti" by Hubert Cole, the author writes, *"...in the spring of 1793...the struggle between whites and mulattoes had reached such extremes of savagery that the whites paraded a captured mulatto leader through the streets in a cart with his feet nailed to the floorboards before breaking him on the wheel and burning his broken body alive, while mulattoes ripped open a pregnant white woman and threw her unborn child to the hogs, and then decapitated her husband and sewed up his severed head in her womb."*[11] The black slaves were no angels, in their bloodlust for revenge they murdered, raped, and brutalized their former masters, and there was no love lost between them and the mulattoes either.

So much has been made of black slavery in the Americas that people forget that Native Americans and Whites were also in bondage. Black slavery only became popular when the Native Americans of the Caribbean began to die in massive numbers because of their inability to live a life of oppression and their susceptibility to European disease. It is ironic to note that the Catholic priest, Bartolomé Las Casas, considered one of the earliest advocates of universal human rights, was the one who suggested the idea of using Africans instead of Native Americans for slaves, something he repented of later.

It is a little-known fact that many of the early imported slaves to the Americas were white and came from Britain and Ireland. White slavery was popular back in the 1600s where criminals, prostitutes, beggars, and prisoners of war were rounded up and deported from Britain to America and the West Indies. The logic seemed impeccable. Get rid of all the unwanted riffraff from Britain and turn them into productive slaves in the Caribbean. It was a win-win situation.

Then there was the matter of the pesky Irish. Consider that as a result of the Irish Rebellion in 1641, 80,000 Irish intellectuals were rounded up, deported to the West Indies, and served as field slaves. [12] Between 1641 and 1652, 300,000 Irish citizens were sold into slavery, with many sent to America, Barbados, Antigua, and Montserrat. As a matter of fact, during the mid-1600s, Irish slaves constituted 70% of the population of the island of Montserrat! [13]

---

[11] p40, Christophe: King of Haiti, Hubert Cole, Eyre & Spottiswoode Ltd., 1967
[12] Back cover, To Shed A Tear: A Story of Irish Slavery in the West Indies, iUniverse, 2001
[13] p255, Ohio Confederate Connection, Curtis and Gloria Early,

Too Much of a Good Thing

My apologies for deviating what seems to be a chapter on church discipline into a history lesson, but my point is that there was a time when human rights were as real as the unicorn. What a privilege we have to live in a society where we have the right to vote, determine our future with peace and security, where little girls have the right to live a normal childhood without the fear of marriage, and where even running water and electricity is seen as a right. These are things we take for granted, and the thought has never crossed our minds.

The problem with living in a society where we take rights for granted is that many now believe the freedom to do anything we want to do is a human right. Gay marriage is now a human right in most Western nations. As a matter of fact, in Germany, the German Ethics Council, a government-backed organization, a few years ago, were pushing lawmakers in the nation to abolish incest laws. In a statement, the Council said, "Criminal law is not the appropriate means to preserve a social taboo... ***the fundamental right*** of adult siblings to sexual self-determination is to be weighed more heavily than the abstract idea of protection of the family."[14] (emphasis mine)

Society is degenerating into a moral free-for-all. This paradigm shift has brainwashed many members of society to feel that it is their right to do anything they want to do without the fear of repercussions and consequences. A good case in point is the right to protest. While I agree that peaceful demonstrations and protest is a human right, it is not a right to riot, destroy property, and to act in a way that brings harm to others.
Consequently, one of the results of this push to ever-increasing rights is the decrease in personal responsibilities for our actions. My right to have as many sexual partners as possible diminishes my responsibilities for the unwanted children produced, the abortions, and the STDs transmitted to others. My right to happiness diminishes personal responsibility to the others hurt in my attempt to gain pleasure.

In a world where the word 'rights' is the mantra of the day, the word 'responsibility' has gone out the window along with the archaic words 'brabble', 'monsterful', 'groak' and 'hugger-mugger'. The consequence of this is seen when it comes to church discipline.

---

[14] http://www.telegraph.co.uk/news/worldnews/europe/germany/11119062/Incest-a-fundamental-right-German-committee-says.html

The Twisted Perception of Church Discipline

There was a time when church discipline was a natural occurrence in the life of the everyday church, but today it is a marginalized aspect of church life and, in many cases, confined to a time gone past. As Christianity Today puts it, *"Today, church discipline is feared as the mark of a false church, bringing to mind images of witch trials, scarlet letters, public humiliations, and damning excommunications."*[15] That is, in today's world, church discipline is a breach of human rights. How dare the church or anyone for that matter stop someone from doing what he or she wants to do!

Perhaps the most significant "breach" of "human rights" is seen of God Himself. How many times in both the Old Testament and the New, we see God killing people for seemingly innocuous infringements? There is the matter of Ananias and Sapphira, who were killed for hiding the fact that they sold a piece of land for more money than they had told the apostles. Why? Didn't they give most of the money to the church? Even if they didn't give it all, at least it was something.

And an angel struck poor old Herod down when other people proclaimed him to be a god. It wasn't his fault that he was such a good speaker that the crowds were impressed. Then there were the sons of Aaron, who God literally smoked for offering up a new flavor of incense. Why can't we try something new now and again? All Uzzah did, as a gesture of goodwill, was to keep the Ark from falling, and what was his reward? He was struck dead. I guess no good deed goes unpunished.

These are the stories that unbelievers use to accuse God of being harsh in His ways towards people. In their minds, God uses the proverbial sledgehammer to smash a peanut. The God of the Bible, they say, is a God of terror who seeks to control people by fear and intimidation. In their minds, church discipline is an extension of that harsh and brutal God, and it is the church's method to use "controlling behavior" as the means of keeping people in line through fear and intimidation. Church discipline, therefore, is made out to be a cultish activity used in keeping those going out of line under control.

This kind of thinking is entirely unreasonable when one considers that in any form of organization, there has to be a code of ethics in its constitution where you deal with breaches. In most companies, employees can be disciplined or even fired for breaking some sort of protocol. Lateness, sloppy work, the

---

[15] Christianity Today, August 2005, Vol. 49, No. 8,

inability to get on with co-workers, and sexual indiscretions can lead to people losing their jobs or placed on suspension.

The purpose of the discipline is to get employees back in line with what is the agenda of the company or organization. In cases where violations have crossed a line, for the sake of the harmony and productivity of the business, individuals will be fired.

We accept that in the secular sphere, but we take a double-standard approach when it comes to the church. Why is that? Is it because the church is seen as a non-entity, an anachronism from the last century, or some kind of happy club?

The reality is when it comes to the unsaved, there is total prejudice when it comes to God and the church. If the wicked are unpunished, it means God is unfair, and if the wicked are punished, it means God is brutal. If there is a free-for-all in the church, then we are hypocrites, and if there is church discipline, we are controlling.

Jesus revealed the fickleness of the unregenerate soul when He said in Luke 7:33-34, *"For John the Baptist came neither eating bread nor drinking wine, and you say, 'He has a demon.' The Son of Man has come eating and drinking, and you say, 'Look, a glutton and a winebibber, a friend of tax collectors and sinners!'"* It is a case of "Damned if you do, damned if you don't."

Establishing the Right View of Church Discipline

As we look into the issue of church discipline, we must point out that it has nothing to do with trying to control people. I wonder if those in the secular world, on the outside looking in, realize just how hard it is to get people to do right much less to control them. I pity the pastor who seeks to make it his role in life to control people because it is an exhausting and fruitless task. In addition to the many hats he has to play, e.g., father, husband, Christian, psychiatrist, motivator, teacher, bus driver, games coordinator, etc. he must now add the hat of a dictator.

When God disciplined people in the Bible, it was for a far greater purpose than terrorizing the lives of individuals. As a matter of fact, despite the slanderous comments of non-Christians, God's discipline of people was done out of love, and when it comes to church discipline, the chief motive behind it ought to be love.

This may seem incredulous to some because when people think of love, they think of a gentle emotion where we do our best not to hurt people, where we are kind and sensitive, understanding, and sympathetic. Therefore, if one is perceived to be harsh or strict, then one isn't operating in love. While I do believe love can be kind, sensitive, and sympathetic, I think that love can be tough, and there is such a thing as "tough love."

There are times as a parent, being kind and sensitive isn't going to cut it, and "tough love" has to be applied. Does it mean that we hate our children? Absolutely not. Disciplining our children demonstrates that we love them. Hebrews 12:5-7 gives a great biblical example of the discipline of love. *"And you have forgotten the exhortation, which speaks to you as sons: "My son, do not despise the chastening of the LORD, nor be discouraged when you are rebuked by Him; for whom the LORD loves He chastens, and scourges every son whom He receives." If you endure chastening, God deals with you as with sons; for what son is there whom a father does not chasten? But if you are without chastening, of which all have become partakers, then you are illegitimate and not sons."*

We may live in a politically correct world today where the word 'illegitimate' is seen as a degrading word. Still, I have seen this play out in real life where children whose parents don't care one iota allow them to be out on the streets all hours of the night, to hang out with undesirables, do all kinds of destructive things, do drugs, get drunk, skip classes, and drop out of high school. The 'freedom' to let a child do whatever he or she wants to do is not love. The parents who love their children make sure that they are in at a decent hour, check on who they associate with, admonish them for poor grades, and see to it that they grow up to be respectable citizens. Thus, parents who love their children do discipline them.

King Solomon wrote in Proverbs 13:24, "He who spares his rod hates his son, but he who loves him disciplines him promptly." I wonder if when he wrote this in mind, he thought of his half-brother Adonijah of whom it was said, according to 1 Kings 1:6, that "…his father had not rebuked him at any time by saying, "Why have you done so?"

Adonijah grew up doing whatever he wanted to do without his father disciplining him at any time. As a result, he grew up thinking he could do whatever he wanted to do, and although he knew that Solomon was to be king, he would not be denied and anointed himself king, which almost cost him his life. Yet he still didn't learn from his mistakes and indirectly sought the kingship again by asking for his father's youngest concubine in marriage, a request that sealed his doom. A lack of fatherly discipline ultimately caused the untimely death of a son.

In my last two years in Jamaica, I had five young men that passed through my church in Mandeville end up in the local jail. In all five cases, they were all illegitimate, with only one having a slight relationship with his father. In most cases, their mothers were the only ones involved and treated them like little princes. None of them could take correction from me whenever I asked the question, "Why have you done so?"

The first one had the habit of calling me his father, but to my irritation, he never listened to anything I said. (It took me a while to realize when I'm called 'father' and my wife 'mother' it is because they are hoping we will support them financially the way we do our natural children.) I sat him down in church once and said, "You say I'm your spiritual father, and so, as a "father", I'm going to correct you on a few things…" I warned him that if he didn't change his ways, he would end up in prison. He didn't like what I had to say and left church.

Fast-forward three weeks later and he is in the local lockup where he was caught stealing a cell phone. Jails and prisons in Jamaica make correctional facilities in the West look like hotels. In this local lockup, men sleep on the hard floor with nothing but a few newspaper sheets as bedding. It is under the police station, so there is no natural light, and being in the tropics, it can get unbelievably humid and damp, and the smell of urine overpowers the senses. Prisoners have been known to die in custody, and violence between fellow inmates is common. You can forget about three square meals a day. If you want to get decent nourishment, you must request it from friends or family members who can only visit on Sundays and Tuesdays.

While this young man is in jail, he somehow gets a phone text through to me saying, "Pastor, I need your help. Can you bail me out? Also, can you bring me some cooked food, one loaf of bread, a bottle of syrup, soap, rag, towel, toothbrush, toothpaste…I don't like it here. It's not nice. Please help me. You are my spiritual father, and the only one I can depend on."

When I rebuked him the first time, I did it out of love because I knew what was going to happen to him if he continued down the path he was going. I could have easily left him alone to his own devices and been indifferent to his issues. I guess that's what counts for "love" these days, i.e., just to leave people to their devices, smile in their faces, and pretend that you care. But to confront and deal with their issues is to be uncaring and harsh.

But what else can you expect from a society where the family structure is increasingly breaking down? And this isn't just in Jamaica, but also all across Western civilization, where one significant consequence of the dysfunctional home has been a loosening of discipline. Personally, the most significant proof of the link between the breakdown of the home and the loosening of discipline can be seen within Afro-Caribbean and Afro-American families, families that were once known as no-nonsense disciplinarians.

There was a time when children who got in trouble at school also knew that they were in trouble at home. A few whacks of the principal's cane were coupled with a few belt strokes at home. Teachers and parents were allies in the training and admonition of children. But that was when the family structure was intact. In today's society, however, a rebuke from a teacher will result in a furious parent storming the school gates, ready to attack the teacher. Nowadays, children know that they can do what they want in school, with little repercussions as parents no longer view discipline the way they used to.

Therefore, it is only fair to say that you can understand why people today would have a problem with any kind of church discipline, as discipline in the home is almost non-existent.

The Righteous Justice of God

In the Bible, we see God confront wrongdoers many times resulting in severe chastisement for their behavior. While unbelievers may think that God is harsh for doing what He did, Psalms 7:11 says, *"God is a just judge,"* meaning that with God, the punishment fits the crime. God is not a human judge that gives a twenty-year sentence to a man who steals a bottle of milk but gives six months to a rapist. God grants true justice, and so the issue isn't the sentence that God gives but understanding the severity of the crime committed.

A great case to examine can be found in the book of Numbers, where Balaam, the prophet for hire, saw that he couldn't curse Israel and earn the wages that Balak, the king of Moab, had put aside for him. Not wanting to leave without being paid, Balaam realized that if he couldn't curse Israel, then the only solution was to get Israel to curse themselves. So he advised Balak to send in hundreds of sexually attractive Moabite women to the camp of the Israelites and get them to fornicate and, in so doing, curse themselves.

The plan worked exceedingly well, and as a result, a plague spread amongst the people killing 24,000 in the process. The plague only came to an end when Phineas, the grandson of Aaron, the high priest, took a spear and thrust it through the fornicating couple of Zimri and Cozbi.

Why this couple? Because according to Numbers 25:6, "...one of the children of Israel [Zimri] came and presented to his brethren a Midianite woman [Cozbi] in the sight of Moses and in the sight of all the congregation of the children of Israel, who were weeping at the door of the tabernacle of the meeting." Firstly, it was the brazen audacity of this man to bring the woman he was fornicating with right into the presence of the congregation who were crying over the sins the people were committing.

Secondly, both Zimri and Cozbi were children of leaders and thus examples. Numbers 25:14-15 says, "...Zimri the son of Salu, a leader of a father's house among the Simeonites...Cozbi the daughter of Zur; he was head of the people of a father's house in Midian." What brought the judgment was their influence and their brazenness. And as a result, they were judged, and the entire nation was spared.

Unrepentant Sin – The Spiritual Cancer of the Church

Cancer is one of the evilest of disease, and it occurs when cells in our bodies mutate and grow uncontrollably, creating tumors. It can spread throughout the body, ultimately killing its victims. You can't treat cancer with Aspirin or Pepto-Bismol, and when cancer reaches a particular stage, the best remedy for it is Chemotherapy. This treatment is almost as bad as the disease itself as it kills both healthy and diseased cells alike.

When you use Chemotherapy, you lose your hair, you tire frequently, you get sick, you can't keep your food down, you lose weight, and at times you look like death.

Why would a doctor treat you with such a severe remedy? Why would he prescribe medication that looks like it is making you worse than you were before? Why? Because the sickness is so bad, the only solution is a radical cure. If there were a more natural way to get the desired results, it would have been taken. No one takes Chemotherapy unless it is needed to deal with cancer. Think about it, if it were a simple case of influenza, the doctor would have prescribed Ibuprofen, and if it were heartburn, he would have recommended Nexium. But for the doctor to prescribe Chemotherapy means that the sickness is so bad there is no other choice.

Imagine if you were a seven-year-old child, and your mother told you that she was sick with something called cancer, but the doctor managed to catch it in time, and with the proper treatment, she will be cured and be back to normal.

As a seven-year-old, even though your mom looks okay, you take her word for it, but then you notice every time she goes to the doctor, she gets worse. At first, she tires easily, then she gets sick, then she can't eat, and she loses her hair. What is a seven-year-old supposed to think? It is quite likely that you would think that the doctor is making her sick and because you love your mother, you don't want her to go back to that mean old nasty doctor.

You would be forgiven to think in such a way because you didn't understand as a seven-year-old how serious cancer is, and as a result, you didn't realize just how radical the treatment of Chemotherapy was.

In the same way, some sins are devastating if they are allowed to run amok in the church, and thus, the treatment to contain those sins is drastic as well. You would conclude that God is harsh when you see things from a spiritually immature point of view. Still, if you were spiritually mature and understood the issues that preceded the judgment, you would see things entirely differently. When you are a seven-year-old child, you will hate the doctor for making your mother suffer, but when you are a twenty-two-year-old adult, you would be so grateful.

Paul – The Apostle of Tough Love

Consider Paul, a man with a passion for the church and a love for the people of God. There is no question that he sacrificed much for the cause of the gospel and ultimately paid the price for the gospel with his life. In almost all of his letters, one fact he points out is that he labors in prayer for them, and you can see that he was a man always checking up on the churches he started to see if they are holding on to Jesus.

He said disappointingly in 2 Corinthians 12:15, "…I will very gladly spend and be spent for your souls; though the more abundantly I love you, the less I am loved." The fact that his love for the Corinthians was not reciprocated didn't stop him from loving them and doing his very best for them. He didn't just love them because they loved him. That is the mark of true Christian love, of which Paul is a great example.

It is the same Apostle Paul who spoke of love so eloquently in 1 Corinthians 13:1-3, "Though I speak with the tongues of men and of angels, but have not love, I have become sounding brass or a clanging cymbal. And though I have the gift of prophecy, and understand all mysteries and all knowledge, and though I have all faith, so that I could remove mountains, but have not love, I am nothing. And though I bestow all my goods to feed the poor, and though

I give my body to be burned, but have not love, it profits me nothing."

And yet, this is the same man who spoke seemingly harsh words of instruction to the Corinthian church when it came to church discipline. 1 Corinthians 5:1-5 (TLB) says, "I hardly believe the report about the sexual immorality going on among you – something that even pagans don't do. I am told that a man in your church is living in sin with his stepmother. You are so proud of yourselves, but you should be mourning in sorrow and shame. And you should remove this man from your fellowship. Even though I am not with you in person, I am with you in the Spirit. And as though I were there, I have already passed judgment on this man in the name of the Lord Jesus. You must call a meeting of the church. I will be present with you in spirit, and so will the power of the Lord Jesus. Then you must throw this man out and hand him over to Satan so that his sinful nature will be destroyed and he himself will be saved on the day the Lord returns."

I am sure that many would consider these words "drastic". Consider the statements – "...you should remove this man from your fellowship." "...I have already passed judgment on this man..." "...you must throw this man out..." "...hand him over to Satan..." Can this indeed be the same man who speaks about love eight chapters later? How can a man who claims to love the church so much be so ruthless? Yet it is because he loves the church and the individual disciplined that he says what he says.

Before we go any further, I want to point out that church discipline is administered in different ways and for various reasons. There is no one size fits all approach. While there are guidelines in dealing with church discipline, we must be sensitive to the Holy Spirit's promptings.
We will get to these ways and reasons in due time. But because sexual immorality is perhaps the most significant reason for church discipline and it is the issue dealt with most clearly in the New Testament, this is the first area we will look at. Also, regarding sexual immorality, I will look at the theory behind the discipline, and afterward, I will highlight a few practical applications to make things even clearer.

Please note that many of the ideas expressed when dealing with sexual immorality will also be relevant in dealing with the other issues worthy of discipline.

Please also bear in mind that this is a mere chapter on discipline and not a book. There are so many different issues that can't be addressed in just a few short pages, but hopefully, what is written will be an essential guide for getting the ball rolling.

The Impact of Sexual Immorality on the Church

Paul continues in 1 Corinthians 5:6-7 (TLB) by saying, "Your boasting about this is terrible. Don't you realize that this sin is like a little yeast that spreads through the whole batch of dough? Get rid of this old "yeast" by removing this wicked person from among you. Then you will be like a fresh batch of dough made without yeast, which is what you really are."

The idea Paul illustrates is that unrepentant sexual sin in the church can spread like yeast through dough. If the "yeast" isn't removed immediately from the dough, the whole lot will be contaminated.

Here was a man utterly relaxed about being in church and sleeping with his stepmother. He feels no way about it even though non-Christian people would think his behavior disgusting. The church is proud of itself for showing how tolerant they are of people involved in sexual deviancy. How graceful they are! How kind and compassionate! The reality is that they don't see just how spiritually immature they are and how they have made the entire church vulnerable to one man's sin.

As a pastor, I have seen first-hand just how devastating sexual sin can play out in church. A couple fornicating in secret can open a door and release the demonic into the church. All of a sudden, other couples are struggling with lust and temptation, and some fall into fornication themselves. What on earth is going on? Why is all this craziness happening?

I can recall one occasion when I was a new pastor pioneering in Manchester, England, where a number of the men told me of their recent struggles with lust. I could understand one or two at different times, but when it was a number of them at the same time, I knew something was up. Sure enough, there was a dating couple in church fornicating in secret. Sadly, there was no need to discipline as they had already backslid in their hearts and with the truth revealed they left the church. But interestingly enough, the temptations these young men felt were suddenly gone.

The other problem in tolerating sexual sin in the church is that people in the church will follow their example. "Why should my girlfriend and I live in sexual purity when that guy is allowed to sleep around?" Pretty soon, everyone is doing it, and such a lifestyle becomes entrenched. Holiness is thrown out the window, and everyone becomes immoral while praising the Lord at church.

Isn't this what we regularly see in the church world? Some pastors live with women who they are not married to, and no one bats an eye. Choir members having children yet have no husband, and it is not seen as an issue. No one has a problem with a common-law relationship where man, woman, and children born outside of wedlock come every Sunday to worship.

No wonder church discipline is seen as so alien and foreign. How intolerant we must be of people's situation. The interesting thing is that churches that operate in this fashion do not see the destructive dynamic of sexual immorality that churches with a standard of holiness do. When several church people are involved in sexual immorality, there is not much more that another fornicating couple is going to do to it.

Living in Jamaica, one of the sad things I saw regularly is mentally challenged people living on the streets having nowhere else to go. They are frequently dirty and dressed in rags. Now, if I were to throw a cup of coffee on their clothes, it wouldn't make a difference, as their clothing is already filthy. I doubt anyone would notice there is a difference before or after. But had I thrown a cup of coffee on someone wearing all white, you could instantly see the difference.

It's a simple analogy, but it does explain the difference between a church with a standard of holiness and one without. Sexual immorality in a church already seeped in fornication doesn't make a difference in certain dynamics. However, sexual immorality in one that has a standard of spiritual cleanliness does. This is not to say that sexual immorality creates more dysfunction in a church known for holiness than a liberal one. The free-for-all church has all kinds of issues going on. Still, from a spiritually effective point of view, sexual immorality can impact church with a good standard of righteousness.

Disciplining the Unrepentant

Thus, when a church with a standard of holiness is 'infected' with the sin and cancer of unrepentant sexual immorality, there is no other remedy but spiritual Chemotherapy. The immoral person(s) must be removed, and in removing this individual from the church, the church accomplishes two things – (1) It protects the church from further spiritual infection and (2) it opens the door for the unrepentant sinner to be brought to repentance.
But before we go any further, I must define what is meant by unrepentant.

There is a vast difference in how we deal with repentant people and those who are unrepentant. I will give a more detailed definition of true repentance later but briefly, what I mean by repentant are those who have fallen into sin but recognize their faults and want to get things right. By unrepentant, I mean those who have fallen into sin, who may or may not acknowledge their faults, but do not want to get things right. They either want to continue doing what they are doing while enjoying all the benefits of church life or falling into the same sin without making serious efforts to stop.

There are three things necessary in dealing with the unrepentant sexually immoral. Firstly, the church has to judge the unrepentant sin of the person(s) involved. The apostle Paul said in 1 Corinthians 5:3 (TLB), "For I…have already judged…him who has so done this deed." The church has a responsibility to call a spade a spade. There can be no ifs or buts when it comes to certain types of behavior in the church. We are to call it what it is and not to try and sugar coat it or diminish its seriousness.

Judging the Sins of the Unrepentant

This is where even good churches struggle because they know that judging sin can create unwanted blowback. What if people in the community should find out? What if this leaks out on the Internet? What if the local newspaper gets a hold of it? Many good churches want to do the right thing but are afraid of the unwanted attention it may bring. Even Satan can get in on the act and deceive the unsaved (and members of the congregation) into thinking that this righteous act by the church is, in fact, unrighteous and un-Christian.

I think the irony is lost on non-Christians, as they pontificate to the church what they feel is real Christianity without having any clue as to how the Bible defines authentic Christianity. Possibly the most quoted verse in the Bible by non-Christians is, "Judge not". Don't ask them what goes before those words, don't ask them what comes after, and don't ask them to tell you where exactly in the Bible those words are, but they will say to you with great zeal and conviction, "The Bible says 'Judge not.'"

If they did know the Bible, they would realize that it gives certain conditions by which we can and should judge. The apostle Paul continues in 1 Corinthians 6:2-3, "Do you not know that the saints will judge the world? And if the world will be judged by you, are you unworthy to judge the smallest matters? Do you not know that we shall judge angels? How much more, things that pertain to this life?" Also, Christ clarifies His "judge not" statement in the rest of Matthew 7:1-6 and then adds in Matthew 7:20, "Therefore by their fruits you will know them." What He means is simply this, we know an apple tree because we can see the apples growing on it and while many citrus trees look alike, we can know for sure which one is which when we see the oranges, grapefruits, tangerines, limes, and lemons growing on them. In the same manner, we can determine who someone is by what they do. That's a fact.

The reality is that we all judge, including those who quote Matthew 7:1. There is no responsible parent in the world that will ask a total stranger from off the street to babysit her children while she goes out for the night. No right-minded investor will hand over his hard-earned cash to a shady looking businessman promising a 100% return on his investment in two weeks.

Any well-adjusted and right-thinking person will have to evaluate, assess, and ultimately judge when making certain decisions in life regarding people. You will have to make a decision, and sometimes you are right, and sometimes you are wrong, but you will have to judge whether someone is genuine or fake, trustworthy or unreliable, honest or dishonest. This is just an everyday part of life.

Businesses all across the world are involved every day in judging. When a manager interviews several people for a job vacancy, he or she will have to sit down and judge which of the candidates would be best suited for the job. If an employee violates specific protocols, a committee is consulted to look through the violations and judge as to whether that person should be fired, put on probation, or given a warning.

Yet when it comes to the church, everyone gets spiritual and says, "Judge not." The church doesn't only have the right but even more so than the world to judge because the spiritual destiny of lives is at stake. While a company is concerned about financial profits, the church is concerned about eternity. The stakes are much higher.

Let me make it clear that there is a difference between judgment and condemnation, and this is where the unchurched are confused. When we judge those who have fallen into sin, it is ultimately with the hope of restoration. To condemn is different, as it means to completely write off an individual giving them no hope of restoration.

That is why when we judge, we must judge correctly. Just as it is unfair to give a twenty-year sentence to a man who stole a loaf of bread, it is unfair to issue harsh discipline to those who could have been restored with far easier measures. We must judge whether the person who has fallen into sexual sin is truly unrepentant or if there is hope for repentance.

I have had individuals come to me who have fallen into fornication, and they come broken, humbled, and disgusted with themselves confessing what they have done. I will discuss church discipline for such people like these later, but restoring such individuals has been far easier. While as a pastor, we may have the right to be angry that they could do such a thing, we need to be very careful that we don't go into overkill and make matters worse.

"Quarantining" the Unrepentant

The second thing the church has to do after judging is to "quarantine" the unrepentant individual from contaminating the rest of the church. The apostle Paul said in 1 Corinthians 5:7 (TLB), "Get rid of this old "yeast" by removing this wicked person from among you."

Again, this is where the church faces fire from those who don't understand spiritual truths. It would be absurd to quarantine someone with a slight sniffle from public spaces. It would genuinely be a case of heavy-handedness. But if someone came down with a case of Ebola in the middle of New York, Tokyo, or Mexico City, it would be the responsible thing to separate that person from the rest of society to stop the disease from spreading.

No one is perfect, we understand that, and there is not a person in church who has not sinned at some point in time. A brother may have lost his temper and said something he shouldn't have or a sister might have resentment in her heart against a perceived slight or insult, but that isn't enough to put someone out of the church, even if they are unrepentant. But there are certain sins that when an individual commits there is no other choice but to do what the apostle Paul said in 1 Corinthians 5:5 (TLB), which is, "...you must put this man out..." Paul makes it clear that sexual sin is not like any other sin (1 Corinthians 6:18). For the sake of the health of the church, specific individuals have to be put out.

Let me just say that I don't find any pleasure in throwing someone out. As a pastor who has pioneered three times, I can honestly say that I want to see people come, and the last thing I desire is to see people leave. I can't believe any pastor who has a heart for people would ever want to tell someone that they can't come back for some time. I have not had to do it often, but the few times I have done it, I have done it with a heavy heart and much prayer.

I don't find any pleasure because I know that throwing the person out may be just the beginning of my problems. There are people in the church who don't understand my agony of telling someone they have to leave the church and believe that I, as a pastor, am unsympathetic and unloving. These may be friends or family members of the person being "kicked out", and they, in turn, end up leaving to find a more "loving" church where individuals will not be treated so harshly.

Then some may not have left but upset with me in their hearts, thus causing a breakdown in the relationship between them and me. This bitterness may stay there for many months or even years. When some other unfortunate incident happens in the future, the bitterness explodes, causing further trouble later on down the road. The funny thing is that those who have an issue with the discipline don't know that I have already calculated the possible fallout, thinking that I have done it without realizing the consequences.

Removal from Fellowship

The third thing Paul informs the Corinthian church to do is "...hand him over to Satan so that his sinful nature will be destroyed and he himself will be saved on the day the Lord returns." [1 Corinthians 5:5 (TLB)]. Many people fail to recognize the spiritual protection they have by being a part of the church. A few years ago, people were protesting in Britain over the vast sums of money spent on terrorism prevention. The logic was that since there was no attack on British soil, it meant spending all that money was a waste. Then-Prime Minister Tony Blair looked incredulous and said that it was because so much money was spent on preventing terrorism that there was no attack (Many changed their tune a year later when London suffered the terrible 7/7 terrorist attack in 2005 where fifty-two persons were killed and over 700 injured).

We fail to realize just how much protection God gives us behind the scenes. As a result, we come to the wrong conclusion that there are no such attacks, and we have nothing to fear. Paul tells the church to "...hand him over to Satan..." so that this man will feel what it is like not to have the protective power of the church over him. Then he will see what he had been taking for granted all that time.

The result is that the unrepentant man is going to feel the consequences of his sin, and Paul hopes that when Satan brings the heat, the offender will repent. Kicking someone out the church or in other words, handing him over to Satan, is the church's last option in getting a backslidden brother to repent. It is the drastic chemotherapy treatment of the spirit, only to be administered when every other option has failed. "...hand him over to Satan so that his sinful nature will be destroyed..."

When I put someone out of the church, it isn't a case of "good riddance to bad rubbish". It is with the hope that being out there in the world will make the unrepentant sinner feel the weight of his sin and feel what it is like being outside of fellowship. It is that he may feel very much like the prodigal son and like him come to his senses and realize how much he or she has lost due to his sinfulness and repent.

In the story Jesus gives of the prodigal son, He said in Luke 15:16-18, *"…he would gladly have filled his stomach with the pods that the swine ate, and no one gave him anything. But when he came to himself, he said, "How many of my father's hired servants have bread enough and to spare, and I perish with hunger! I will arise and go to my father, and will say to him, "Father, I have sinned against heaven and before you…"*

That is the hope the apostle Paul had, and that is the hope every real pastor has. As harsh as Paul's words may seem, it was for the ultimate good – his soul. "…hand him over to Satan so that his sinful nature will be destroyed and he himself will be saved on the day the Lord returns." [1 Corinthians 5:5 (TLB)]. Sometimes the only time you can help someone is by hurting him. It's not what you want to do, but for the greater good, you must. Paul says in 1 Corinthians 11:31, "For if we would judge ourselves, we would not be judged."

There is a slogan made famous by Tupac Shakur that says, "Only God can judge me." And the idea is that you can do whatever you want to do and no one else should be able to say anything to you. It is a foolish concept to live by because once God judges you, it is final. It is better man judges you here on earth so you can get your heart right and repent and so that you won't have to be judged by God. Better to face the discipline of the church here on earth than the judgment of God in the afterlife. As Paul in 1 Corinthians 5:5 (TLB) says, "…his sinful nature will be destroyed, and he himself will be saved on the day the Lord returns." By being judged here on earth, that man would be saved in heaven.

Discipline as "A Necessary Evil"

However, the sad truth is that many pastors and churches do not want the fallout of having to discipline people. Thus, they give the illusion of caring for people by allowing people to continue living in their sin without repentance. They project themselves to be loving, compassionate, and tolerant, and the world applauds them. Yet those under their care don't realize that their souls will be lost in eternity.

The courage of conviction lacks in many of today's churches, and that has made any church that genuinely cares about the souls of men vulnerable to attacks and criticism. But what we need to motivate and encourage us in these times of assaults is that we are saving lives, and when it is all said and done, the light and momentary afflictions we face will be worth it as we inherit the crowns that come with being soul winners for Jesus.

As I was writing these notes, a brilliant book written by Malcolm Gladwell called "David and Goliath" came to mind. Gladwell wrote about the origins of the cure for childhood leukemia and gave credit to two doctors – Dr. Jay Freireich and Dr. Tom Frei. During those days (the 1950s), Leukemia was an incurable disease, and the unfortunate children who contracted it bled to death. They would bleed out of every orifice in their bodies, soaking their sheets in blood. Internal bleeding into the liver and spleen would result in excruciating pain. Nurses would start their shifts in white uniforms and leave at the end in crimson red. Staff turnover was particularly high on the leukemia ward, as every child died an agonizing death. As one doctor said, "I would come home every day, completely destroyed psychologically."[16]

The cure for Leukemia was a mystery for many years because the children bled to death before a proper analysis of cancer could be diagnosed. But Dr. Freireich was a completely different doctor whose grating personality was such that people thought him callous and unfeeling. But his philosophy about being a doctor was about giving people hope. He said, "I was never depressed. I never sat with a parent and cried about a child dying."

To cut a long story short, Dr. Freireich firstly solved the problem of children bleeding to death by the radical idea of blood transfusions, convinced that bleeding lay in the children's blood and if given the blood of a healthy person the bleeding could stop. At first, the hospital refused to give blood from the blood bank, and so he went out and recruited his own donors. The bleeding stopped.

Then Dr. Freireich went about treating the cancer. There were only a few drugs at the time that had any effect on cancer, but it wasn't long-lasting, and in a very short time, the symptoms would return. The authoritative view then was that "drugs did more harm than good and they just prolonged the agony. The patients all die anyway."

What Freireich and Frei did was to combine all the cancer drugs (hence "cocktails") with the understanding that each drug attacked the cancer differently. They had nothing to lose since all the children would die

---

[16] p143, Chapter 6, David and Goliath, Malcolm Gladwell

nevertheless. This radical idea of using a cocktail of drugs was initially condemned as inhumane, and Freireich thought of as mad. There were so many side effects like paralysis, depression, and even comas, and one consequence for sure was the complete wiping out of the immune system.

Gladwell writes, "For their parents, it was agony. In order to have a chance at life – they were told – their child had to be brought savagely and repeatedly to the brink of death."[17] Freireich and Frei's gamble paid off, and Gladwell continues, "Today the cure rate for this form of cancer is more than 90 percent. The number of children whose lives have been saved by the efforts of Freireich and Frei and the researchers who followed in their footsteps is in the many, many thousands."[18]

I said all that to say this; there was a time when Leukemia was not treated because it was just too painful a disease to treat. The best thing was to be humane and comfort the sick as best as you could until the victim died. Freireich and Frei would have none of that. They had hope that they could beat the disease even if it made the victims go thur a living hell. While the "humane" doctors saw only the suffering, the "inhumane" Jay Freireich and Tom Frei saw beyond the suffering and saw it as a means to an end. They did it even if it meant having the entire medical profession against them.

As pastors and church members, we have a more critical role than curing cancer. We have been given a mandate by God to help people make heaven their home. People with Cancer may be cured of their sickness, and we thank God for that, but eventually, they too will die. The souls of men live on forever either in heaven or hell, and we must do our utmost to make men go the former and never the latter, even if it means subjecting them to something as harsh as church discipline.

In 2002, Dr. Robert Courtney was sentenced to thirty years in prison for selling diluted chemotherapy drugs. He made millions over the years diluting drugs and selling them to people who had a good chance of dying of cancer, knowing that the doctors treating the victims would never suspect that the drugs were diluted.

A few of his patients were happy with his treatment, as they didn't feel sick when they took the medication and, along with his charm and good manners, thought he was a good doctor. But the more experienced patients began to suspect something because they knew Chemotherapy should have its side

---

[17] p153, Chapter 6, David and Goliath, Malcolm Gladwell
[18] p154, Chapter 6, David and Goliath, Malcolm Gladwell

effects. It was the presence of side effects that would let them know that the drugs were working and when there was none, they began to have serious doubts.

The naïve and unsuspecting thought this doctor was doing them a favor, but those who understood how Chemotherapy should work, recognized something was wrong. Many naïve people attend churches that leave them in their sin, and they think that they are loved and cared for when they are neglected. It is those with a sense of discernment who know otherwise.

Disciplining with a Right Heart

While it may be a tall order, as much as it is possible with you, the ones who are going to feel this discipline must know that you love them. Church discipline must be tempered by love. It may be difficult to see or comprehend considering the discipline, and you may even be accused of hypocrisy, but the hope is one day they will understand what you are trying to do.

Love is essential because the discipline isn't supposed to be retribution, but a means to repentance. A friend of mine once told me that in the church he grew up in as a teenager, there was a case where a woman who confessed fornication was brought before the church board for discipline. This was an old-school legalistic holiness church where discipline was done in public, and though the woman was repentant and wanted to get her heart right with God, the church kicked her out permanently. What imprinted on his mind was the remorse of this woman and the cold-heartedness of the church board.

My prayer for us as a fellowship is that we would retain our tough stance on unrepentant sin without losing our compassion and love for the sinner.

Receiving Back into Fellowship

Church discipline is for redemption, not damnation. Sin must be revealed and addressed, and once the correction is given, sin must then be concealed and forgotten by extending forgiveness and mercy to the repentant. Once again, Paul provides us with an example of how to receive back into the "fold" the repentant sinner.

2 Corinthians 2:6-8 says, "This punishment which was inflicted by the majority is sufficient for such a man, so that, on the contrary, you ought rather to forgive and comfort him, lest perhaps such a one be swallowed up

with too much sorrow. Therefore I urge you to reaffirm your love to him."

Some wonder if Paul alludes to the incident we looked at in 1 Corinthians 5 or a new incident in a lost epistle. Whatever the case, the principles are still the same, meaning forgiveness must be extended to the repentant. We can see that this man is repentant because of the sorrow he has shown for his sin. He has now seen the light. He has seen how his sin has affected him, affected the church, and affected his relationship with God, and the revelation of these truths has caused him to grieve for his sin.

Paul emphasizes that we demonstrate our love for him through forgiveness and comfort to remind him that for all the tough discipline he had to endure, the people of God were still for him and wanted him to come back home. But he also gives another reason: while he may be genuinely sorrowful for his sin, Satan can exploit the situation and make him feel that he is too unworthy to return and that the church hates him for his sinful behavior. As a result of personal unworthiness, he would wrongfully perceive that he was unwelcome to return to the church or God.

In 2 Corinthians 2:10-11, the Apostle Paul says, "Now whom you forgive anything, I also forgive. For if indeed I have forgiven anything, I have forgiven that one for your sakes in the presence of Christ, lest Satan should take advantage of us; for we are not ignorant of his devices."

I have personally experienced this. There was an occasion when I had to throw out a young lady in her late teens for fornication. I had a few sisters check on her during the six months I had put her out, and after the six months, I rang her to see how she was doing, if she was living right, and if she wanted to come back. While she was doing right during that six months, she was angry with me feeling that I didn't care about her at all, as I hadn't spoken to her all that time, but after that phone call, she returned to church and became my biggest 'fan'. She saw that I did care, and as a result, Satan had no more lies to make her believe that I wanted nothing further to do with her.

Let us never forget that we do not operate in a spiritual vacuum. There are spiritual forces at work, and Satan would seek to exploit such situations for his purposes. We must not be "ignorant" but rather operate in wisdom if we are to right the wrongs of sexual immorality. While Satan is used by God to destroy the flesh, it is possible that he can go too far, and that is where a wise pastor functioning in love and forgiveness can keep the devil from going overboard.

God's people must also be prepared to receive back the repentant sinner. There are two types of church people that hinder the process of church discipline and restoration. The first is the borderline antinomian that fails to see the seriousness of specific sins. As a result, he thinks that the pastor is strict, unloving, and ungracious and should demonstrate the love of Christ by overlooking the violations of the sinning brother or sister believing that their "love" will make everything right. As John Lennon said, "All we need is love." It is 'love' like this that caused individuals like those in 1 Corinthians 5 not to repent. These are the ones that hinder church discipline.

The second is the legalist who views the fall of a brother or sister as committing the unforgivable sin. Such vile sinners should never step foot in church again. For the pastor to involve himself in the restoration of such individuals would make him, at the very least, a compromiser. Legalists may respect his authority as a pastor to allow the repentant to return, but don't expect them to make these "sinners" feel welcome. As a result, they give the repentant the cold shoulder and the icy stare. Should they turn up at the wrong fellowship, they receive a frosty reception. If they missed a church service, they would be reminded, "You of all people should know better after what you did." Thus, they can make the restoration of the repentant hard work indeed and are a hindrance to church restoration.

The Marks of True Repentance

There are three things I look for to see if someone is truly repentant. Unless these signs are seen, getting someone to mend their ways truly is going to be a long, painful, and possibly fruitless effort. Sometimes in our desperate hope to see someone restored, we can overlook things we ought not to, fooling ourselves that they would "get it" soon enough. Such wishful thinking may just prolong the agony and make things worse.

The first thing I look for is godly sorrow for their actions; godly sorrow as opposed to its counterfeit version, worldly sorrow. 2 Corinthians 7:9-10 states, "Now I rejoice, not that you were made sorry, but that your sorrow led to repentance. For you were made sorry in a godly manner, that you might suffer loss from us in nothing. For godly sorrow produces repentance leading to salvation, not to be regretted; but the sorrow of the world produces death."

Worldly sorrow is when someone is upset that they got caught, and the truth of what they did has been revealed to the universe. It's the woman who took naked selfies and sent them to her supposed boyfriend, who sent them to all his friends, the young man who made ridiculous statements on Facebook, causing him to be publicly mocked, the teenage girl who got herself pregnant while going to high school. Had things not played out the way they did, they wouldn't have regretted what they did.

But godly sorrow is when someone is genuinely sorry for what they did regardless if others found out. If no one else knew what he did, the fact that he disobeyed God was reason enough for him to be sorry. When someone has godly sorrow, the fact that she has sinned against God is more punishment than any consequences that came her way as a result of the sin. This leads to the second thing, and that is how people respond to discipline. Repentance is simply agreeing with God regarding our sin. When it comes to church discipline, we are dealing with sins that bring violation to the body of Christ, and as such, those who are genuinely repentant are those who see just how damaging their sins were. It isn't just a trifle that we can dismiss as if were nothing. Those who are genuinely repentant, therefore, are those who accept the discipline.

Thus, the question to ask yourself is, "Is there any evidence to show that the discipline was received correctly?" Some people, while they may admit they were wrong, can hit the roof when you suggest anything sounding like church discipline. They want you to treat the violation as it didn't happen or like it was a minor issue, and you can see they are not genuinely sorrowful because they do not see the gravitas of what they have done. Thus, dismissing the discipline as unnecessary shows that the full significance of the sin is not realized. The danger of that is the sin will most probably be repeated. If you can't honestly see the importance of the mistake you have made, it's most likely it will be made again.

When the prophet Nathan confronted David for his adultery with Bathsheba and his subsequent murder-by-proxy of her husband, Uriah, he repented of his sins. In Psalm 51:3-4, David cries out to the Lord, "For I acknowledge my transgressions, and my sin is always before me. Against You, You only, have I sinned, and done this evil in Your sight – that You may be found just when You speak, and blameless when You judge."

These aren't just cute words written to appease the righteous anger of a holy God. He truly meant these words because one of the disciplines David faced for his deception, adultery, and murder was the death of his son. 2 Samuel 12:14 says, "However, because by this deed you have given great occasion to the enemies of the Lord to blaspheme, the child also who is born to you shall surely die."

David, like any good father, tried to change God's mind through prayer and fasting beseeching for the life of his baby son. God would have none of it, and the child died, but David wasn't bitter or mad at God but accepted the ruling unbelievably well. 2 Samuel 21-23 says, "Then his servants said to him, "What is this that you have done? You fasted and wept for the child while he was alive, but when the child died, you arose and ate food." And he said, "While the child was alive, I fasted and wept; for I said, 'Who can tell whether the Lord will be gracious to me, that the child may live?' But now he is dead; why should I fast? Can I bring him back again? I shall go to him, but he shall not return to me."

These are powerful words that show the conduct and the attitude of the truly repentant. David didn't get into a huff and puff, trying to dismiss the seriousness of his actions. As much as it grieved him, he took the discipline like the man of God that he was. Yes, he made some serious mistakes, but he also took his punishment well.

This leads to the third sign; that is, you know when someone is truly repentant when they change. Zacchaeus, the tax collector, was willing to refund everyone he had cheated, the prodigal son was willing to work as a servant for his father, and Abraham was willing to put out his eldest son Ishmael. Those who are genuinely repentant are willing to put the effort in to complete their restoration. It may be painful, hard, and challenging, but they are eager to work hard to get back to where they were spiritually.

Many fail to realize just how much particular sins can impact their lives on a spiritual level. Fornication and adultery are sins that cause you to lose your moral compass, and you no longer see things as clearly as you used to.

Those who fall into sexual sins are unaware of the spiritual destruction that occurred in them. Over the years, I have observed individuals who have fallen to sexual immorality degenerate in other areas of their lives. While odd and erratic behavior isn't just the forte of the sexually immoral, it does seem to go hand in hand.

Coarse language, laughing at crude jokes, inappropriate speech, and out of character behavior seem to mark those who have fallen into sexual sin, and these activities can continue long after repentance. It does take a while before individuals can recalibrate themselves back to the people they once were. Restoration to one's former self, before the sin transpired, can take months and even years. For many Christians, we seek to go from strength to strength in our walk with Christ, but for those who have fallen into sexual sin, just getting back to who they used to be is a victory in itself.

Discipline and Ministry

This is one of the reasons why we ask people to step down from ministry when involved in sexual immorality. It's not simply a matter of shaming them in the eyes of their peers, but they genuinely need to be restored spiritually, and it is going to take much time and effort. The restored believer must reconnect and spend as much time with Jesus for his spiritual life to get back on track. It is a recalibration of the soul and spirit so that the Christian will be able to see the issues of righteousness, truth, and morality as clearly as they once did. It takes much prayer, reading of the word, fasting, soul searching, and communion with Christ to get back on track.

The process may take a while, but with hard work, it is more than possible in Christ. Recovery isn't a walk in the park, and it does take significant work on the part of the individual to get things back to the way it should be.

There was a time when Christian leaders who got caught up in adultery would do the honorable thing and resign. This would not only limit the damage caused, but it would also cause the leader to be able to reconnect with Jesus in a way he was unable to in the months (possibly years) he was in sexual sin. How can he effectively lead the people if he needs direction? How can he instruct people to do right when he has been doing wrong? How can he judge sin when his sin has not been judged? How can he give wise counsel when his moral and spiritual bearings have been eroded?

It takes a monumental amount of will power to give oneself over to true repentance, to receiving discipline, and to make the changes necessary for restoration. Ministry at this time is only a distraction. Sometimes a car can still run when there are all kinds of lights blinking on the dashboard, but the best thing to do is to bring it to the mechanic's repair shop and let it stay there for a while until all the issues are dealt with. Some people think that as long as it can still run, it doesn't matter until they find themselves at the side of the road on a lonely street with the sun setting over the horizon.

Since I'm on the topic of the disciplining of church leadership, I deviate slightly. A while back, I watched on the Internet a sermon of one of the most famous televangelists in today's church world. This was at a time when several moral failures regarding high profile pastors were revealed. There was much outrage and harsh criticism by people in the Christian community, and rightly so in some cases, as some of the pastors refused to step down from their large churches.

But in this sermon, the televangelist focused on the outrage and caustic denunciation of the people. We are the only soldiers, he said, that kill our wounded. He spoke eloquently and with great emotion of the need for forgiveness and love and compared the outrage of the people to a hostile mob running loose and destroying everything in its path. He may have swayed the crowd that night with the use of illustrative similes and metaphors, but I wondered how many would have thought as to why people would act like a hostile mob?

Mob justice is a frequent issue in Jamaica. Praedial larcenists, burglars, murderers, and pickpockets raise the ire of the local citizen, and often when the crowd catches such individuals, they are killed either by being beaten or chopped to death with a machete. But one of the main reasons why mob justice is so popular is that the justice system in Jamaica is inept in dealing with the escalating crime problem. According to statistics in 2014, less than half the serious crimes for that year remain unsolved.[19] When statistics are that bad people take the law into their own hands knowing that unless they do something about it, the criminals will walk free.

My point is that people act like a hostile mob due to a lack of justice. In the church world where pastors who are involved in adultery, homosexuality, fornication, and pornography are left where they are, with no form of discipline, people are going to believe there is no justice—the voice of the mob rises. Even in the church world, at least when it comes to leaders, people want to see that there is some sort of discipline enforced.

The Wisdom of Damage Control

Church discipline can be a messy affair, and Satan will use such issues to create as much havoc in the church as possible. There have been several occasions where I have heard people say, "I didn't like how the situation was handled," and the truth is that when it comes to sexual sin, especially adultery, we are dealing with a mess. There is no perfect way to "handle" such situations. Sin is messy, and Satan is always on the lookout to make things even messier.

If there is a more effective way to deal with church discipline, I would like to know because I often didn't like how the situation was handled either. There are so many variables outside of my control. So many spiritual IEDs that Satan detonates at all the stages through to restoration. Just when you thought you got the handle on things…"BOOM!"

---

[19] http://jamaica-gleaner.com/gleaner/20140711/lead/lead9.html

There is no such thing as the perfect church because there is no one in the world who is entirely without sin. It only shows just how fallen a world we live in because the truth about righteousness is that living in it makes life so simple, and yet the world has not managed to figure that out. Sin is what complicates matters, and we see just how lost people are by the complicated lives that they live.

When you find sin, you find a mess, and you also find that Satan is not too far behind. As long as people are in church, you will always encounter issues, but the greater the sins, the more complicated church life becomes, and sexual immorality is one of those issues that bring great complications.
As ministers of the gospel, it behooves us to pray for our churches and pray for our members that they fear God and have a revelation of sin so that they can live righteous lives and keep complications down to a minimum.

As pastors, we have to preach on sin, not because we have an ax to grind or give churchgoers indigestion before their Sunday afternoon meal but because we know just how more comfortable life can be when people live clean.

But I also believe we need to preach and teach on church discipline regularly. We may not have to make it a whole sermon every time but enough to keep people informed and aware. It is better to prepare people beforehand before there is even a whiff of sexual immorality in the church so that when it does come (and believe me, it will), the church will be equipped to handle it. Unpreparedness opens the doors to ignorance, and ignorance is the devil's playpen.

We may not be able to convince everyone about the importance of church discipline and restoration. The apostle Paul himself couldn't (2 Corinthians 2:6). But we may be able to convince the majority, and in so doing, they will work with us when it comes to administering the discipline and also when it comes to restoring the fallen.

Another thing a pastor can do to limit the damage of unrepentant sexual immorality is to walk in wisdom to deal with this sin. I have met some overzealous pastors in my time who, in their zeal, make matters far worse than it already is. They are going to let their church and the sexually immoral know how they are not going to be like the lukewarm churches in the flaky religious world that tolerate that kind of stuff. No, sir, they are going to knock this thing on the head and let everyone know that they are real men of God who stand up for righteousness.
This is a disastrous mindset because inadvertently, a David-Goliath syndrome is created where the pastor is Goliath, and the sexual immoral is

David. While the pastor may be right, the reality is you can make the person under discipline look like a victim, and I don't care what part of the world you come from, everyone supports the underdog, even if the underdog is in the wrong.

The ancient Roman historian Tacitus gives a great illustration that back in the late first century AD, "Nero charged and tortured some people hated for their evil practices – the group popularly known as "Christians." The founder of this sect, Christ, had been put to death by the governor of Judea, Pontius Pilate when Tiberius was Emperor. First, those who confessed to being Christians were arrested. Then, on information obtained from them, hundreds were, convicted, more for their anti-social beliefs than for fire-raising. In their deaths they were made a mockery. They were covered in the skins of wild animals, torn to death by dogs, crucified or set on fire – so that when darkness fell they burned like torches in the night…As a result, although they were guilty of being Christians and deserved death, people began to feel sorry for them. For they realized that they were being massacred not for the public good but to satisfy one man's mania."[20]

Though the ordinary Roman thought that Christians were evil and worthy of death, they earned his sympathy because of how Nero treated them. Those in the church who know that the sexual immoral must be disciplined can be swayed when the pastor acts like Goliath (or Nero). Thus the danger of going in too militant is that you make a "cause célébré" of the individual, which can cause the opposite of what you hoped to achieve, and that is the person no longer has a desire to repent because of all the moral support.

Never forget that as ministers of reconciliation, we carry a scalpel, not a sword. A scalpel is for surgery, and surgeons use it to cut unwanted tissue out of the body like tumors and ulcers so that the body can heal and function normally again. A sword is for war and is used to bring death and destruction.

People root for the underdog; so, don't make the person you hope to discipline look like a martyr because this is one battle you will lose if you do not use wisdom. You must learn to operate in wisdom and take the sting out of the situation; otherwise, Satan will have the advantage.

General Examples

From time to time in the ministry, you will find either an individual or a

---

[20] Tacitus, Annals 15.44

couple involved in sexual immorality. Obviously, with the individual, he or she is involved sexually with someone outside of church. It could be that the individual was involved in a sexual relationship before he or she made a decision for Christ. Still, the other person in the relationship chose not to become a Christian.

If that individual is a recent convert, as a pastor, I give a bit of time for that new believer to come to terms with that relationship, even working with the unsaved person in the relationship. Still, there comes a time when enough is enough. A decision needs to be made whether that individual will live for Jesus or continue the relationship.

A decision has to be made because somewhere along the line, things will get messy if you don't. Many new converts know in their hearts that having a sexual relationship outside of marriage is a no-no for the church, and they don't have to be reminded of that truth. But the time will come if a decision isn't made when the individual starts to become comfortable living a dual lifestyle and lose the conviction he or she originally had.

It is at this junction in the road that an ultimatum needs to be made. He or she will either have to leave the other person or have to leave the church. As much as we love them and want to see them make it to heaven, the reality is that living in fornication means they are no longer saved. The apostle Paul makes that very clear when he said in Galatians 5:19-21, "Now the works of the flesh are evident, which are: adultery, fornication…of which I tell you beforehand, just as I also told you in time past, that those who practice such things will not inherit the kingdom of God (emphasis mine)."

Living in fornication is practicing 'such things'; therefore, those who do so 'will not inherit the kingdom of God'. With this person choosing to continue to live such a lifestyle, we have lost the battle for their soul (hopefully temporarily), and now we have to move into damage control mode, that is, stop the infection from spreading. Sadly, it is easy for others in the church to misinterpret the grace shown to a new convert as a license to sin. As a result, people in church need to see that there is a standard of holiness that must be maintained and that sexual immorality will not be tolerated, even though we are trying to reach out and help people. In the battle to save one, we can't afford to lose others.

Then some unmarried individuals have been in church long term who somehow have fallen into a sexual relationship with someone on the outside. It may seem contradictory because it can seem harder and easier to deal with at the same time. It is harder because of the possible bonds of friendship and fellowship you had with such an individual. At the same time, it is easier because they already know the standards for sexual immorality.

How do you help a woman attending church for years but despair of her chances to get married? What happens when she meets someone on the outside, whether at work, at school, or play, through a family member or friend? Desperation is a powerful thing, and it can lead to deception. As a pastor, thinking with a clear head, you know that the odds are that the relationship will not last, and there is a possibility she will become a single mother, but that's information she is not willing to receive. This is perhaps, in her mind, her last chance at happiness.

I can recall such an incident when a long-term sister fell for a low life snake-in-the-grass. This man already had a few children with different women and just three years previously tried to seduce a young fifteen-year-old girl in our church. I pointed out to her that she was going to be his next "baby-mama" if she wasn't careful, something that she reported back to him, and as a result, I received a tirade of personal insults from the man via text messaging.

At this point, I had to put the sister out the church, and the "gentleman" pointed out to me that she was doing fine in the church he was attending and that the people in his church were far more loving than we were and 'supportive' of her. It didn't take too long for her to get pregnant, and he is no longer on the scene. Her dream of marriage failed to materialize, she is no longer at his church, and she is a single mom. Sadly, it was an accident waiting to happen. Perhaps the only good to come out of it was that others saw and took heed.

One of the joys I have, as a pastor, is to see a young couple come to church and give their lives to Jesus. This being the age that we live in, the age of cohabitation, it is not surprising to find out that they are not married, but no problem, I have high expectations that they will make right decisions and why not? As a pastor, I must have hope for people. And I have seen couples in similar situations turn things around and make things right with each other and with God, and go on for Jesus. Just because they are a couple doesn't mean that they should get married because people can be together for a myriad of reasons. But I have to make it clear that they can't be living together and still be a part of the church.

Again, it's not because I want to be a bad guy, but understanding the dynamics of leaven, and at the same time wanting to see this couple make it, I am living under tension. In one direction, I am pulled by the spiritual health of the church. In the other, I am drawn by the potential of this couple. But it is a tension that can't go on forever. In this time of tension, my prayer is that they will get enough of Jesus in them so that they can see for themselves that they can't go on like this.

My first bit of advice would be to tell them to split up for a while and let them individually focus on Jesus. I think this is a good idea. If they do have a future together, it would be right that the first love in their lives would not be each other but Christ. It makes a world of difference in a relationship. But even if they do not have a future together, at the very least, they would have established a personal relationship with Jesus.

I have seen, over the years, couples who did not disconnect from each other and connect with Christ, and in many cases, as the months went by, they ultimately disconnected from each other and sadly never connected to Christ. Sexual relationships outside of marriage are transient, and while we may fear the reproach of breaking a couple up, the odds are that the relationship would have broken up anyway. It is easy to blame a church over something that given time would have fallen away nevertheless.

Then some come to church strictly to prey on vulnerable individuals. I have had several guys, especially in Jamaica, who came to church simply to look for young girls. They sit like zombies through the service but come alive afterward, and when they think no one is looking, they ask the young ladies for their phone numbers. I will be straight up with them and tell them in no uncertain terms that while they are welcome to come, under no circumstances will they be allowed to talk to the young ladies, and if they don't like it, they can leave. As a pastor, I have a responsibility to protect those who come to my church.

When I first started the church in Jamaica, we had several young men coming at the very beginning. Then we had our first female, which we prized, and tried our best to work with. She was from a religious background; her stepfather was a pastor, and she always had bible questions to ask, which made me assume she was very keen. The problem was that the boys were all fighting over her, which I thought was because she was the only female in the church.

Unbeknownst to me, she was not only seducing them individually but also playing them against each other. I only found out when one of the boys told me what she was up to, and her stepfather, who told me of her frequent rendezvous with men, confirmed this. Here were young men giving their lives to Jesus only to be sexually exploited by someone in church. I had to put her out, and I told her she could not come back until she repented of her immorality (She came back to visit eighteen months later, but by then, the church's dynamics had changed, as we had a batch of young women coming. On seeing that she was no longer the only female in church, she never returned).

Disciplining the Repentant

Much of what I have written in the pages previously can be gleaned to find the necessary information to help those who have fallen into sexual sin but are repentant. There is no need to go over the principles of godly sorrow, having a positive response to discipline, and a willingness to change. But there are a few things I would say in addition to these principles.

While we are not to condone sin, at the same time, we don't have to declare them from the rooftops either. What I am saying is that keeping things quiet doesn't mean we are covering up sin. Some people think that unless the indiscretions committed by individuals in church are exposed to the general congregation, it must mean that we are trying to keep it on the hush and pretend as if nothing is going on. To them, it stinks of hypocrisy.

My answer is if an individual is repentant and feels the shame of what they have done, what benefit is there to expose him or her to more disgrace? Whether we like it or not, certain actions can mark people for life. Even though they may have repented, changed, and moved on, some people are like elephants, that is, they never forget. Some will never allow those who have fallen but restored to move on. Failures made five or ten years ago are relived in gossip as if it were yesterday.

Church discipline is a means to an end, and if the end is accomplished, there's no reason why the world needs to know. Wisdom dictates that some things be kept private. Otherwise, they become distractions. It's bad enough that the individual and Satan will remember the mistakes, so why should we make things worse by informing the church busybodies (every church has them)? Therefore, apart from a few individuals on a need to know basis like a church council, things that can be kept quiet should be kept quiet.

Wisdom would also dictate that it is best never to talk casually about people who've been put out of the church to those who are in the church because we are ministers of hope. Our comments can filter to the ears of those who have been put out, making them less likely to return. The message we must give to the church by our actions is that we never write people off.

Don't give the negative a platform. Never give the negative the attention it doesn't deserve. At any given time, any church already has a myriad of issues that it is dealing with, and we don't need to increase it with unnecessary nuisances.

The Hope of Church Discipline

After one revival service at a church I had previously pastored, I talked with a lady who had been there since her late teens. She reminded me jokingly that I had thrown her out of the church many years before for sexual immorality, and I had almost forgotten about it until she reminded me (To be honest, I felt a bit weird and uncomfortable when talking about it). Then I remembered throwing her out, and I remember being sad at the time because she had brought more people to church than any other person.
I asked her what was going on in her mind when I told her to leave for six months. Bear in mind that she was no longer an insecure teenager looking for love in all the wrong places, but now in her 30s, married, a mother, a university graduate, and a department store manager.

She said, "I don't think you treated me horribly. I think you did what you felt was right for the church, and I understand that. You have to remember, Pastor, all that I have been through and where I have come from. The Potter's House and the people in it were all that made sense. I never knew what it was to really serve God till I came to the Potter's House, and when I got the revelation before backsliding, I said I would never go to another church. The church didn't save me, but the church helped me to remain saved. I think in regards to church discipline, people are different, and people will take it in different ways. The person has to have a real understanding of God's word and what church discipline is all about. You have to remember, Pastor, that it's best to kick that one person out than them poison the whole church. I thank God you did discipline me because I had my time in the world, and it's not nice. My life is a testimony of how great God is; nothing I have can I claim as a work of my hand because my life is a living miracle. Today (her birthday) has been a day of reflection for me and how blessed I am in more ways than one. And I thank you, Pastor, for never giving up on me. For that, I'm forever grateful."

Ultimately it is the salvation of the soul that matters, and while I have had my fair share of criticisms, testimonies like these are the ones that encourage me that I am on the right track.

Other Vital Areas

There is much to learn about the discipline and restoration of saints who have fallen into sexual immorality that can be used in other areas. Another main area in which the New Testament addresses the issue of discipline is when it comes to false doctrine.

The apostle Paul made a similar declaration to the one in 1 Corinthians 5 when he spoke to his disciple, Timothy, about an issue he had to deal with. In 2 Timothy 2:16-18, he says to Timothy, "But shun profane and idle babblings, for they will increase to more ungodliness. And their message will spread like cancer. Hymenaeus and Philetus are of this sort, who have strayed concerning the truth, saying that the resurrection is already past; and they overthrow the faith of some."

In a very similar theme, the apostle pointed out that false doctrine is just as deadly an issue as sexual immorality. While the word picture he uses for sexual immorality is leaven and that for false doctrine is cancer, the idea is one and the same – they are destructive forces that can spread quickly and, if not contained, can bring havoc and destruction.

Hymenaeus and Philetus are men, previously in the church, who got caught up in error, teaching that the resurrection has past and as a result, they destroyed the spiritual lives of the naïve and undiscerning who took heed to their message. When Paul heard about it and confronted Hymanaeus, he was unrepentant, and as a result, the apostle had to bring spiritual discipline. Paul wrote to his young disciple in 1 Timothy 1:19-20. He said, "…having faith and a good conscience, which some having rejected, concerning the faith have suffered shipwreck, of whom are Hymenaeus and Alexander, whom I delivered to Satan that they may learn not to blaspheme."

In 1 Timothy, Paul expresses the same idea as we had previously seen in 1 Corinthians 5. Because Hymenaeus wouldn't repent (no doubt due to pride, as many bound by false doctrine, seem to have), Paul had no choice but to put him out of the church and, therefore, out of spiritual protection for Satan to whip him into repentance.

Like sexual immorality, false doctrine is an issue we still have to contend with in churches today. Being evangelical churches reaching out to the communities and town centers in our cities, we are bound to attract people who have kooky ideas and beliefs. Moreover, genuine converts can pick up funky teachings from an acquaintance or the Internet and bring that nonsense into the church. Over the years, I have had to deal with all kinds of dangerous and damaging doctrines such as Calvinism (Reformed Theology), Seventh Day Adventism, Oneness Pentecostalism, Black Hebrew Israelites, and all sorts of self-created and warped beliefs.

I must say that unlike sexual immorality, there is usually an agenda with false doctrine. In most cases of sexual immorality, those involved have no other thought than to be with each other. As far as they are concerned, it is a situation that affects only them, and what makes them mad is the idea of the church getting involved in what seems to be a private matter. In false doctrine, there is an actual plan to spread that teaching to as many people that can be reached.

In many cases, you will have individuals looking for churches in which they can express their ideas. For those on the outside seeking to have expression within, it usually happens in only a few ways. They look for smaller churches, either pioneer works or churches that have seen better days. In both cases, the leadership structure is much smaller, and the church less organized, and as a result, there is less cohesion within the church. In both cases, the pastor or elder(s) do not have the respect and trust of the people. In a pioneer setting, this is usually because most of the attendees are new in the faith, have no real understanding of the pastor's role, and lack relationships that would inspire trust in the leadership. In older decaying churches, many issues have happened over the years, and as a result, the church is now vulnerable.

I can recall pioneering my very first church and seeing this take place. We had four visitors, two married couples, who made it a point to visit and attempt to deviate the services in their direction. In the regular services, they sat with a glazed and vacant look but come alive at the end of service.

In the mid-week Bible studies, they would try to turn the study to what they wanted to talk about. It didn't matter what the topic of discussion was that night, they would seek to veer the conversation off course, and I would have to bring it back. I was only a new pastor in my second year of ministry and didn't have much experience in that sort of thing, and so it was a bit of a tug and war initially.

Their biggest bone of contention was that I was working a job while pioneering, which meant that I lacked faith in God's ability to provide. It was a hard battle trying to convince them, but by the grace of God, I learned that the older couple had convinced the younger couple to sell their home, and all four were living off the proceeds. Armed with this revelation, they were discredited in the eyes of my converts. Had it been now, with many more years of experience in the ministry, it wouldn't have gotten that far, but I was able to at least keep damage to a minimum.

Another church up the road wasn't so lucky, and these folks were able to create all kinds of mayhem. It was a church that had revival years before but had been decimated by infighting. A lack of cohesion created the perfect atmosphere for this couple to do their wicked work (I learned a few years later that this same older couple had destroyed one of our pioneer works in London).

Then you have others who look for larger congregations to go about their nefarious activities because, in larger churches, you can hide in plain sight. About two years later, when the church had grown significantly, I had a Seventh Day Adventist visit a few times, and it was at his second to last visit, I heard he was trying to teach the Sabbath to the new converts. The next visit was his last as I publicly rebuked him in the presence of the entire church. I told him his false doctrine would not be tolerated and that he would be asked to leave if he kept talking nonsense. He got the message, left, and never returned.

I usually don't name and shame people in public, but I had to do it for the sake of the new converts. This man was covertly trying to find naïve and undiscerning people to sway, and I had to expose what he was doing before everyone. He knew what he was doing, and he had to know that as the shepherd of that congregation, I was looking out for God's sheep.

Personally, it is a waste of time to try and convince someone who has believed false doctrine for a long time and has come to the church intending to "enlighten" the pastor and everyone else. Maybe on the odd occasion, as the Spirit leads, one could, but in most cases, the best thing to do is to show these people the door. You aren't going to convince them, and hopefully, they won't convince you, but more importantly, leaving them in the church will only allow them to influence others. You may be able to watch them during the church service, but anything can happen outside those four walls between Monday and Saturday. You'd be amazed at how naïve new converts can run into these people during the week, and because they met in church and hearing how "spiritual" they sound, in naïveté, they will give them all the time they need to share their spiel. Then you will be shocked to find out your best new convert is now in the Oneness Pentecostal Church.

While I said these people are almost always agenda-driven, sometimes they are not aware of the agenda they are driving. While some come intentionally, others come, not realizing Satan has sent them. There have been times when I have seen such people come to church, genuinely like being there, but they are full of funky teaching that they can't help but share. In most cases, we will never convince them, and while we may be full of compassion for them, we need to remember that the converts come first, and it is best to tell them to make it like a tree and leaf.

It is easier to deal with false doctrine from those without, but what happens when the issue is within? What happens when a good convert goes funky? What happens when that young disciple gets influenced by a Reformist rapper? What happens when your song leader starts believing in a post-Tribulation rapture? What do you do then? This isn't some weirdo off the streets. This is someone with relationships and influence within the church.

I believe prevention is better than cure, and while I cannot give a spiritual silver bullet to deal with this issue once and for all, the first thing I suggest is arming yourself with the knowledge of God's word. I have learned over the years that credibility with people comes by knowing what you are talking about. While I am no scholar, I have made it my business to know what the Bible teaches about fundamental doctrines of the faith and to preach them so that people are convinced that I know what I believe.

But that is not enough. You need to establish real relationships with people within the congregation and not just the superficial greeting of people during services. Relationships lead to trust. As a result, when someone with false doctrine comes in, because people trust you, they will also trust what you have to say, even if they don't fully understand the issues.

Whenever false doctrine spreads through people in the church, you can be sure that the infrastructure driving the false teaching forward is relationships. Thus, the critical ingredients needed to avert spiritual disaster is a greater level of relationships with people and a superior understanding of the word of God.

Not just that, because you may succeed in removing the offender from the congregation, but the relationships he or she has with others will cause others to leave. As far as possible, let us not get so caught up in church duties and activities that we lose sight of the people we claim to be ministering to. Proverbs 27:23 says, "Be diligent to know the state of your flocks, and attend to your herds..." I understand churches can grow to such a size that it is impossible to build relationships with everyone in the congregation adequately. Therefore, build solid relationships with the men and women who do most of the heavy lifting in the church and, in turn, instruct and teach them to build equally solid relationships with others below them.

The wise pastor is the one who is not so caught up in legitimate kingdom affairs that he neglects to keep his finger on the pulse. Spiritual intuitiveness and discernment are critical ingredients in damage limitation. The ability to see potential land mines before they blow up is a great gift indeed. I would also say be on the lookout for bitter, resentful, and unforgiving people as that can be an open door to false doctrine. In such people, the issue isn't even the doctrine but rather some grievance they have, and sub-consciously they have embraced false doctrine to create contention and spiritual sabotage to the church.

But let us suppose the worst has happened and that a good disciple has gone sour. What do you do? We know the apostle Paul said in Titus 3:9-11, "…avoid foolish disputes, genealogies, contentions, and strivings about the law; for they are unprofitable and useless. Reject a divisive man after the first and second admonition, knowing that such a person is warped and sinning, being self-condemned." But rejecting such an individual is going to lead to severe repercussions.

This is where pastoring gets tough, and we have two choices – not a good one and a bad one, but a bad one or an even worse one. The bad one is dealing with the issue head-on and dealing with the potential fallout, but the worse one is putting your head in the sand, leaving it, and letting the radioactive teaching contaminate the entire church.

Dealing with Less Drastic Issues

In the New Testament, there are very few examples of church discipline other than those outlined. Still, I believe a general rule of thumb when considering church discipline is facing issues that affect the body of believers within a church. Certain issues may require little or no discipline, and we have to differentiate between that and real issues affecting the congregation.

Just because there are individuals who dislike the pastor or are obnoxious and have behavioral issues, it doesn't mean that they have to be put out of the church. Granted, some people need a good talking to, but it may not necessarily be a major issue. I have heard of pastors throwing people out of the church for no other reason than those people have a problem with headship. I understand rebellious people can be an issue that must be dealt with as they can affect the body in general, but sometimes, the issue doesn't have anything to do with the church but some kind of conflict between that person and the pastor.

Pastors can overstep their biblical authority simply because their egos have been bruised. The Lord knows that I have met people over the years in my ministry who have rubbed me the wrong way, who have been obnoxious, rude, and disrespectful. Not only to me, but people within the congregation, and yet their violations have not reached a level where being put out is justified.

Just because someone disagrees with your decision in a building project or a church strategy doesn't mean that there should be an inquisition. Ringing up members of the congregation just to hear what John Brown said of his displeasure at you moving the summer outreach across town is overkill. Rebuking men in the church for disloyalty, who heard John Brown say what he said, but never reported that back to you is way over the top.

We have to make a distinction between what is just an irritant on our part and what affects the body of Christ. Believe me, there are real battles to fight so it would be wise on the pastor's part not to be fighting on the wrong battlefield. It is possible to use a sledgehammer to smash a walnut when a simple nutcracker would do.

Unwise pastors misuse their authority and, in so doing, build up animosity amongst good people in their churches. As a result, when people leave over what seems to be a minor issue, the pastor fails to realize that it was simply the straw that broke the camel's back. He, however, doesn't learn from his mistake, having failed to see his flaws, concluding that those people were rebels and bad people to begin with. Being "El Pastor" doesn't make you infallible, and you should tread very carefully with the people God has given you the privilege to shepherd.

The apostle Paul gives us some help for issues not as dangerous as false doctrine or sexual immorality, but more serious than whining church members. In 2 Thessalonians 3:6, he says, "But we command you, brethren, in the name of our Lord Jesus Christ, that you withdraw from every brother who walks disorderly and not according to the tradition which he received from us." This is something I have rarely seen practiced in any church because withdrawing from anyone seems rude on our part, and we don't want to be seen as rude.

In context, the apostle Paul is dealing with lazy individuals with questionable work ethics. Still, I believe the principle applies to those who are disorderly in other areas of Christian living. Being created as social creatures, we crave and feed the relationships we have with others, and nothing affects our psyche than being disfavored by the collective. The point of this discipline is not to make anyone feel like scum or a pariah but to point out to them the errors of their ways and to let them understand such behavior won't be tolerated in the church setting.

The apostle further explains in 2 Thessalonians 3:14-15, "And if anyone does not obey our word in this epistle, note that person and do not keep company with him, that he may be ashamed. Yet do not count him as an enemy, but admonish him as a brother." We are not to ostracize those individuals but to let them know that while we love them, there is a price to pay to have good relationships, and part of the price is to keep in line with God's word.

Spiritual relationships are a big deal in the Bible. One of the reasons for that is just how easily unrighteous people can corrupt good relationships. 1 Corinthians 15:33 says, "Do not be deceived: "Evil company corrupts good habits."" You would be amazed at how good people become twisted and cynical by associating with the wrong people in church. As a result, the Bible gives drastic cures for bad associations.

Consider the apostle John's words in 2 John 2:9-11, "Whoever transgresses and does not abide in the doctrine of Christ does not have God. He who abides in the doctrine of Christ has both the Father and the Son. If anyone comes to you and does not bring this doctrine, do not receive him into your house nor greet him; for he who greets him shares in his evil deeds." Talk about serious! And yet, once again, the seriousness of the apostle's words shows just how grave the situation is! We can't just have a blasé attitude towards church issues and hope that love will make a way.

While I understand that pastoral abuse is real, I have to say that the ignoring of discipline is a far bigger issue in the church today. The reason for that is while pastoral abuse makes its way into the headlines, lack of church discipline isn't even recognized as a problem. In today's church, both members and leaders know the various spiritual and moral dysfunctions running riot in the church but have a "leave it to Jesus" attitude. They spiritualize their cowardice by saying, "We are leaving it to the Holy Spirit" when the word of God clearly instructs us on what to do.
If leaving it to the Holy Spirit is the right thing to do, then why did the writers of the New Testament instruct the various churches to get a grip on these issues?

Closing Thoughts

Ultimately, church discipline is the last resort in our attempt to keep harmony in the church. The apostle Paul goes through great lengths in the New Testament to speak about the harmonious church. When he speaks of those "who walks disorderly," he speaks of individuals who, according to the Greek, are "out of line", "out of place", and in a military sense, "out of the ranks".

One of the most impressive things to watch in a Russian military parade is how in step all the soldiers are. Imagine if one in the ranks begins to practice his moves amidst a field of harmony? It is a given that all eyes will focus on what was once a well-coordinated effort to the aberration in the midst.

A harmonious church is a healthy church; it is a growing church; it is a vibrant church that reflects the nature of Christ and shines a light into this dark world of disharmony and sin. In a sense, the pastor is the conductor whose role it is to keep the orchestra together playing beautiful music. But all it takes is for one violin to play a different tune, and while every performer is doing their best, one wrong note can veer the entire symphony off track.

Many times, the undiscerning public may subconsciously realize something is not quite right. Still, it is the trained ear of the conductor who can know precisely where the deviation is coming from and therefore address it.

The truth is that everyone wants to be in the orchestra, but some want to play their own tune. It is our role to make sure that the music of Christ is being played and that those who want to be involved are playing it. The church is not a free for all for individuals to be doing their own thing. A culture must be established in the church where people know that there is a part expected of them. I am always amazed at people who like what we do but who don't want to be who we are. The only reason we do what we do is because we are who we are. They like the music but fail to realize if they don't play the same tune, the same music they love will be done away with.

I once heard a definition of a good coach is getting athletes to do what they hate to create what they love. No boxer enjoys getting up in the cold at 4am for a morning run, and they hate having to live solely on chicken breasts and vegetables to make weight. But when the final bell is rung, he loves to have his hands raised in victory with the championship belt around his waist. It is the coach's job to get them to do what they hate to create what they love.

Everyone wants a healthy, growing, and vibrant church. What they don't know is the hard work it takes to create such an environment. We have to take our eyes off the possible dislike for our methods, knowing that what we do will create the very thing the people need. It is by no means a walk in the park, but it must be done. If pastoring was easy, everyone would be doing it.

James Bartholomew, a columnist for the Spectator magazine, a weekly UK publication on politics, culture, and current affairs, is the inventor of the phrase 'virtue signaling'. He did this back in April 2015. He defines it as "…the way in which many people say or write things to indicate that they are virtuous. Sometimes it is quite subtle. By saying that they hate the Daily Mail or UKIP [United Kingdom Independence Party], they are really telling you that they are admirably non-racist, left-wing, or open-minded. One of the crucial aspects of virtue signaling is that it does not require actually doing anything virtuous. It does not involve delivering lunches to elderly neighbors or staying together with a spouse for the sake of the children. It takes no effort or sacrifice at all."[21]

The phrase has taken a life of its own in the last few years. More and more, we see people who have no interest in making tough choices, saying things that may appear to be nice and wonderful. These are the people who march for the environment and yet leave trash on those same streets. These are the politicians who pontificate about global warming and yet travel by private airplanes.

These are the ones who talk about how mean and oppressive the church is, in so doing making themselves out to look like the good guys, and will do absolutely nothing about the issues that are devastating the church. If you ask them for a solution, they can't tell you because they don't have one, but what does it matter? What matters is that they are seen to be the nice guys.
We ought not to fear those who have kind words but no real love for people. Let our passion for the church, for righteousness, and for the glory of God be the driving force to help us shepherd a people ready to meet Jesus.

---

[21] https://www.spectator.co.uk/2015/10/i-invented-virtue-signalling-now-its-taking-over-the-world/

4 LAY-PREACHING AND CHURCH PLANTING

When I first got saved and had the early rumblings of the call to preach, I wrestled in my mind if I could do a degree with physics as my major and theology as my minor. I automatically assumed that to preach, I would have to enroll in some kind of college course. In all my run-ins with Christianity, it never crossed my mind that you could be a pastor without formal theological training.

You can imagine my surprise when Peter Ajala, then the main disciple in the church, told me of discipleship as a path to preaching. He never used the term at the time, but what he meant was lay-preaching. I initially thought it odd. Was there a kind of a Bible school that Pastor Stephens ran? Is he the only lecturer? How do you get on that program? Isn't a bit odd that he has a building for his Bible School and yet the church was meeting in a rented space?

As I grew in Christ, I began to learn that lay-ministry was not a new thing. Lay-ministry had been around from the very beginning of the church and even before. The prophets of old were not men formally trained in theology. The last person I would ever think who would be in Bible school would have been Elijah. We know Elisha wasn't enrolled either. Amos was a sheep-breeder and farmer.

The Rise and Fall and Rise Again of Lay-Preaching

In the New Testament, we see a similar thing. The Twelve were not scholarly men but ordinary fishermen, tax collectors, and so on. There is no record of

Christ starting a Bible college for His men, but rather it was through discipleship that He trained them to be able ministers of the gospel. They, in turn, trained up men to preach the gospel, like the Apostle Paul, who trained such men as Timothy, Titus, Silvanus, and Luke.

What history tells us, however, is that over time, as the church grew in numbers combined with the rise of heresies such as Gnosticism, Sabellianism, and Arianism, she began to organize herself into training ministers of the gospel.

Nineteenth-century German scholar, Karl Krumbacher, wrote, "There was always the possibility that the lay preacher, unskilled in theological polemic and with undisciplined enthusiasm, might commit himself to dangerous positions, playing into the hands of the heretical sects and leading the people astray. The "liberty of prophesying" was checked, and by the middle of the second century, it is probable that lay evangelism, except in missionary fields, was almost abandoned…With the downfall of the Roman Empire and the adoption of Latin, fast becoming a dead language, as the language in which the Bible was to be read and liturgies to be performed, lay preaching became more and more impossible. The ministry demanded a scholastic training; liturgical practice usurped the place of preaching; and the layman was reduced to the position of a submissive hearer. Yet throughout the middle ages, the lay preacher sprang up sporadically and had a hearing, for he at least could talk to the people in their own tongue, and whenever there was a movement of spiritual revival, there was a reappearance of lay preaching."[22]

While lay-preaching was more or less dead for a thousand years or so, the ebbs and flows of lay-preaching continued in Britain from the time of John Wycliffe and the Lollards in the fourteenth century until the time of John Wesley in the eighteenth century. John Wesley initially was against lay preaching, as he was a clergyman ordained by the Church of England through his studies at Oxford University. Still, there were quite a few things Wesley changed his stance on during his ministry that caused him to deviate from Anglicanism, and lay-preaching was one of them.

There was an occasion where he left young Thomas Maxfield to look after his church while away on business. He was aghast to find out that while gone, Maxfield took it upon himself to preach to the church. Maxfield couldn't help it. There were no clergymen around to cover for Wesley, and he had no choice but to preach. Wesley went back to London to put Maxfield in his

---

[22] The New Schaff-Herzog Encyclopedia of Religious Knowledge, Vol. XII, Baker Book House, Grand Rapids, Michigan

place but was persuaded by his mother to hear the young man preach. After hearing Maxfield preach, Wesley changed his mind, and he became one of the very first lay preachers in the Methodist church.

This didn't mean that all of a sudden Wesley began to train up lay preachers, but as the Methodist revival began to spread, he found himself in need of preachers, and there were a limited number of ordained ministers at his disposal. He discovered that lay preachers were handy in ministering to the spiritual needs of the many converts being won to Christ. He got a lot of criticism for making lay-preaching popular, but he stuck to his guns. I like John Wesley a lot. He didn't always get it immediately, but once he did, he latched on to it with a passion.

Karl Krumbacher continues, "The Methodist lay preachers were the means by which Methodism spread so rapidly not only over Great Britain, but also over the United States and throughout the English-speaking world. They were the advance guard of Methodism; cottage meetings and open-air meetings, supplied by lay preachers, prepared the way for chapels, which were the permanent garrisons of the districts occupied. The "traveling preacher" might have ten to thirty chapels and mission-stations under his oversight, and, with thirty to fifty lay preachers "on the plan," he arranged quarterly for all the pulpits to be filled, while "mission bands" of lay preachers carried on aggressive evangelistic campaigns in towns and villages as yet unoccupied. The lay preachers were drawn from all classes-university graduates, country gentlemen, business men, artisans, and agricultural laborers being on the same "plan." This promoted fellowship, and saved the Methodist Church from being divided into class cliques to the extent that has happened in some other churches."

The Dangers of Bible College

We owe much to John Wesley and the Methodist movement to bring back something that started with the early church. However, while lay-preaching has a place within the church world today, the preferred route to the pulpit is through the Bible school. At first glance, it would seem that there is much use for the Bible school. Where else would you find so many teachers who are experts in various aspects of theology under one roof? A young student can be educated by the best of the best and come out full of knowledge and understanding.

Now I am not saying that there aren't people who have been helped by Bible school. I will be a liar if I deny the fact that there are good preachers out there who have been formally trained in theology. But I can say that after many years in the ministry, looking back, I still wouldn't choose the route of the Bible College. I am not anti-intellectual by any stretch of the imagination, but the idea of being cooped up in an institution, away from the real world, studying day and night, cramming to pass exams to be accredited and then going out into society and ministering to people I have been disconnected from for so many years, and trying to reach a sinful generation I have been separated from with no understanding of their everyday struggles, just doesn't appeal to me.

It may be a cliché, but it still is true today that through Bible College, it is possible to be so heavenly minded that you are of no earthly good. And I'm talking about saved kids who desperately want to answer the call of God, live for Jesus, and help people.

Then you have those at a Bible College who have no desire to live holy lives. Pastor Greg Mitchell, in his sermon "The Heavenly Vision", explains why Pastor Wayman Mitchell has such an aversion to Bible College. He said Pastor Mitchell, "...packed up the family and moved to Los Angeles, California, to attend Life Bible College. It was not at all what he expected. For one thing, many of the students he went to college with were not even saved! They were getting in trouble, so their parents sent them to Bible College hoping that it would do some good...The other discouraging dynamic was the unbelief of the professors. They were teaching the Bible and yet did not believe what it said. They did not believe in the rapture, in speaking in tongues, or in healing. He spent most of his years at Bible College arguing with his professors that the Bible was true. It also began to dawn on my dad that none of his professors were successful pastors. The reason they were teaching was because they had never been able to build a church. They were trying to teach people how to do something they were unable to do themselves. All this caused my dad to be disillusioned with the whole concept of Bible College."[23]

As bad as it is for men who teach the Bible but don't believe it, it can get progressively worse in the Bible school as we now have atheists as professors of theology. It's interesting to me that the concept of Bible school was created to train men in right theology, and yet it has now been hijacked by men who don't even believe in God. Higher Criticism initially taught in German theological universities in the nineteenth century, did much damage to Protestant Christianity in reducing the Bible from the word of God to an ordinary human book. (Higher Criticism, in short, is using present-day

---

[23] p3, Still Taking the Land, edited by David J Drum, Kidwell Publishing, 2012

reasoning to assess the legitimacy of the scriptures. If we consider that present-day thinking is awash with atheism and evolution, we can see that there is no way these so-called "experts" can objectively assess the word of God.)

It was through Higher Criticism, taught in theological universities, which brought about the belief that Moses did not write the first five books of the Bible, that Daniel's prophecies were written after the time of Daniel and not before, and that there were "three different Isaiahs" who wrote the book, that is, proto-Isaiah, deutero-Isaiah, and trito-Isaiah. As Bible-believing Christians, we find that bizarre, but you would be amazed at how much of Higher Criticism has filtered through the church world today, and churchgoers all over the western world believe this stuff but have no idea where it came from.

In an online article entitled "Can faith survive Bible College?" by Justin Brierley, he highlights an observation made by Dr. John Hayward, a Mathematics lecturer who also researches church growth trends. Hayward mentions that churches with liberal theology die out. They never experience church growth of any type. The only churches that experience growth are conservative. Nevertheless, liberal churches survive due to Bible school because inadvertently conservative kids end up going there and turning into liberals.

Brierley writes, "Part of the reason that liberal churches continue to survive, according to Hayward, is because a proportion of the evangelicals who go to theological college end up adopting a liberal theology. Conservative churches turn out to be indirectly ensuring the survival of liberal churches this way - a proportion of their ordinands become more liberal and go on to pastor liberal congregations, or turn evangelical churches into liberal ones. He cites the Welsh chapel he grew up in as an example: 'In common with many Welsh Presbyterian churches, it was rooted in the conservative evangelical theology of the 18th-century revivals. When the 1960s started, a liberal minister came, who taught people to doubt the orthodoxy they had received. In ten years, the church emptied from a few hundred to a handful of members, as people left and found other conservative churches. After another decade the church was closed.'"[24]

In other words, Bible schools are like viruses. The work of a virus is to turn healthy cells into replicas of themselves. Viruses are not living organisms.

---

[24] https://www.premierchristianity.com/Past-Issues/2014/February-2014/Can-faith-survive-Bible-college

They can't naturally reproduce like a living organism. They duplicate rather than reproduce, and they do so by hijacking a cell, making it duplicate the virus' genetic code, and then sealing the newly-formed viruses into protein shells called capsids. Without a host, a virus cannot duplicate itself. You can get many viruses from just one healthy cell being invaded.

Liberal theology, like a virus, is not a living entity. It doesn't have a Spirit-given life. Left to itself, it cannot do anything unless it finds a host. It is, therefore, parasitic. It "lives" only if it can find Bible-believing Christians to infect. Most Bible Colleges are liberal in nature. Justin Brierley continues in his article and explains why we shouldn't give up on Bible school. He infers that the Christian student must work harder to keep from being infected with liberalism. They have to recognize that their faith will be challenged, and they will have to make sense of it all.

But my question is, "Why put yourself in that position?" Why should I go to the strip club to prove to myself that I am faithful to my wife? In other words, why would you deliberately put yourself in a place where you will be challenged for what you believe in, in a place initially created to help you develop in your faith but has now been hijacked by those who don't have faith? Why put yourself in a situation where those in authority are committed to making a non-believer out of you by using your desire to know God against you? Why would a patriot put himself in a room full of traitors just to prove that he is loyal to his nation?

It just doesn't make sense. No one else would do such a thing in any other arena of life, and yet it would seem Christians would. Jesus was right when He said in Luke 16:8, "For the sons of this world are more shrewd in their generation than the sons of light."

As bad as it is for any Christian to want to enter such an atmosphere, let me put it another way. What godly parents, in their right minds, would want to put their children in such an environment? We wouldn't leave our little children with pedophiles, and yet we would leave our young adult children in the care of wolves in sheep clothing. They may come out with a degree but lose their salvation in the process.

Pastor Greg further stated in his sermon on "The Heavenly Vision", "Many of the young men that were getting saved began to catch a vision of being used by God. Several came to Pastor Mitchell to get direction, and he gave them the only option that he knew, which was going to Bible school. He sent two young men off so that they could be trained to be men of God, but both of them lost the fire and started to believe strange things. It had ruined them.

My dad knew there had to be another way. God began to show him the plan for reaching the world is through the local church."[25]

We know modern secular universities are a hotbed of immorality, but you have more chance of surviving intact than in a Bible College where there is the potential damage due to secular sin, but more so the potential damage due to ecclesiastical sin. Damage done to the individual because of church can be far more crippling than damage done in the world. Much church growth is a result of broken sinners from the world looking for refuge in Jesus. But I have seen the damage done to people by the church, and I can honestly say that they don't fare as well.

Now I am not saying that all Bible Colleges are liberal, but most of them are and the ones that aren't don't prepare potential ministers for real life. Ministry is about people and being able to take the gospel and put it in the context of everyday life. I'm sure there may be ways in which a Bible College could adapt to that, but in most cases, they don't function in that manner.

Then you also have to look at the dynamics of how Bible School would fit in. Imagine that we get a young man saved who feels the call of God to preach. Fantastic! When do we send him to Bible School? A month after he is saved? Six months after? How will he pay for it? Will he have to get in debt? Can his parents afford it? Will he have to work and study? Is he married? Will his wife and kids have to relocate to where he is going? When he finishes, then what?

I'm sure someone can come up with an argument to counter that, but from a logistical point of view, the Bible College model for discipleship is a very difficult one. Who is going to teach passion for souls? Passion is caught and not taught, and it is only caught in an atmosphere where there is a push to reach the souls of mankind. Is evangelism, therefore, an academic issue, or is there real interaction with people at a Bible School? Were the lecturers successful in ministry, or are they merely talking theory?

It just seems to me that if you want to be like a church manager, someone who keeps things ticking, preserving an already existing church, then Bible School is for you. But if you want to reach the world for Jesus, if you have a passion for souls, if you like being around the lost and pointing them to Christ, I can't see how being in Bible College will teach you that.
Even as a pastor in our Fellowship, we can get so bogged down in the church's every day running that if we are not careful, we can lose our passion

---

[25] p7, Still Taking the Land, edited by David J Drum, Kidwell Publishing, 2012

for souls. We can become disconnected to the sinners in the world, being surrounded by church people all the time and doing all kinds of Christian stuff. Imagine a young Christian being separated from the real world for three or four years? We in the ministry know when we have gone off-track and know how to get back on track because, in our formative years, we were discipled. What about young Bible College students who never had that reference point and built up the worst habits in the years that should have been used to establish good patterns of discipleship?

Bible College removes the dignity of the local church. When you send your men to Bible School, you strip the local church of its importance. The local church must raise up and send out couples, not an institution. If you give me your children to parent, you are telling me you can't raise your children properly. If you send your converts to Bible College, you are saying that you can't train them properly. The apostle Paul said in 2 Timothy 2:2, "And the things that you have heard from me among many witnesses, commit these to faithful men who will be able to teach others also." How can we have four levels of disciples in the local church if we send those men to Bible College?

The Need for Discipleship

I believe the answer for the future of the church is discipleship. The protection we have against liberal Christianity is discipleship. We are the ones who are growing, not them. Rather than keep liberals alive by giving them converts, we need to train our own. We need to raise up our own preachers and workers for the field. This is where we take a page out of John Wesley's book and tweak it to suit the needs of today.

While John Wesley had lay-preachers working under ordained Bible College approved ministers, we are lay movement altogether. We are a Fellowship that trains men for the ministry while living in the real world. It means that church is more than church, it is a training center. This is what makes our church different, and this needs to be stressed.

When we pioneer a church, we are not merely trying to establish a work, and then that's it, job done. No. The anti-thesis of the virus is the cell. While a virus is non-living, a cell is living. A cell doesn't replicate; it reproduces itself. Living things reproduce. It's what living things do. A healthy growing church needs to reproduce, and this is where the local church becomes more than a church but a training center for the ministry.

It means that the men in the church are not just men you would find at other churches. It means there are going to be demands made on them that would not usually be placed at other churches.

This is something that needs to be communicated by the pastor to the church; otherwise, people will be confused. There are times when people, ignorant of the principle of discipleship, think that the pastor has groupies and sycophants. It looks as if a pastor has men who will answer to his every beck and call. Or they may think there is an elite group of men, an exclusive company of individuals who are treasured above all, and the rest are just unimportant people in the congregation.

We know the word 'pastor' means 'shepherd,' and that is our duty. We are to tend and care for God's sheep. We must love the people in our congregation, pray for them, check upon them, and be a blessing to their lives. But the pastor is not a glorified social worker or, on the other extreme, a motivational speaker. This is the impression being communicated in the church world nowadays.

Ephesians 4:11-12 says, "...He Himself gave some to be apostles, some prophets, some evangelists, and some pastors and teachers, for the equipping of the saints for the work of ministry, for the edifying of the body of Christ..." The pastor's role is to equip the saints for the work of the ministry, the ministry being the work done to build up the church. It means he has to train people that things get done because he cannot be in every place at the same time. This is why the church needs to work with the pastor as he works with men.

The ideas of discipleship, raising up of leaders, and church planting needs to be woven into the church's fabric. This is not a one-off weaving but continuous, as the dynamics of the modern church are such that if left neglected will cause the church to degenerate. For this to happen, the vision of these principles needs to be imparted. It first needs to be communicated over the pulpit through preaching, but it needs to be seen on a practical level. This is where national and international impact teams, men's discipleships, victory rallies, and conferences come in.

As individuals within the local church are exposed to the bigger picture, that ethos will be imparted into their lives. They will "get it," and that will, in turn, become the culture of the church. It's incredible to see people change during an overseas impact team, as they see the vision in action in a foreign setting. As they say, the penny will drop, and these teams do as much for the individuals who attend as it does for the church who receives them.

Discipleship is then embraced because we see what we are trying to accomplish – the evangelization of the world through men and women being raised up and answering the call of God. Larger churches may get their sense of dignity by their size and professionalism (nothing wrong with a larger church or being professional; let's try to get both). We get ours by understanding that God could use our lives to impact a city or a nation with the gospel. It is a mind-blowing thing for a young man off the street to come into a church and learn that his life could make a difference. You can't get that from a Bible College program.

The catching of the vision means that people within the local church will work with disciples. For example, you may have a situation where a church member is sick and asks the pastor to visit. In another church, the pastor may not be able to go and may ask if it is okay to send a brother to pray. But people can be funny, and if the pastor isn't able to come, they don't want anyone else. But when we understand the idea of training men, people understand what the pastor is trying to do when he sends a disciple. They know that the pastor isn't a caretaker or someone who is just trying to keep the church ticking.

The church understands that a disciple is a man in training. He is going to make mistakes. He is going to blunder from time to time. He won't be able to articulate when he first gets an opportunity to preach. He may blow an altar call. He may mess up the organizing of an impact team or concert. But the church is patient because they understand the idea of discipleship. If image and professionalism were the church's priorities, then he would never get a chance. He would have to be behind the scene for years before given an opportunity.

A church without a vision, a church without discipleship, doesn't have much purpose. There may be goals, but they aren't lofty goals. They may have people, but there isn't much of a challenge presented to the people. They may have an abstract concept of evangelization and reaching the world, but there are no practical steps seen.

Discipleship means we believe in the men we are training. Do you know what it means to a young man written off by the world to come into a church and find out that people are willing to invest in him? Do you know what it means to a young man who has been faithful, and someone hands him a key to the building to open up for church or prayer? Discipleship doesn't only give dignity to the local church; it also gives dignity to the people who submit to the process of discipleship.

The apostle Paul speaks to his disciple in Titus 1:5 and says, "For this reason, I left you in Crete, that you should set in order the things that are lacking…" Paul left Titus in Crete to sort things out. Paul believed in Titus because Paul trained and discipled Titus. Most churches won't take the risk and disciple men. There is just too much to lose. It's better to send him to Bible School where he is polished and trained up, and then they will have him. But we let guys have an expression, who could blunder or say the wrong thing, but it is because we believe that one day, after being correctly discipled, he will get it.

The idea that we can spend thousands of dollars on a man and send him to pioneer or take over a church is mind-blowing. I'm sure some of the guys in South London still have a tape of Pastor Carnegie's first sermon in Tucson in the mid-1980s. It was horrible! It is nothing like the man today, and yet Pastor Warner spent thousands sending him to Jamaica to pioneer. Who does that? Who would invest so much on an unproven man?

The Danger of Anti-Intellectualism

The danger in lay-preaching, however, is if we are not careful, it can lead to anti-intellectualism. With the apparent and present danger of the liberal Bible College, we can throw the baby out with the bath water and go the opposite direction and become shallow. From the very beginning, Pentecostals have been distrustful of university-trained theologians, and there is something to be said of that idea still having some kind of unconscious expression in the psyche of many.

Also, there is the fact that a significant amount of our converts are not the university types. I'm not saying we don't have them, but if we are honest, we have a lot of converts who were lucky to have graduated from high school. That's not a problem. Better to be a high school dropout and have your name in the Lamb's Book of Life than have your name on a diploma but be on your way to hell. Thank God for the brothers and sisters who know they are messed up and need Jesus rather than being an educated but self-righteous person who think the universe just created itself and have no need for God.

The apostle Paul points out in 1 Corinthians 1:27-30, "God has chosen the foolish things of the world to put to shame the wise, and God has chosen the weak things of the world to put to shame the things which are mighty; and the base things of the world and the things which are despised God has chosen, and the things which are not, to bring to nothing the things that are, that no flesh should glory in His presence."

However, people who have had no desire to read before salvation have a limited willingness to do so afterward. I'm not saying this is true for everyone because I have known people personally who rarely picked up a book before salvation and yet now are great readers. Pastor Courtney Lowe is one such person. He has dyslexia and, as a result, never did well in high school, but after salvation, God helped him to become one of the most profound thinkers I know.

I am not saying there is an epidemic in apathetic readers in our Fellowship, but there are quite a few and enough to make you wonder what will become of us in the future. The ministry is time-consuming, and there is much in the ministry that demands our attention. We have outreaches to attend, follow up, telephone calls, events to organize, bills to pay, people to meet, and all kind of logistical endeavors that are the behind scene projects that help the church run smoothly. Outside of our devotional time, the other major area that gets neglected is reading.

Take it from someone who has been reading since he was two years old. I could read a newspaper at four, so my father told me. I have been reading books for years, and I rarely ever throw one away. I'm not trying to brag but make a point. I am a man with limited talents. I can't sing or rap, I'm not Marty Carnegie behind the pulpit, and I can't sing and clap at the same time without having to think hard about it. But I can read, and I can remember what I read. Books are my world and let me tell you from personal experience, despite all that, when you face the pressure of having a family, having to work a job and run a church, it is very easy for reading to get neglected.

As I write these words this very minute, my mind reflects on a book I am currently reading – "How to Survive the Titanic or The Sinking of J. Bruce Ismay," by Frances Wilson. A fascinating read, but I haven't picked up in a week because I have to finish writing this book. I looked at it longingly last night and wished I had the time. If I, an avid reader, can struggle to find time to read, what about the man who has a limited desire to learn?

When I got saved, many of the converts in the South London church were young people from the lower end of the social spectrum. No disrespect to them, but that's who we were, and as I said before, I was told that I would backslide because I read too much. Those guys have grown out of that kind of thinking, and they are good readers in their own right, but this is an idea that if people aren't careful of it, it will play like a background app in the subconscious. The idea is this – reading is unspiritual. Therefore, the more you read, the more unspiritual you will become. There is the idea that the only book you should read is the Bible.

I admit that the foundation of all reading is the word of God. Going back to my friend Courtney Lowe, when he got saved, he knew he needed to read God's word, and so he trained himself to read with the Bible. The other books he began to read started from him learning to improve himself by reading the Bible. We need the Bible, and if there is only one book in the world, it should be the word of God. Sometimes, however, people mistake reading everything else under the sun and neglect the word of God.

The idea that reading is unspiritual is like a demonic spore circulating in the wind. You can't pinpoint it, but when it finds a home with the right conditions, it turns into mold. What are the right conditions? It is the individual who hates reading combined with the idea that reading is unspiritual. Add to both of those busyness, and you find a pastor or disciple who never takes time to pick up a book and educate himself.

As a result of a lack of reading, the ministry suffers. For one, you become a hobby-horse preacher. Because you never took the time to read and to learn new stuff, you become stuck on the few things you know and like. Hobby-horse preachers have a handful of favorite topics that they rotate over and over and over and over again. He never sees that he is continuously repeating himself because he sincerely believes that what he knows is everything there needs to be known about the faith.

It's the same reasoning why some people don't pray. Why do we pray? Because we recognize that we haven't got all the answers in ourselves, and we need divine help to get things done. When prayer is not our default position, it is because we think we are self-sufficient. That is the root cause of prayerlessness. This is why a new convert finds difficulty in prayer because he or she doesn't know what to pray for. They have been so used to doing their own thing all the time they don't know what to pray. Prayer is dependency, and when our default position is on our knees, it is because we know our sufficiency is not in ourselves.

The same is true with reading. Men who don't read are those who don't think they need to read. Why should they read when they know everything? Now, they won't say that, but that's the root cause, just like the root cause of prayerlessness is self-sufficiency.

Once again, it comes out in their preaching, and they repeat themselves because that's the only thing they know. It never dawns on them that they are boring the socks off their congregation. Now I have met men who can deliver a message, and if you have them for revival, they could really do a good job, but you can only have them for one revival because the next time they come they are going to repeat the same things, albeit with a different text. Okay, I exaggerate, but you get my point.

One such brother I know, who loves Jesus, is passionate about the ministry, loves his wife, family, and people, and is the embodiment of a man who is sold out for the gospel, however after hearing him over the years, I have come to realize he goes around in circles, so much so that people in his congregation complain that he is boring.

Let me illustrate what I mean. It is a bit simplistic, but I'm sure you will get my point. Imagine a man who is writing a sermon on faith but doesn't read. His text is Moses parting the Red Sea – "Tell the children of Israel to go forward." Because he doesn't read, he needs to find illustrations from the only book he reads – the Bible. His illustrations are Elijah and the widow of Zarephath, Elisha and the widow with the jar of oil, Jesus and the feeding of the 5,000, the faith of the paralytic, the lepers visiting the enemy's camp, Jonathan attacking the Philistines, etc. It's a great one-off sermon. But the next time he preaches on faith, his text is Jesus and the feeding of the 5,000, and his illustrations are Moses and the Parting of the Red Sea, and so on.

After a while, it is just a recycling of the same points. It's like a treadmill going around and around but not going anywhere. It gets boring after a while. Pastor Carnegie always used to say to us as young disciples – "Preaching is saying the same things in different ways."

If you read enough, you can always find illustrations for topics instead of using other stories in the Bible that could be for another sermon. This way, the Bible stays fresher in people's minds. We will always need to preach on faith. Perhaps many times through the year, if the need arises. But you could use the main text from the Bible and from reading, to use stories that you have read from others' experiences. The next time you preach on faith, find another text, and use other stories. You will find that while you are repeating yourself, which you need to from time to time, it is fresh. We all need bread, but I would rather have fresh bread every day than eat a stale loaf.
Reading gets you to think thoughts you wouldn't usually think left to yourself. Reading gives ideas that you would have never thought about on your own. There are authors that I read that I have disagreed with, but they have helped me work out my position on the topic by considering why I am not in agreement. While I may not agree with their position, they have taught me how to look at things from a different angle. Then some authors have stirred my faith and caused me to look beyond the struggles and issues I am

addressing right now. These are books that help you to see a bigger God and make you aware that the circumstances of life you are presently in are confining your perception of God.

Then some books will teach you stuff you need to know. Let me tell you from personal experience; knowledge is power, and knowledge gives weight. When you know what you are talking about, it gives you validity, and people listen. I'm not saying we will know everything, but reading helps you to know things that can be invaluable in getting people to hear what you have to say.

The last thing any disciple wants to have is a pastor who can't answer his questions regularly. The last thing any new convert wants is a Bible study leader who can't answer a fundamental question about the Bible. I have heard guys mutter all kinds of Bible jargon to get those who ask the questions to back off. You know what I mean. If you use big theological words, even if it is incoherent, the hope is that the one who asks will be too embarrassed by his ignorance and keep quiet. But the thing is, people aren't fools, and while they may not say it to your face, they know you have nothing to say. Ultimately, you are only kidding yourself with your ignorance.

Reading the newspaper is good. It's good to be informed, but that can't always be the inspiration for your sermon. Sermon illustrations on the Internet can be handy, but "cut and paste" isn't real preaching. I heard someone say years ago that preaching should be like cows chewing the cud. Cows spend nearly eight hours every day chewing cud, and so the milk produced from a cow comes from much digestion. "Cut and paste" preaching is like biting off blades of grass and spitting it out on the congregation. Reading and meditating is the digestion of spiritual truths that we convert into milk to feed the flock.

In the beginning stages of pioneering, it may not be necessary to know much. We are not trying to reach church types, and the people we tend to attract are stone-cold sinners. Even with the little a pioneer pastor knows, new converts may think he is a Bible professor. That's okay for a while, but what happens when these stone-cold raw sinners start to grow in Christ? What happens when they need more from you than what you can deliver? Yet still, what happens when your church grows and the university types come in?

Nothing turns a smart sinner off more than a preacher who doesn't know what he is talking about. Britain is in England; South Africa is a continent, Louis Armstrong was the first man in space[26], and so on. It doesn't mean

---

[26] Yuri Gagarin was the first man in space

people won't forgive these mistakes, but after a while ignorance turns people off. If you don't know the basics, how can anyone trust you with the word of God? There are men out there who couldn't defend the doctrine of creation to an evolutionist or coherently explain the position of the pre-Tribulation rapture. It is, therefore, imperative to invest in our men theological along with logistical training.

The Natural Progression – Church Planting

The climax of discipleship is church planting. I don't think that the anticipation people have on Friday night at a Conference is manufactured. Church planting is the natural progression of discipleship, and it makes perfect sense. It is what we are aiming for. While we do understand discipleship is necessary for the well-being of the church in general as not everyone will be a pastor, nevertheless, discipleship finds its full expression in church planting as a church cannot outdo the gospel.

Whatever else a church may do – schools, community daycares, homework clubs, moms and toddlers groups, etc., if evangelism l is not paramount, the church will inevitably die. Church planting is the ultimate expression in fulfilling the great commission as outlined by Jesus in Matthew 28:19 when He said: "Go therefore and make disciples of all the nations…"

Therefore, we don't just plant a church for church-planting sake. It is not just something we do. We do it because there is a lost world out there. There are sinners desperately in need of the Savior, and we are the means to reach them for Jesus. Church planting means forming a new spiritual family in the heart of a different community, city, or country with the same ethos and spirit as the sending church.

We see this principle at work in the church at Antioch. Acts 13:2-3 reads, "As they ministered to the Lord and fasted, the Holy Spirit said, "Now separate to Me Barnabas and Saul for the work to which I have called them." Then, having fasted and prayed and laid hands on them, they sent them away." When Barnabas and Saul were sent out, they had a fantastic adventure planting churches all across the Roman Empire.

Notice also that Barnabas and Saul didn't volunteer to go out; they were sent. I find it amazing when I hear of stories of people leaving the home church of their own accord to start another church in another city or area. They go with no financial and emotional support, no accountability, no blessing from the local congregation, and without seeking any direction or advice. They are literally on their own.

I remember the first time I went to Manchester on my own to spy out the land. I wish I could say I was as brave and bold as I was on the Friday night of the conference, but I was gripped with fear and apprehension. In the following months, it didn't get easier, but knowing that I had a church supporting me financially, in prayer, and with regular impact teams, it made the difference in not just the success of the pioneering work but our mental and spiritual well-being.

The problem with some who have known nothing else besides a CFM church is the belief that every church functions like ours. Every conference is free; every missionary is on support; every pastor is put up in a hotel and given a decent love offering for preaching a revival. I have known men who have left and have had to face a tough church world that has little regard for their ministry. Some men complain about their mother church, and while in a few cases there may be justifiable causes, in general, they have no idea how good they have it.

I have seen independent churches out there, and in many cases, they are scary places to pastor. A critical factor in church planting is the relationship between the one being sent and the sender. I can honestly say that there have been times when I have someone over me, directly responsible for the church I pastor that has helped me through difficult patches. Not only financial help and spiritual wisdom, but knowing that headship is behind me when I have to make critical decisions in the church that some people will not like. Let me see the independent guy try to make those hard choices without having anyone backing him.

When I was in Manchester, there was an independent church I got to know quite well, as the daughter and son-in-law of one of their elders went to my church. This elder was a very godly man, but he was in a church that had seen better days and was in a dramatic freefall. To cut a long story short, the replacement pastor had enough of pastoring spiritually dead people and left. This godly elder took up the pastor's position, even though others in the church wanted it.

Now he used to visit us from time to time, especially revivals, and saw the church grow from a handful of people to a dynamic functioning church, and he liked how we did things, especially evangelism. He liked what we did so much that he decided to implement what we did in his church. It was the biggest mistake of his short pastoral career. One of the brothers rose up against him, poisoned the rest, staged a coup and kicked him out. He left the church he had served for many years a defeated man. You can't do what we do unless you are what we are. But that's what happens when you don't have anyone behind you. You better be glad, pastor, that you aren't a volunteer. (not sure what you are saying here…maybe "autonomous" would be a better word?)

We also need to realize that church planting is hard work. Some churches explode in growth, others take time, and yet others don't make it for whatever reason. It isn't an exact science, and we can't see into the future. Therefore, it means that church planting is a long-term plan with the willingness to sacrifice financially on the part of the sending church and also sacrifice on the couple being sent. There are no guarantees in the kingdom.

Paul started two great churches in Macedonia – Philippi, and Thessalonica – but it was a project that never started well. He was beaten and thrown in prison before he saw any breakthrough. Sometimes it takes effort to dig up the fallow ground. Sometimes it takes time for the community to know you. Sometimes all the conditions for revival are right there just waiting for someone to step in.

I would like the potential pioneer-pastor also to bear this in mind. Sometimes as a pioneer, you can be intimidated at the established churches around you. You can look at your basic equipment, storefront building, and simple sermon and say to yourself, "How can we compete with that?" You can fail to realize that there are people out there who are tired of the status quo and would have nothing to do with the established church.

Quite a number of the people I have worked with over the years would have never given an established church a look, even though the church is just outside their front door. When I moved to Manchester, my old boss in London got me a job interview with a friend who had a business in the area I was pioneering. When I told the man why I was moving to Manchester, he said, "Not another church in Moss Side." It was true, but there were a significant number of people in that area who had nothing to do with the churches there whatsoever.

You would be amazed at how much a church plant can make a difference to the people who have slipped through the cracks.

The other thing about church planting is that it is counter-intuitive. As many churches struggle to find capable people, it would seem illogical to send out your very best. It doesn't make much sense, but that is what we do because we give God our best. Our main objective isn't to our ministries but to reach the world for Jesus Christ. We see the bigger picture. It isn't about us. It is about Christ and Him being glorified in the earth.

It doesn't mean that because we do this good thing that somehow things will right themselves automatically. The potential negative thing in church planting is filling the void left by the couple that is sent. When a church is planted, there is now a gap that needs to be filled. This is where it gets tricky because it can be a good thing or a bad thing.

In a good case scenario, a couple rises up to meet that challenge. For some men, they see the gap as an open door, an opportunity to rise up and do something. It is like when a large tree is removed from a forest. The gap created allows sunshine to come in and allows the smaller trees to grow. Friday night at conference can do wonders for the men in the body. It can stir them into action as they see one of their homeboys going out into the field to do something for God. They think to themselves, if God can use him, there is a chance for us.

But then you have others who haven't got a clue as to what's happening. They are happy for the couple who got sent but somehow assumed things are just going to continue like they always did. I have seen churches collapse at the sending out of their best couple. It's not uncommon for the sent-out couple to have also been the best givers and the best workers in the church.

I am not an expert on the dynamics of church planting, and so I am speculating. I would leave the expert analysis to Pastor Mitchell and Pastor Warner. It could be that the rest of the church isn't mature enough to handle a couple being planted. It could be that the ethos of discipleship, lay-preaching, and church planting hasn't been woven into the church's fabric. For whatever reason, it is something that has to be considered as the church begins to think about sending out workers.

Let me also add this; there is a serious financial cost to reaching the world for Jesus. I have heard criticism of our churches that we are always asking for money. Yes, we are. But we are not building monuments to ourselves to impress the world. Reaching the world for Jesus is an expensive endeavor. Many people have no idea of the financial implications of planting a church. Looking back at my time in Jamaica, the South London church invested a staggering amount of money into the work.

Why do we preach entire sermons on money, stewardship, and giving? Why do we have a mini-sermon with the offering every service? It is because preaching the gospel takes money. Impact teams cost money. Overseas impact teams cost a lot of money. Planting a church costs money. Missionary work costs a heck of a lot of money. Hosting conferences to teach and train disciples so that the vision can be imparted to reach the world cost money.

This area of church planting needs to be woven into the fabric of our churches well before planting a church. Every well-thinking individual knows that it takes money to raise a child, and it is only wise to make sure he or she is prepared to look after that child before the child arrives. I think in the early days of the church and especially as converts start multiplying, while they are still young in the Lord and have a passion for the things of God, that the principle of giving to world evangelism should be implemented. When people get old and set in their ways with all kinds of responsibilities, it is a lot more difficult to create new habits.

Planting churches without finances is like raising a child in poverty – the child has needs, but you can't do anything for him or her. As a result, the child struggles to develop, and it takes a much longer time to get to maturity than it would had he been provided for.

We challenge people to tithe, which we should, but tithing is linked to an individual's prosperity and for meeting the needs of the local church. What we fail to communicate and weave into the fabric of the church is that reaching the world for Jesus is a separate issue from the tithe. What happens when we plant a church and the people don't make that connection? The offerings don't go up and providing for the church plant suffers that's what.

A point must also be made to the ones sent. The home church isn't an ATM with an unlimited amount of resources. While the pioneering work needs support, you have to make it happen. Necessity is the mother of invention, and it is incredible how much you can get done with little. It causes you to trust God and step out in faith. It gets the supernatural involved, and it makes you and your ministry stronger. Some men with less do far better than some men with more.

Ed Stetzer, who researches and writes on church planting, observed, "The churches that received more funding for longer periods of time were overall less effective than churches that received less funding for shorter periods of time." He also noted that, "Church planters consistently complained that they were underfunded. Those who received part-time funding indicated that they would have been more successful if they received full-time funding. Those who received full-time funding wanted start-up funds. Those who were full-time with startup wanted additional staff. It is fair to say that funding was never enough for the church planter."[27]

All in all, church planting is the opportunity of a lifetime as there are sinners everywhere. In every location, there is an exciting chance of being used by God and given the privilege to help transform lives and impact generations to come. Note also that there are always going to be problems with the ministry. As long as there are people involved, there will be problems. As long as Satan opposes the will of God, there will be problems. But as we look at the bigger picture, of reaching the lost and desperate in the cities and nations of the world, there is no greater privilege than being a disciple of Christ used by God to populate heaven.

---

[27] p22, An Analysis of the Church Planting Process and Other Selected Factors on the Attendance of SBC Church Plants, a NAMB self-study, May 2003, Edward J Stetzer.

5 MALE LEADERSHIP

The Great Divide

It was something that struck me again and again. Something I saw every Sunday for over six years straight, over 300 Sundays, and yet the profundity of it never wore off. They say that Sunday is the most segregated day in America when it comes to race. I don't know if that is still true, but I do know that in Jamaica, where my family and I served as missionaries for six years, segregation is practiced every Sunday. In this case, it wasn't the segregation of the races; it was segregation of the sexes.

Every Sunday morning, in towns across Jamaica, there would be scores of women on their way to Church all dressed in their finest and every Sunday evening, as the sun sets, there would be scores of men coming off the soccer fields, all muddy and sweaty, on their way home. The contrast never failed to impact me, and there was never a Sunday where it all became normative. The stark reality of the oppositeness and the divergence of the values of each sex never lost its impression on me.

So strong was the impression that in every Church that I have seen in Jamaica, the first thing I did when I went in was to do a quick ratio of men and women within the congregation. In many cases, the proportion of men and women was at best 1 to 3, with many times 1 to 7 or 8. One service I went to was 1 to 20, where roughly 250 people were in attendance.

Churches in the U.K. and the USA are only doing marginally better. According to the U.S. Congregational Life Survey (2014), 61% of church attenders were women compared to 39% men. That is a difference of 22%. The survey was also keen to point out that it wasn't because women live longer than men as the ratio was consistent throughout all age groups. In the book, "The Black Church in the African American Experience" by C. Eric Lincoln, the attendees of a typical black church are 66% to 80% female, which is a ratio of 1:2 at best and 1:4 at worst. He points out that in his survey of 2,150 churches, the average male attendance was around 30%.[28]

According to a survey done by the UK Christian charity Tearfund in 2007, when it came to regular church attendance, 65% of British women went to Church while only 35% of men did. It is a ratio of almost 2 to 1. Another Tearfund survey done in 2011 reveals that in the last 20 years, 49% of men aged less than thirty have left the Church. It has been estimated that by 2028 men will have altogether disappeared from the U.K. church. [29]

There is something profoundly wrong in Western Christianity, and it is seen in the increasingly disjointed ratio of men and women going to Church. It seems more and more men are dropping out of Church and doing other things. And while I will go into detail later on in this chapter, it appears that there is something about western Christianity that doesn't appeal to males. What is it? Why are things so off-putting to men?

What is an even greater indictment against western Christianity is just how popular Islam is with men. The proportion of men in other religions is far higher than it is in western Christianity. There is no such gender gap in Islam, Buddhism, Judaism, Sikhism or Hinduism. It amazes me that despite all the bad press Islam may have received over the years, many young men have converted to Islam and are increasingly sympathetic.

In Britain, the "2008-2009 Citizenship Survey: Race, Religion and Equalities Topic Report" by Chris Ferguson and David Hussey, pointed out that only 25% of men who classified themselves as Christians had an actively practicing faith while 78% of men who classified themselves as Muslims did.

William Kilpatrick, in his book "Christianity, Islam, and Atheism: The Struggle for the soul of the West," says, "Today, sociologists are worried about the contracting role of men. As a result of feminist victories, some women have become stronger and more independent, but others have found themselves dependent on the government. Moreover, an unseen consequence of government paternalism is a general slackening in the

---

[28] p304, The Black Church in the African American Experience, C. Eric Lincoln, Duke University Press, 1990
[29] https://www.ministrytoday.org.uk/magazine/issues/55/424/

willingness of men to shoulder the responsibilities of marriage and family. *The irony is that the absence of men from key social roles may pave the way for a form of patriarchy far more restrictive than feminists of the Betty Friedan era could have imagined.* As males in the West retreat into self-absorption and self-indulgence, Muslim men are increasingly convinced of their religious right not only to rule over women but to rule over the world. The culture of male sensitivity is in danger of submitting to the culture of male supremacy."[30] [Emphasis mine]

While I disagree with the theological dispositions of Malcolm X, one area I have great admiration for him was his ability to win men to himself. How was he able to do that? Why is that so difficult in today's church culture? What is it with western Christianity? What has altered our spiritual DNA were within our core, there is something that repulses men? Let me put it like this, what has caused western Christianity to become so overtly feminized?

Yet, that issue isn't only seen in Church but in Western civilization where it seems men are increasingly dropping out of society. In Britain, 2018, the University and Colleges Admissions Service (UCAS) pointed out that 367,300 women applied to university compared to 269,660 men. That is a difference of 97,640, showing that nearly 100,000 more women than men applied to university.[31].

In 2017, according to the U.S. Department of Education, 56% of students on campuses will be women compared to 44% men, which means, in numerical terms, 2.2 million fewer men than women. They estimate that by 2026, the stats will go up by a percent to 57%. If you compare this to the 1970s, you will see that it is almost a statistical reverse where it was 58% of men who were at university compared to 44% of women.[32]

While in Jamaica, I attended the graduation ceremony of undergraduates from one of the nation's universities. That year, I counted 41 men graduating compared to 450+ women. It was a ratio well over 1 to 11. While I expected a high proportion, I didn't expect anything that dramatic. No one seemed to realize just how devastating this would be on society. Let us just say hypothetically that one of the men who graduated married one female graduate. What would happen to the other ten? Who would they marry? The gardener? The road sweeper? The bus driver? Don't get me wrong; I am not saying that such men are not good men, but from an intellectual point of

---

[30] p164, Christianity, Islam, and Atheism: The Struggle for the Soul of the West by William Kilpatrick, Ignatius Press, 2000.
[31] https://www.independent.co.uk/news/education/gender-gap-university-students-men-women-applications-uk-a8442941.html
[32] https://www.theatlantic.com/education/archive/2017/08/why-men-are-the-new-college-minority/536103/

view, what do you talk about? Then there is the issue of finances and social circles? There are so many dynamics that would be at play.

The Disappearing Act

Nicholas Eberstadt, in his book "Men without work: America's invisible crisis" points out that between 1965 and 2015, American men in work has been on a downward trajectory with more than 7 million jobless men between the ages of 25 and 54 who aren't just unemployed, they are not even looking for work. Many of them are either on some form of government subsidy or dependent on a wife, girlfriend, or family member.

Using the statistics he provides, it is estimated that by the year 2050, one in three American men between the ages of 25 and 54 will be out of work. It is a crisis, he says, hiding in the shadows, and people are mostly unaware of this downward trend. Post World War 2, men between the ages of 25 and 54 in the workplace were at 98%, whereas in 2015, it was 88%. According to the Pew Research Center, the share of men in the USA between 25 and 34 living with their parents rose from 15% in 2006, to 22% in 2014.

In Britain, the Office for National Statistics (ONS) pointed out that in 1971, 8% of children were raised in single-parent homes, but in 2011 it increased to 22%. I must point out that 97% of these single-parent homes are mothers, which means that fathers are absent in one out of five homes across the United Kingdom. In the USA, according to the U.S. Census Bureau, nearly 25 million children, roughly 33% of all children, do not live with their biological father.

This rises to a staggering 73% in Afro-American households according to 2015 data, showing that nearly three out of every four fathers in Afro-American homes are missing. Before anyone brings up the reason of slavery, it is interesting to note that according to census surveys from 1890 to 1940, a black child was slightly more likely to grow up with married parents than a white child. Note also that in 1965, out-of-wedlock births for black women were at 25% compared to 73% in 2015. The statistics are a bit better for Hispanics, where in 1980, the rate was 24% to compared to 53% in 2015. For whites, it stood at 5% in 1965 and 25% in 2015.

I digress for a moment to make a point. With the business of life, it is easy to overlook that things are no longer what they seem to be. One day it dawned on me that I hardly ever saw bees and butterflies like I once did. Even when I went back to Jamaica, I noticed the same thing. And yet without bees and butterflies, how will the plants that produce our food be fertilized? It is incredible how something so important can be overlooked. However, the overlooking was not intentional. It was a very subtle decrease over time that went unnoticed as we were so busy and preoccupied with our lives.

I have not given those statistics to make people feel depressed or to condemn men but to make a point that we in the West are setting ourselves up for disaster if things continue the way it's going. The sad thing is that the modern Church seems to be hand in hand with the world. It is as if the world is the Pied Piper, and the Church has been mesmerized by its tune. Male involvement/leadership has to be consistent on our minds and in our methods if we are to keep the world from affecting us the way it has the church world. We have to see the problems as clear as day if we are going to create any real solutions to this mess.

What we are seeing is a subtle but increasing withdrawal of men in today's society. It is a withdrawal from responsibility and influence in a productive way. While we may not be able to cure society's ills, we can, at the very least, take preventive measures to keep the spirit of this age out of our churches.

We must ask ourselves the question, how did we come to this? Why is the Church such an aversion to modern men? How is it that an organization founded by Christ nearly two thousand years ago that attracted men is today one that repels men?

The Consequences of Feminism in Modern Society

There is a common thread between what is happening in western Christianity and the western world, and it is something I have hinted at before, radical feminism. It only goes to show once again how the world has been influencing the core of Christianity. Feminism has aggressively forced its way, not only into western society but also the western Church.

Before I go further, I want to say that women having rights is not the issue. Women should have the right to vote, the right to work, and a say in their own lives. If a woman wants a top job or a university education, then I say more power to her. But what we are seeing in society today isn't an issue of equality but an aggressive spirit that seeks, not equality, but to dominate men and render them weak and emasculated. Any strong man who has a sense of identity and plays his role as a man, whether it be an employer, employee, father, husband, or a man of the community, he is increasingly seen as a "toxic male" and a threat to the world at large.

The strong male is seen as a stereotype of an older generation. He is associated with the macho man, the wife-beater, the dominating man, and as a threat to a forward-thinking society. For a strong man to give his opinion on any particular subject, he is "mansplaining", which is now an accepted word in modern-day English considering it did not come up as a wrong word on spellchecker as I was typing it!

The thing about feminism is that it is not about gender equality but the destruction of what they see as masculinity. Emily McCombs from the Huffington Post writes, "Little boys want nothing more than to love and be loved. Then toxic masculinity slams down on them like the giant mousetrap from that game "Mouse Trap," and everything changes. As a feminist mom to a 5-year-old boy, I fear the day when the "man" part kicks in."[33] This is coming from a woman who declared via Twitter on December 29, 2017, that her New Year's resolutions were "1. Cultivate female relationships" and "2. Band together and kill all men." [34]

Jody Allard, in her Internet article said, "I'm done pretending men are safe (even my sons)", written on July 6, 2017, "If the feminist men—the men who proudly declare their progressive politics and their fight for quality—aren't safe, then what man is? No man, I fear. I have two sons. They are strong and compassionate—the kind of boys other parents are glad to meet when their daughters bring them home for dinner. They are good boys, in the ways good boys are, but they are not safe boys. I'm starting to believe there's no such thing."[35]

When mothers view their teenage sons as potential rapists, you can see just how destructive feminism is. To say that all men are misogynists and that in their very core are exploiters and abusers of women, man as a whole is beyond redemption. If there is no such thing as a "safe" man, then why shouldn't they be exterminated off the face of the planet? Such a ridiculous belief is not only tolerated; it is also promoted.

Feminism started innocuously – the right to vote and other basic human rights – but it has since revealed the demonic agenda behind it. It is not about equality, as I said earlier, but the domination of masculinity altogether. In the West, men have recognized certain inequalities and their part in their creation and, in turn, have made room for women in society. But now we are seeing

---

[33] https://www.huffingtonpost.co.uk/entry/how-to-raise-a-feminist-son_us_598344b8e4b06d488874aa4d
[34] https://www.inc.com/suzanne-lucas/huffpost-editor-says-new-years-resolution-is-to-kill-all-men.html
[35] http://www.rolereboot.org/culture-and-politics/details/2017-07-im-done-pretending-men-safe-even-sons/#.WV5zqH_7FTl.twitter

the projection of false guilt condemning real masculinity as toxic and something to be feared. The use of false guilt is to make man feel guilty of his manhood and further backtrack.

While there is truth in the #MeToo movement, it is a movement that has been high-jacked by feminists. The agenda is not merely for women to be treated with the respect and dignity they deserve but to further project the guilt of some men upon the entire lot.

Just like a cold, damp atmosphere allows mold to grow on walls, the moral climate of the times allows social cancers like trans-genderism, homosexuality, socialism, fascism, and radical feminism to thrive. What we are now seeing is a snowball effect. As more men retreat from society, the more aggressive feminism becomes, causing more men to retreat from society in meaningful ways.

Distorted Masculinity

There are four main ways in which feminism has negatively impacted masculinity in recent years. These are not always distinct from each other as there is some overlap, but in general, you can see these four having some impact on the modern man.

1. The MGTOW movement

There is a new modern-day men's movement called "Men Going Their Own Way" or MGTOW for short. According to Tim Patten in his book, "MGTOW building Wealth and Power: For Single Men only", MGTOW is "…the modern men's liberation movement, delivering men as a gender from subjugation. MGTOW is a lifestyle that frees men from patriarchal traditions regarding expectations for dating, living entanglements, and marriage. It liberates men from a life of tiresome labor, waste of personal resources and costly emotional exhaustion often devoted to toxic mates, girlfriends, or wives."[36]

MGTOW are bitter and resentful men who see women as having the best of both worlds in today's society, a kind of having your cake and eating it as well. They believe that women desire to be looked after by men and, at the same time, be in charge. They think it is unfair that women can claim to be independent of men and, at the same time, demand that men meet their every

---

[36] p1, MGTOW building Wealth and Power: For Single Men only by Tim Patten, iUniverse, 2016

need. Such a relationship, to them, is a one-way street.

MGTOWs are men bound by self-pity and, as a result, are not able to see what is going on. While we do see an attack on masculinity, it doesn't mean that women have everything their way. Most women are not having their cake and eating it but are suffering under increasing pressure from feminism. The so-called freedom that has been promised is an illusion.

2. Irresponsible masculinity

The pressure many modern women face today is due to the second negative impact that feminism has had on masculinity, and that is the rise of irresponsible males.

It has been said that the women's liberation movement didn't bring freedom to women but rather gave men freedom from responsibility. Many men today love independent women because it means she doesn't have to be a burden on him. I have seen women repeatedly aim to find a "non-threatening" male, only to regret it later in life, having to do everything themselves.

She pays all the bills while he spends his money on whatever he likes. She has to discipline the kids when they misbehave while he ignores them. She is the one who stresses when the debts pile up while he hangs out with his friends. Initially, she may feel that she was independent, but as life catches up with her, she becomes tired, burdened, and worn out.

But it isn't only the wives and girlfriends of deadbeats who suffer burnout. Normal wives experience severe stress when they are told they can be domestic goddesses and professionals at the same time. Many women today suffer from all manner of psychological issues like anxiety and depression due to believing the lie that she can have it all.

It has been my experience in over twenty-one years of ministry to learn of wives pulling out their hair, as the rent and other bills are well overdue, but hubby has spent a good chunk of his month's salary on the latest cell phone. And he is mad that she is mad. I never fail to be amazed at how a man can justify such blatant irresponsibility.

As a result of his negligence, she has no choice but to take all responsibility in her own hands, which causes more irresponsibility. Things get from bad to worse, as the wife crumbles under the pressure, and he has no idea why she is falling apart.

Men are now free to do what they want, and why would they want to go back to their fathers' ancient paths when they can play Peter Pan? Why engage in meaningful conversation when you can spend the night playing the Xbox? Why work hard, save and buy your own home when you can rent an apartment with two or three of your best buddies, and live the life of eligible bachelors?

3. Emotional males

One of the reasons I love Jamaica is that it is a great nation to study human behavior. Jamaicans are not pretentious, and what you see is what you get. They make lousy hypocrites because they can't help be who they are. It is entirely different from England, where the people have perfected the art of wearing masks. It doesn't mean you can't understand human nature in England, but Jamaica surely makes it easier. In England, people can smile in your face and yet have all kinds of negative feelings towards you, whereas, in Jamaica, you always know where you stand with people.

One of the things I got to study in-depth was the effect of dominant femininity on the male psyche. According to one survey done in 2002, 45% of all Jamaican households are headed by a woman.[37] That, I am sure, is far worse today, and the effects can be seen on the young men growing up without fathers in their formative years, only having their mothers as reference points to learn from.

For one, these young men grow up as little princes in the eyes of their mothers. Young Johnny can't do any wrong, and if, God forbid, that he gets into trouble at school, mom will give that teacher a piece of her mind. Young Johnny can get away with anything that his sister can't. Johnny will get his mother's last dollar while his sister will have to do without. Johnny can hang out with his pals while his sister has to stay at home to look after the younger siblings, cook dinner, and wash the clothes.

The paradox of that is that his sister grows up to be an independent young woman who knows she has to look after herself because no one else will look after her. She has the will and determination to make things happen, and it isn't surprising that she educates herself to degree level while her brother dropped out of high school and depends on mom to provide him with money.

The other consequence of growing up without a father is that the mother's

---

[37] https://www.unicef.org/jamaica/parenting_corner.html

femininity stamps itself on his psyche. These young men have grown up being highly emotional, and when combined with natural male testosterone, it creates a very dangerous explosive. While my evidence may be anecdotal, it was something I repeatedly saw in the six years I was there. Men would lash out at the slightest provocation, unable to contain their emotions only to regret their actions after. There was no man around to teach them how to control and regulate their emotions. It was amazing to see how a slight rebuke could emotionally crush them where they would sulk, wallow in self-pity, and isolate themselves for days on end.

Now, let me state that having emotions is not just a feminine thing or that sulking, self-pity, and all kinds of negative emotions are feminine. I'm not saying that at all. I'm saying that when being treated as special, having no ability to control oneself, and being in an atmosphere where emotionalism is rife, being feely-touchy is normal.

Perhaps the most sobering revelation of the overly emotional male was a young man I was working with for several years. He was a lady's man extraordinaire and troublemaker, but a very sharp brain – perhaps the most naturally intelligent individual I met in my time there. He was a real leader of men, charismatic, handsome, and smart, yet he had the Achilles heel of being super emotive. I can remember being with him on several occasions where he would lash out at individuals who "dissed" him.

I remember meeting him with his mother for the first time, and it blew my mind how this tough guy could suddenly switch his persona to be that of a little boy. "Mommy, mommy, I want you to meet my pastor. Yes, mommy, I'm going to Church now." It was the voice of a little boy who desperately wanted his mother's approval.

I recall once meeting him outside our church building for lunch, and he came dressed in a pink shirt, tight white shorts, classic white sneakers, and a sailor's hat, and I nearly fell on the street laughing in hysterics at just how camp he looked. He was a playboy for sure, but he seemed so effeminate, and what made it funnier is that he genuinely didn't know why I was laughing.

Less than four years later, this same young man was in prison for murder. The ex-boyfriend of his girlfriend "dissed" him, and he stabbed him to death. He stabbed him 83 times with most of those stab wounds occurring while the rival was still alive and with him looking his victim directly in the eye. It's not surprising that his mother spent every penny she had on lawyers knowing that her son was indeed a murderer, but hey, he is her little prince. Funny enough, his sisters have gone on to graduate from university, paying their way to get there.

I have not said that to say that Jamaica is worse than anywhere else. It is to simply highlight something seen there that goes on everywhere else, albeit not to such a dramatic extent. Young men today are highly emotional and, as a result, are unable to contain their natural male aggression.

London today is struggling with an epidemic of knife crimes, and all the government seems to think will solve the problem is spending more money policing youth. No one seems to want to address the real root of the problem, which is fatherless homes, where there is no dominant male figure in the lives of these young men that can help keep them in check.

But the manifestation of emotional males isn't just in the area of crime and violence but also seen in the home. Many men today, growing up in fatherless homes, cannot cope with life's demands. There are genuine men out there who start out wanting to be different from their fathers but are ill-equipped to cope when the pressure is on. It is an increasing but disturbing thing to see men pick up and leave their homes altogether because they just can't cope as they succumb to all manner of negative emotions of fear, despair, hopelessness, and depression. And I'm not talking about only men who run off with a new woman somewhere else, but men who had disappeared off the grid completely, not because of a sexual rendezvous, but unable to handle the responsibilities of manhood.

4. Emasculated males

Perhaps the most "celebrated" of neutralized masculinity is the rise of the emasculated males. Much has been said about the emasculated male, and I won't try to rehash what has already been said, but I think a few points should be made.

In the last twenty-five years or so, we have been hearing that men should be in touch with their feminine sides. Now let me just say that when we hear that, all we usually focus on is the fact that there is a push for men to be feminine. Let me point out the deeper meaning of that phrase. It is saying that emotions are strictly in the feminine realm and that masculinity is unemotional. It is, therefore, suggesting that there is something fundamentally wrong with masculinity adding to the idea of "toxic masculinity" and that femininity is the right thing.

Jesus is the most masculine of men that ever lived, yet He showed many emotions in the three years of His ministry. Jesus wept at the grave of Lazarus

(John 11:35), He was in agony (Luke 22:44), troubled, sorrowful, and deeply distressed (Mark 14:33-34) in the Garden of Gethsemane. He marveled at the faith of the centurion (Matthew 8:10), angry and grieved with the Pharisees' hardness of heart (Mark 3:5), had compassion for the people (Matthew 9:36), and rejoiced (Luke 10:21).

The central idea of men being in touch with their "feminine side" is for them to be more self-aware of how they behave. It is social engineering on a huge platform. Men must learn how to tone down their masculinity. While they should work for a living, they shouldn't be too aggressive and dominant in the workplace. While they should be thoughtful and sympathetic, they shouldn't be condescending. Of course, men should have some sort of intelligence but not show arrogance in displaying their knowledge.

All this is subjective and relative. How aggressive is aggressive? It may be aggressive to one and yet normal to the other. What may genuinely be sympathy can be treated by another, bound in insecurities, as condescending and what may genuinely be insight can be condemned as mansplaining.

As a result, many well-meaning men find themselves confused and on the back foot. A curveball could occur any minute and from out of nowhere. He is ashamed of his masculinity as society has brainwashed him into thinking that way. He doesn't know if he opens a door for a woman if he will be treated with contempt for assuming she can't open the door, or if he doesn't, she will think he is a jerk. The result is many men just give up and try their best to keep from offending the new social norms. They have emasculated themselves and have channeled their energies to navigate through the politically correct environs they now inhabit and hope for the best. They have turned themselves into wimps without any kind of conviction or personal standard of conduct but blow in the direction society tells them at any given time.

How this translates into relationships with the opposite sex is that confusion reigns. These are men who won't reveal their masculinity to their wives because they are afraid that being assertive or dominant will cause their wives to leave. They dance and skirt around issues when in reality their wives just want them to simply show some backbone and make a decision. The irony about such men is that their wives get frustrated and will pick an innocuous fight, prod and poke just so that they can get some kind of reaction.

Society is made up of individuals and as individual males succumb to this modern indoctrination, western culture has degenerated into a society of impotent men. The dramatic drop in western's society's birth rate is an excellent analogy of that impotency. The great fear of the loss of European culture is the Islamization of the West through mass immigration when in fact another very important factor is the drop in the birth rate.

According to the U.K. left-wing newspaper, the Guardian, the average fertility rate for Muslims is 2.6 compared to 1.6 for non-Muslims. The article also pointed out that the proportion of Muslims under the age of 15 is 27%, while that of non-Muslims is 15%, nearly double. [38]

The article uses data from the Pew Research Center. According to the report, if mass immigration were to stop, by the year 2050 Europe's Muslim population would increase from 4.9% to 7.4%. [39] In 2017, the name "Muhammad" became the eighth most popular boy's name in the U.K. Just a decade earlier, it was the forty-third.[40] It seems that literally as well as figuratively speaking, the increasing impotency of a secularized Europe is threatened by the potency of Islam.

Whether you like Islam or not, one thing you can't disagree with is that their men are anything but effeminate or androgynous. Much furor has been made about the child-grooming outbreaks in England where organized gangs of young Muslim men have exploited vulnerable under-aged girls and also in Germany where on New Year's Eve, December 31 2015, there was mass sexual assaults all over the country by Muslim men. While I agree those things ought not to have been done, the fact is that local men are no longer the protectors and defenders of women. How could they be? They are either emasculated or have abandoned their homes and thus abandoned their wives and daughters to exploiters of any background. I could be wrong, but I do not think such a thing could be attempted en masse in the American mid-West.

I find it very interesting that with the rise of radical feminism and the vitriol against anything masculine in the West, those same feminists do not display the same rage against fundamentalist Islam. It's incredible to me to see feminists defend the "right" for Muslim women to wear the hijab; the greatest physical symbol of women's oppression.

Jordan Peterson once said in an interview, "I read this quote once…'men tested ideas and women test men'…obviously it is an overgeneralization, but we also don't know to what degree women test men through provocation. If

---

[38] https://www.theguardian.com/world/2017/nov/29/muslim-population-in-europe-could-more-than-double
[39] https://www.pewforum.org/2017/11/29/europes-growing-muslim-population/
[40] http://fortune.com/2017/09/22/muhammad-william-popular-baby-names/

you want to test someone…you poke the hell out of them and say "Okay, I'm going to go after you and see where your weak spots are."…One of the things I really try to puzzle out and it's not that I believe this but I'm just telling you where the edges of my thinking has been going, is that you have this crazy alliance between the feminists and the radical Islamists that I just do not get. Why are they not protesting non-stop about Saudi Arabia is just completely beyond me? I do not understand it in the least and I wonder too…this is the Freud in me, is there an attraction that is emerging among the female radicals for that totalitarian male dominance that they have chased out of the West? That is a hell of a thing to think but after all I am psychoanalytically minded and I do think things like that…As the demand for egalitarianism and the eradication of masculinity accelerates there is going to be a longing in the unconscious for the precise opposite of that. The more you scream for equality, the more your unconscious is going to admire dominance."[41]

That is a lot to think about but the point, I believe, is correct. Women ultimately despise the emasculated male and for all his effort to acquiesce he will fail to achieve the goal of pleasing females. When the mouse is running on the floor, the woman doesn't want her man to accompany her on the kitchen table screaming in unison, but for him to kill the mouse.

I knew someone years ago whose father and mother separated due to domestic violence. She went on with her life and in an attempt to rebuild and empower herself, she studied hard and got herself a doctorate. That was good on her part. What wasn't wise was marrying soon after to a man who was working as a low level, minimum waged employee. My friend didn't feel right about that and asked for my opinion and I agreed. It wasn't that the man was a bad guy or a bum, far from it. He was a great guy. But it was a mismatch because she felt like a powerful alpha-female and she chose him because he wasn't a threat to her. He was a man she could dominate and not be intimidated by like her previous husband.

I knew it would end in disaster, but it was far worse than I thought because eventually, mixing with high society due to her position, she became ashamed of her poorly educated husband. One day she announced she was going to leave and so he killed her and then killed himself.

Now I know that is an extreme case, but women ultimately resent the emasculated male. He may be a smooth looking metrosexual but if you scratch below the surface you will find nothing. I have seen with my own

---

[41] https://www.youtube.com/watch?v=-vT86SjrISk

eyes women who find it difficult to respect a man who spends the day looking after the children while she is at the office surrounded by alpha males. Initially all may seem well, but it is when a woman needs her man the most that she will find out that the man she thought was her soul mate was really just a shell of a man.

The Damage Caused by the Welfare State

When I was pioneering my first Church in Manchester, England I met a man who was a former Assemblies of God pastor. He and his family had visited one of the concerts I had and we struck up a friendship. He was in his late 40s, enrolled in a local Bible college and working towards a degree. As a result of being a full-time student he found himself in serious debt. He went to the social services who offered him a deal. He could either face bankruptcy or he could leave the family home and the state would pay the rent and financially provide for his wife and son.

He chose to face bankruptcy rather than have his home split, but this is the insidiousness of the welfare state where the state now takes the role of the father. I can see the reasoning behind the creation of the welfare system, but its implementation created a lot of unintended consequences such as the contribution to the degradation of the nuclear family. With the state taking responsibility for women and children, what need is there for a man?

Up until very recently in the U.K., a teenager who found herself pregnant was given an apartment and various other state benefits. This was the solution the government created to deal with the fallout from the sexual revolution of the 1960s. What they didn't realize is that it wasn't a solution but an incentive to further promiscuity. "Do you mean I get my own place and money without having to get a job if I get pregnant and I'm not married?"

While this has been clamped down in recent times as mass immigration has resulted in an immense strain on social services, the culture of male irresponsibility has been exacerbated. Why should any young man have a sense of responsibility? He doesn't have to feel guilty for not providing because where he falls short, the state will foot the bill. There is no need to work because the state will provide.

A culture of dependency was ingrained in the psyche of many, especially in the north of England. In my time in Manchester, I have seen state dependency at its worse with generations of men not working and having no intention to work. Living in government housing and claiming unemployment benefits every two weeks, they scratch out an existence on cash-in-hand jobs to supplement their meager benefits. This is so ironic considering that Manchester was one of those small market towns that boomed due to the Industrial Revolution.

It doesn't matter how hard the government tries to fight state dependency, as radical leftists do their uttermost to undermine the mission. A similar case can be made in the USA where free money has fortified the ghetto and it is no coincidence that these areas primarily support the Democratic Party, the very people who keep them poor and dependent. It is ironic that black Americans depend more on government subsidies today than they did back in the 1960s.

I have previously pointed out that out-of-wedlock births for black women were at 25% in 1965 but exactly fifty years later it is 73%. For ethnic minorities the welfare system has done unbelievable destruction. Whereas at one time children from single-parent homes felt ashamed to go to school because everyone else had their fathers at home, nowadays having both father and mother at home is seen as weird. The paradox is that a system that was created to improve people's lives has now made it worse.

The Consequences of Feminism in the Modern Church

Not only is the family and society at large struggling due to this imbalance, but the Church is struggling as well. Nowadays in the western Church, women are overrepresented while men are underrepresented. Women have more expression in the Church than ever before, and men have less expression. For many women, they see it as a sign of progress but is it?

For one, the average man doesn't like to be dominated by a woman and even if only on a subconscious level, a church in which most of the expression is by women is a put off. Men want to be where men are free to be themselves. This could be the bar, the basketball court, or the football field. If a church is dominated by women, then that's the last place they feel comfortable. If they do stay in that atmosphere, they are either governed by women or passive in their involvement.

It has been my experience over the years to see men who have larger than life wives are they themselves emasculated. Masculine men, in such a church atmosphere, are viewed with covert hostility and met with invisible resistance. This in turn causes men who are not emasculated to be as involved as little as possible. It's incredible to find such men who are as exciting as a blank piece of paper become so creative and energetic outside the walls of the Church. Whether it is conscious or unconscious on their part, they have learned to back off in order to avoid contention.

All this serves to do is to keep men out of the Church or cause them to have a hands-off approach to church activity. Any young man coming into such an atmosphere dominated by women feels like a fish out of water and more than likely will not be making a second visit. This secures the gender imbalance and it sends a message to men that Church is not the place to be. Over the years of evangelizing the unchurched, whether in Jamaica or Britain, there has never been a time where young men have seen the Church as anything but a feminine organization to avoid. It was something I always had to be aware of when pioneering, especially in Jamaica.

The second problem is this, if one out of three, four, or five members of a church is a man, who are the other one, two, or three women going to marry? In Jamaica, I always mused to myself, whenever I was invited to a service, just who these women are married to, if they are indeed married. The fact is if they were married their husbands weren't Christians. The joke in Jamaica is that on Sunday mornings, husbands drop their wives to Church where they will be filled with the Spirit. But the husbands go to the bar where they will be filled with another kind of spirit.

And in a country that has more churches per square mile than any other nation, yet having an 86% illegitimacy rate, you can guarantee that many of them are living in fornication. And so while the women may be preachers, prophetesses, and deaconesses, the truth of the matter is that many are either married to unsaved men or living in fornication. How does that make a church effective?

Years ago, a friend of mine told me of a common occurrence in his old Church, a church packed with single eligible females but very few males. It always amused him that when a young man answered an altar call, there was an immediate rush by mothers, inviting him home for dinner to introduce him to her daughter. Such was the desperation in the Church due to the lack of men. (It didn't do well for the Church in terms of those men staying because as tough as it is to answer an altar call, I hardly think any young man would like to be press-ganged into marriage.)

The truth is that for many women, the Church is the only place where they can feel a sense of dignity and empowerment and yet it is only a sense and not the real thing because in the spiritual realm, Satan has no respect for uncovered women. In a misogynistic society like Jamaica, men have not given their women dignity and respect and so they go to the Church and believe they can find it in a position. As men withdraw from society, they also too withdraw from Church and with all manners of needs in Church, the Church looks to women to fill the gap and they do so gladly. As a result, while the temporal needs are met, it creates a long term problem where the gender gap increases.

It is a vicious cycle in so many different ways that we haven't got time to go into. I would also like to add that as young boys grow up in an effeminate church, every service is a nail in the coffin for future church involvement, and as soon as they are of age, they go out the door, never to be seen again.

Being Mindful of the Issues

What we need to realize is that this spirit behind feminism is nothing new but something released from the original curse invoked on the original couple where in Genesis 3:16 God said to Eve, "Your desire shall be or your husband, and he shall rule over you." In this case, the term "your desire" doesn't mean only attraction or affection. In Genesis 4:7, when God warns Cain to do right, He says to him, "If you do well, will you not be accepted? And if you do not do well, sin lies at the door. And its desire is for you, but you should rule over it." It is the same type of sentence construction and we know sin doesn't have affection for the sinner. Its desire is to control and dominate and that was a part of the curse where women would desire to control men and men would seek to dominate women.

The battle of the sexes is a direct fallout from the fall of man into sin. What was once a harmonious union of male and female ended up becoming a tit-for-tat war for dominance. Something that was once simple has now become a complicated issue, and where God's desire was for a productive relationship between the two has now in our generation become a significant stumbling block to the wellbeing of society at large. In the battle between two sides that were created to work together, no one wins.

Believing the Lie

In any pioneering work in the western world, one has to appreciate that we are not starting from scratch like a missionary to Mongolia or Kazakhstan. Even amongst the unsaved, there is an awareness of Christianity, even if it is on a basic level. Most people know about the traditional Sunday morning service, the role of a pastor or priest, and so on. It is something we take for granted until we find ourselves on the other side of the world struggling to lay foundations that we once thought everyone knew.

While that is good, what is also an issue is the modern interpretation of the Church, a church that has been feminized. How do we seek to bring balance to something that is now viewed as normal Christianity? How do we make it plain to our female converts that they cannot take the lead as they would in another church? How do we get our male converts to "man up"? How do we appreciate Christian mindfulness in the West but tweak it to our advantage?

This is especially true considering the times we live in where the issue isn't just about male and female or "toxic masculinity" but gender in general. In a sense, we are lucky, that for the most part, the struggle in Church is only between male and female. As society moves further away from God, we see an increase in confusion, not only between traditional male and female roles but gender itself.

Something I once took for granted is that there were only two sexes – male and female. This is something that is now breathtakingly brought into question. Now chaos reigns as we are told that there are myriads of sexes, and the list keeps on growing. New York, last time I checked, recognizes 31 different sexes. I know I am repeating myself, but it has to be emphasized that modern society is swept, not with little lies, but lies on a grand scale that boggle the mind with incredulity.

In James Murphy's translation of "Mein Kampf" he quotes Adolph Hitler as saying, "…in the big lie there is always a certain force of credibility; because the broad masses of a nation are always more easily corrupted in the deeper strata of their emotional nature than consciously or voluntarily; and thus in the primitive simplicity of their minds they more readily fall victims to the big lie than the small lie…It would never come into their heads to fabricate colossal untruths, and they would not believe that others could have the impudence to distort the truth so infamously. Even though the facts which prove this to be so may be brought clearly to their minds, they will still doubt and waver and will continue to think that there may be some other explanation. For the grossly impudent lie always leaves traces behind it, even after it has been nailed down…"

Hitler wasn't just a military leader but a man totally under the control of demonic forces and, as a result, had tactics and strategies inspired by hell itself. Just as Hitler used propaganda to control the minds of Nazi Germany, Satan uses thoughts and suggestions to transform the thinking of men and women. Gender confusion is an issue that needs to be addressed in its own right, but I pointed that out because it is something that we will have to face shortly. That confusion is simply the consequence of man stepping out of touch with God and His word and opening the door for sin.

My son was discussing with a schoolmate, and a girl, about transgenderism, when his teacher stepped through the door. There was a dispute as to whether another girl who identified herself as a boy was a boy. My son and his friend said that she was still a girl, which offended the other girl. The teacher interjected and said to her, "Never mind them. They are just confused." My son looked at his friend incredulously and said, "We're confused?"

But that's the generation we live in where right is wrong, wrong is right, light is darkness, and darkness is light. Children nowadays are indoctrinated by schools and the media. Yet they will be visiting our churches in the future. These are the ones who believe that what is abnormal is normal, which implies that we are abnormal.

Several years ago, the nation of Zimbabwe had a severe financial crisis where hyperinflation peaked at 79,600,000% PER month in November 2008. As a result, there was an intermittent service of the essential utilities of water and electricity with frequent power cuts and water shortages. Fast forward to 2010, where customers rang the utility companies to ask if something was wrong. For a whole week in the capital of Harare, they had both water and electric running for an entire week without any water shortages or power cuts. They wanted to know why there was such consistency in the supplies. Were workers sleeping on the job and left the water and electricity to run unsupervised?

This is what happens when the normal is considered abnormal. We may laugh at the story, but in Western society, we see something similar when it comes to male leadership. We are so used to absentee fathers, emasculated and effeminate men, irresponsible males, metrosexuals, and passive husbands. They refuse to leave the nest, and this increasingly seen as normative behavior. Men who lead their homes, work hard, are disciplinarians, play a hands-on approach to parenting, and who are the primary breadwinners are increasingly seen as controlling and authoritative and, therefore, uncomfortable to be around.

All this is the result of modern social engineering. More and more we are hearing about the "patriarchy" and that the relationship between the sexes is a social construct. The wickedness behind that belief is that if the roles of men and women are due to social engineering then it means a re-balancing must be done through social re-engineering. In other words, they will justify creating real social engineering by blaming everything on a fake social engineering. It would be genius if it wasn't so devastating.

But we have to remember that we are not fighting against flesh and blood. Our battle is not against feminism or modern social engineers who are looking to reform society in a way that they see fit. Our struggle is against the spiritual forces that are creating these demonic ideas and agendas. And we have to keep ourselves from being conditioned by false philosophies being propagated in the world and from being sympathetic to ungodly teachings that ultimately will result in the destruction of society. Our role is not merely to passively embrace the dysfunction we see in society and hope to do our best despite it, but to also seek the solution to the problem.

We must realize that in a society that is increasingly disconnected from God, the more demonic lies and strategies will be implanted in the hearts and minds of men and women across the world. The following scripture I am about to share is something I have read for over twenty-five years, but it has never been so profoundly true in my mind as it is today.

The apostle Paul says in Romans 1:18-19; 21-22; 24-29, "For the wrath of God is revealed from heaven against all ungodliness and unrighteousness of men, who suppress the truth in unrighteousness, because what may be known of God is manifest in them, for God has shown it to them… because, although they knew God, they did not glorify Him as God, nor were thankful, but became futile in their thoughts, and their foolish hearts were darkened. Professing to be wise, they became fools… Therefore God also gave them up to uncleanness, in the lusts of their hearts, to dishonor their bodies among themselves, who exchanged the truth of God for the lie…For this reason God gave them up to vile passions. For even their women exchanged the natural use for what is against nature. Likewise also the men, leaving the natural use of the woman, burned in their lust for one another, men with men committing what is shameful, and receiving in themselves the penalty of their error which was due. And even as they did not like to retain God in their knowledge, God gave them over to a debased mind, to do those things which are not fitting; being filled with all unrighteousness, sexual immorality, wickedness, covetousness…"

If that doesn't describe the western world today, I don't know what does. This is a generation that has created the most technological advancements in mankind's history and yet never has a generation been so idiotic as now to think it is possible for a man to be a woman just because he feels he is one (how would a man know how a woman feels having never been one before). This is the generation that believes if you are white, you can make yourself black or Asian. I'm not trying to make fun of anyone who feels they are suffering from gender or racial dysphoria but it is a demonic spirit lying to people and it is spirit that has been given access to the world because of their willful disconnection from their Creator.

In speaking of the end times, the apostle Paul continues in 2 Thessalonians 2:9-11, "The coming of the lawless one is according to the working of Satan, with all power, signs, and lying wonders, and with all unrighteous deception among those who perish, because they did not receive the love of the truth, that they might be saved. And for this reason God will send them strong delusion, that they should believe the lie…" Ultimately he speaks of the coming of the Antichrist, but we can see that the times we are living in people are given over to strong delusion so that they believe things that are utterly false.

We must realize what we are dealing with. These are spiritual forces operating in the world today, and we can't afford to let the lies affect our beliefs. As the world twists things and defines perversion as love and truth to be hate, we can't afford to fall into the trap of thinking that there is something wrong with us why we can't see what they see.

It is one thing for the world to be blind. It is another thing for the Church to be able to see and yet pretend to be blind. The pressure the world is putting on us is like the case of the Emperor's new clothes. Everyone can see that he is naked, but no one wants to say anything for fear of being labeled as stupid. It is no coincidence that Hans Christian Andersen uses a child to expose the lunacy of the king (and the people) because kids say it as it is because they are not beholden to social pressures. This is why we need to stay close to the word and not the world.

Being Reconnected to Jesus

I recall a story of a missionary who lived in a third world country for a few years before returning. He had been using a beat-up wreck of a car whose starter motor had not been working properly for a while. He had no money to get it fixed, but he found a way to get his car to work even without the starter. He parked the car near the brow of a hill, and when he needed to drive it, he would roll the car down the hill until it jerked its way into starting.

It was a bit inconvenient, especially when he had to visit someone or do errands, and the nearest hill was a few blocks away, but for the most part, it was something he got used to. When the new missionary came, the old preacher took him around, and he showed him how he would be able to start the car before he left. He thought he would have been commended for his ingenuity, but the new guy looked at him as if he was crazy. He had a look at the engine, tinkered around for a while. He then turned on the ignition, and the engine roared to life.

The old missionary was amazed. "How did you do that?" The new guy said, "There were a couple of wires loose, and all I did was reconnect them. That was all."

We live in world that is disconnected to Jesus and that is the reason why we are seeing all the issues we are seeing. The problem isn't feminism or any other 'ism' but simply due to the fact that because of sin and apostasy society has walked away from Christ and His words. We need to get back to the word of God and see what it has to say about men and women.

We need to do that because the truth is that for all the negativity we are hearing about male leadership in today's society, without that leadership, families, communities, and societies will fall apart. Modern society may not like it, but it is something they need. And more and more women realize without real men in their lives, things are much harder than they should be. The fictional idealism of the late teens and 20s usually give in to the cold pragmatic realities of the 30s when the consequences of earlier decisions play out.

Anne Bonny is possibly the most famous female pirate of all time. She was married to the notorious pirate John "Calico Jack" Rackham, who was eventually captured at sea when he and his men were utterly drunk. Jack gave up without so much of a fight and was sent to Jamaica to be hanged. His wife, Anne, had given a good fight before she was captured. Before he was hung, she visited him in prison, where she said, "If you had fought like a man, you wouldn't now have to hang like a dog. Do straighten yourself up!" For all her adventure of trying to be a man in a man's world, she escaped hanging by getting pregnant.

Whether modernists like it or not, the Western world was built on strong men who worked hard, loved their wives, took care of their families and responsibilities, and were examples to others. Throwing money at a dysfunctional society is no way to solve long term problems, and the best way to fix society is by empowering men to be men and that empowering comes by connecting men to Jesus.

A Biblical Framework

Clearly Defining the Roles

So how do we iron out the mess we find ourselves in when it comes to Church? The first thing we have to do is go back to the word of God. It may seem redundant to comment, but we are either Christians, or we are not. If we are Christians, then it means we are followers of Christ who said in John 8:31-32, "If you abide in My word, you are My disciples indeed. And you shall know the truth, and the truth shall make you free." It means that we live by the word of God, not the opinions and the dictates of the world, which we know is contrary to the word of God.

So, what does the word of God have to say about male and female relationships? Genesis 1:27 says, "So God created man in His own image; in the image of God He created him; male and female He created them." From the very beginning of the Bible, we see the idea behind the creation of mankind, and it was for mankind to be made (1) in God's image and (2) male and female. We must go back to the beginning because it is there we find God's purpose in our creation.

When Christ addressed the issue of divorce, He deals with it by saying in Matthew 19:4-6, "Have you not read that He who made them at the beginning 'made them male and female,' and said, 'For this reason a man shall leave his father and mother and be joined to his wife, and the two shall become one flesh'? So then, they are no longer two but one flesh. Therefore what God has joined together, let not man separate." Jesus goes right back to Genesis to deal with the complex issue of divorce by highlighting the simplicity of God's word.

I digress for a moment to simply say that for most of my Christian life, I have taken those words to be obvious. The grass is green; the sky is blue, oranges grow on trees, and water is wet. These things can't be helped but be taken for granted. But now, in today's confusing society, it seems that there are certain things you can't take for granted anymore. Is water really wet? Do oranges really grow on trees, or is that what the government tells us? And today, things that we once took for granted, we now, all of a sudden, question.

This is why a verse in the Bible that seems so self-explanatory that it is like stating the obvious is so crucial in today's world. In all the lies and confusion about gender, we can go right back to the very beginning of the Bible, the very start of the word of God, the very foundation of truth. At the beginning of the truth of God's word, we read these words, "...male and female He created them." This truth is our anchor is a stormy sea of confusion, and as society staggers under the delusion unleashed, this truth will keep us from sinking.

This is a chapter on male leadership, so time is not on our side for us to deviate and look into why the obvious is obvious, so we have to take for granted what we have always taken for granted: there is male, and there is female. Many of us are still "old school" enough for us to accept the obvious, so there is no need in this book. But what is not so obvious are the roles and relationships between the sexes. The truth is that we are not "old school" enough when it comes to the understanding that there are certain differences between the sexes. Modern ideas of "gender-fluidity" do have their roots in the idea that men and women are the same, something many of us deep down have been brought up to believe, as feminism made its impact on the world stage back in the 20th century.

As evangelical churches reaching out to lost sinners, we will automatically bring in people who have grown up, consciously or unconsciously, believing this mess. One of the things we have to address – clearly, biblically, and pragmatically – is the reality and importance of gender distinction and roles. We must create a culture in our churches where there is a distinction between the sexes. I am not suggesting that we implement Islamic principles such as women and men sitting in different rooms or different sides of the aisles during services, but in regards to the roles we play, it must be seen clearly.

Why? Men and women are not the same. We may have equal value and worth, but we do not have the same functions in life. A husband and wife may be "...heirs together of the grace of life..." (1 Peter 3:7) but they do not have the same duties and roles. A knife and a fork may be made out of the same materials and may cost the same, but they have two completely different tasks. No one would be happy to have either two knives or two forks to eat with. We take it for granted that while they are both different, they complement each other and that complementary difference gets the job done and makes the job easier. Imagine trying to eat with two forks or two knives. Imagine cutting a steak with a fork and picking it up with a knife.

Using a knife as a fork or a fork for a knife only makes eating complicated and ineffective. Standing up for the rights of the knife saying that it should also be able to be used as a fork because it is of the same value as a fork, not only makes eating difficult, it also diminishes the role that a knife plays in eating. Imagine a world where knives have the fork's role, and forks were left to the sidelines because the days of the "forkiarchy" were over.

As someone who loves a well-cooked T-bone steak, I have no partial preference for either the fork or the knife, which is crucial in my enjoying my meal. I do not see the fork as more important than the knife or the knife more important than the fork. Having one without the other would make my eating experience a very difficult one. Thank God for both the knife and the fork. It is a marriage I would never want to put asunder.

Yet when it comes to the issue of the roles between males and females in today's society, this is precisely what is happening. The role of the fork and the knife are interchangeable, and no one, it seems, sees the problems we are facing in the home, community, and society at large.

There is a reason why God made mankind into two genders; because together, they get things done. As the man plays his part and the woman does the same, both family and the world become better places. But when roles are interchanged, things get difficult, and life gets complicated, which God did not intend. If we are honest, much of modern life is difficult and complicated. In many cases, therein lies the dysfunctional relationship between men and women. This is something many people don't recognize, primarily due to one of man's greatest strengths, and simultaneously, greatest weakness. It is the ability to keep on going in bad situations. While it is possible to make some kind of progress, it isn't effective, and it certainly isn't God's will.

The Role of the Man

God's call for a man is for him to be the leader in his home, his Church, and his society. Having that role doesn't make him superior to the woman but it is a role that he was created for and because of that is more able to effectively handle. 1 Peter 3:7 says, "Husbands, likewise, dwell with them with understanding, giving honor to the wife, as to the weaker vessel, and as being heirs together of the grace of life, that your prayers may not be hindered."

If there were words in the Bible that so-called "Christian feminists" resent and wish they could be deleted it is "the weaker vessel" phrase. Whether they like it or not, it is a spiritual truth just like the truth of husbands and wives "being heirs together". She may be weaker, but Peter goes on to say she is equal. Nevertheless, by implication the man is the stronger vessel and that isn't just a physical attribute but a spiritual one as well. A man's failure to understand and honor his wife will result in the consequence of a spiritually diminished life. This is the protection that God has given the weaker vessel to balance everything.

It is imperative as the pressure of western feminism increases on the Church that we function biblically in order to prevent the dysfunction of the world from impacting us. The spiritual fate of the world rests upon the shoulders of the Church and we cannot allow blindness of the world to cause us to shut our eyes to the truth of the word of God. It is idiotic to let the sick infect the healthy instead of the healthy healing the sick.

This is why the idea of interchanging roles between men and women may be seen as "progressive" in the world but in the Church it is regressive. It is regressive because it is unbiblical. Ephesians 5:22-24 says, "Wives, submit to your own husbands, as to the Lord. For the husband is head of the wife, as also Christ is head of the Church; and He is the Savior of the body. Therefore, just as the Church is subject to Christ, so let the wives be to their own husbands in everything."

The apostle Paul points out that the roles of Christ and the Church are clearly defined. Christ is the head of the Church and the Church is subject to Christ. There can be no interchanging of roles. The Church can never be the head of Christ and Christ can never be subject to the Church. In light of that, the apostle Paul says, "…let the wives be [subject] to their own husbands in everything." Christ died to save the Church. The Church can never die to save Christ.

It goes further. The apostle continues in Ephesians 5:31-32, "For this reason a man shall leave his father and mother and be joined to his wife, and the two shall become one flesh." This is a great mystery, but I speak concerning Christ and the Church." Once again he goes back to the beginning, to Genesis 2:24 and quotes the words of Adam. but Paul in this context, isn't speaking about the relationship between Adam and Eve but between Christ and the Church.

What am I saying? Many times we read these verses thinking that Paul is using the relationship between Adam and Eve as an illustration of Christ and the Church. In other words, Christ and the Church's relationship reference off the original relationship between Adam and Eve. Not true at all. It is the other way around. Adam and Eve's relationship in Genesis 2:24 is a direct result of something God saw in eternity before the creation of man and that was the relationship between Christ and His Church.

Before man was created, the clearly defined role between Christ and the Church was orchestrated and the relationship between a man and a woman was supposed to reflect that. This means any relationship that functions otherwise is a distortion and there are bound to be conflicts and strains rather than peace and harmony.

Male Leadership in the Church

It is no coincidence that when the apostle Paul talks about leadership in the Church he says in 1 Timothy 3:1-3, "This is a faithful saying: If a man desires the position of a bishop, he desires a good work. A bishop then must be blameless, the husband of one wife, temperate, sober-minded, of good behavior, hospitable, able to teach; not given to wine, not violent, not greedy for money, but gentle, not quarrelsome, not covetous; one who rules his own house well, having his children in submission with all reverence (for if a man does not know how to rule his own house, how will he take care of the Church of God?)"

I have heard women preachers say, "I have the authority in the church but my husband has authority in the home." Well, if that is true then it means that a woman does not have to have authority in her own home in order to have authority in the Church. It means a woman can have her cake and eat it whereas a male preacher does not have that liberty. It means that there is one rule for the women and one rule for the men.

The reality is that women who are in authority in the pulpit are also in authority out of it. This was the case with Smith Wigglesworth's wife and any other woman preacher. Someone has to have the dominant role in the household and so if it is the woman then it automatically means the man takes the role of the submissive one. It is unsurprising to see that is the case in the home of many women preachers where she is the senior pastor.

It is unsurprising because if there is a practice that is seen as outdated by most of the modern Church, it is the doctrine of male leadership. Much of the Church is in agreement with the world that such a teaching is bigoted and sexist and as a result "women are being held back from using their gifts and as a result the church suffers". In much of the church world, women have a right to lead just as much as men. After all, didn't the Bible say, "Your sons and your daughters shall prophesy..."? (Acts 2:17)

It can be very daunting to preach on male leadership in our day and age due to the politically correct culture of gender equality where it seems that no one realizes that there is a difference between equality of worth and equality of roles but it must be preached and practiced.

Once again we go to the word of God and to the writings of the apostle Paul who said in 1 Timothy 2:11-15, "Let a woman learn in silence with all submission. And I do not permit a woman to teach or to have authority over a man, but to be in silence. For Adam was formed first, then Eve. And Adam was not deceived, but the woman being deceived, fell into transgression. Nevertheless she will be saved in childbearing if they continue in faith, love, and holiness, with self-control."

Paul does not go back to culture or tradition, but right back to the beginning, Adam was created first and thus has the right of the firstborn to authority. Not just that, but women are more trusting and as a result more prone to spiritual deception and therefore unfit to the role of spiritual leadership. This goes right back to what Peter said about women being the weaker vessel. A woman has a role to play, but it is in the context of homemaking. That may seem sexist to some, but it is a spiritual balance to the chaos we are seeing affecting the world today. I would rather be seen as sexist in the world's eyes if it means having families that are in order and harmony and not struggling with the stresses and strains seen in modern-day relationships.

Years ago when I was in Manchester I was told of a local female evangelist who shared my last name. She was going around various churches developing her ministry but at the same time she was a single mother with a son who was a gang member. I wondered perhaps if she had spent more time with her son maybe she wouldn't have lost him to the gangs. I don't know her and all I can do is to speculate but go no further. I am not her judge. But it was something that I kept at the back of my mind. Interestingly enough, in Jamaica I knew of quite a number of female pastors whose sons were gangsters. I have spoken to such men whose mothers were the preachers in the community. No husband, a handful of kids but they are the pastors of their local Church.

It was then that the Apostle Paul's words were reinforced in my thinking. The Passion Translation translates 1 Timothy 2:15 as, "Yet a woman shall live in restored dignity by means of her children, receiving the blessing that comes from raising them as consecrated children nurtured in faith and love, walking in wisdom." It made perfect sense to me in Jamaica, seeing women raise multiple children from different men, who have lost their self-worth as result, looking to ministry to restore a sense of honor and become so fixated on that, that they lost their children to the devil.

I'm not for once saying that if everything is done right it will result in having saved children, but a woman's first priority is ministering to her children's spiritual needs, not that of a church.

The Ineffective Church

I have already pointed out that a female-dominated church will cause problems for the very females who occupy them. A lack of males means that many of those women will not have Christian husbands. It means that the rest will either be married to men who are not saved, or will struggle with sexual temptation (by men at work or in the community) or will give in to fornication and somehow justify their sinful lifestyle. How can such a church be effective? Oh, yes, there can be much singing and dancing and praising the Lord in the church service, but from a spiritual dynamic, how is there anything effective?

In speaking of covering, the apostle Paul says in 1 Corinthians 11:8-10, "For man is not from woman, but woman from man. Nor was man created for the woman, but woman for the man. For this reason the woman ought to have a symbol of authority on her head, because of the angels." A woman's submission to God's order is something demonic forces observe.

We have to realize once again the spiritual realm in all of this. We can make the mistake and allow ourselves to be conformed to this world and have a peaceful life, but in the spiritual realm, Satan and his forces are watching. We can have the most politically correct Church known to man, but Satan knows we would be completely ineffective. We can sing, shout, and bind the devil all day long when Satan knows we are powerless.

Not only does a feminized church keep men out, it also drives away children. It has been under-reported just how vital the spiritual life of a father must be in order to keep their children in Church. While we thank God for spiritual mothers, they alone are not enough.

Pastors should take note of this because a surefire way of a church closing down in the future is to fail to contend. Without male leadership there will be no men. It is the lazy way to acquiesce to the shouts and screams of the world but what we are in effect doing is driving in the coffin nails. Vision plus conviction in the word of God is necessary to create the discipline needed to enforce this doctrine. The very survival of the Church is at stake.

I would like to share statistics given in a survey commissioned by the Council of Europe's European Population Committee (1994-1995).

Practice of religion by the persons questioned according to the practice of the parents [1994-1995] (%)

Practice of the parents	Practice of the children

Father	Mother	Regular	Irregular	Non-practicing	Total
Regular	Regular	32.8	41.4	25.8	100
	Irregular	37.7	37.6	24.7	100
	Non-practicing	44.2	22.4	33.4	100
Irregular	Regular	3.4	58.6	38.0	100
	Irregular	7.8	60.8	31.4	100
	Non-practicing	25.4	22.8	51.8	100
Non-practicing	Regular	1.5	37.4	61.1	100
	Irregular	2.3	37.8	59.9	100
	Non-practicing	4.6	14.7	80.7	100

We know that church attendance doesn't define the entire realm of spirituality, but it is a good place to start. There is a lot to look at here and for the space of time I would like to narrow it down to a profound truth. If the father is a regular churchgoer and the mother doesn't practice any sort of faith, **AT ALL**, the odds of the child being a regular churchgoer is 44.2%.

If the mother is a regular churchgoer and the father doesn't practice any sort of faith, the odds go down to 1.5%. In other words, only one in sixty-six children from a home where only the mother is a regular churchgoer will be a regular churchgoer! That is a heck of a lot of difference. Even the attendance of an irregular father and a non-practicing mother (25.4%) is more than sixteen times better.

It seems that a father's dedication to Church has such an impact on the child that even the mother's apathy serves as a catalyst to the child's future commitment whereas a father's indifference is like that of a black hole consuming in its entirety the spirituality and example of the mother.

Notice also that if it is only the child's father who goes to Church, the impact on church attendance increases for the child than if **BOTH** mother and father went (44.2% compared to 32.8%). It is a very strange phenomenon indeed.

A Culture of Masculinity

This is why male leadership is not only biblical, it is also absolutely essential. It does not mean women have no part to play in Church, far from it, but men must be seen to lead in order to attract men. There is something subliminal about the church service. There is more to it than meets the eye and it is something the modern Church has failed to pay attention to.

It is possible not to see the forest for the trees. You can be so caught up in church services that you fail to see the impact it is making on an unconscious level. I remember once in Jamaica during our Sunday morning service a woman in her fifties passed by. Her daughter, who was a doctor, was relocating to Mandeville and was looking for a church. She had heard of our Church and came by for a visit. She spent not more than ten minutes before she was out the door. When I asked her why she was leaving she said, "I have never seen so many young people in church before." She felt out of place and intimidated and to be honest, up until then I never saw what she did because I was used to it. A church full of young people is the norm for us.

While that is not a bad thing to get used to, we can get used to a church without men. We can be so caught up in what is the new norm that we fail to see how it impacts our visitors. We can be puzzled when young men come once never to return or when church kids grow up and disappear forever and never connect the dots. We fail to see that there is a culture of femininity that is unwittingly being reverberated through the Church, which is off-putting to men. What we need to do in turn is to create an unconscious atmosphere of masculinity in the Church.

This is why we have male ushers. It's not that having female ushers is sinful, but it is so important that men see men as they step into the Church for the first time. I know that there are some terrific female singers in the church, but having a female praise and worship leader is not going to address the male-female ratio in Church. And the anathema of all anathemas is having a female preacher and pastor, to which there is no coming back from.

Men do not like to be in a place where women dominate. This is why the football fields and the bars are packed with men. Now there may be women present but it is only in a serving role like cheerleaders or barmaids but not in a position where they are making decisions that affect them. In 1 Corinthians 16:13 (ESV), the apostle Paul said, "Be watchful, stand firm in the faith, act like men, be strong." He tells the entire Church to act like men, setting a masculine tone to the Church.

One of the other unconscious areas of femininity in the modern Church is the praise and worship. There are worship songs that make me cringe such as, "You are the air I breathe", "Wrap me in Your arms", and "Never let me go". We sing these songs and wonder why our churches are packed with women and emptied of men. Even saved men struggle subconsciously to sing these songs and song leaders are puzzled why men don't sing in Church. We consciously desire having more men, but unconsciously aim for more women and wonder what's going on.

Where are the "Be bold, be strong" or "Onward Christian soldiers" songs of yesteryear? Today's worship sounds like love songs on the radio. Just tweak the lyrics a little and you could have a hit pop song. I have even heard it being called "Jesus is my boyfriend" music. What unsaved, testosterone filled, twenty-year-old male is going to want to sing that? What unchurched bad boy is going to want to hold hands and sing touchy-feely songs? And with modern songs being sung in high notes, who would even attempt to?

I say this to women all the time, you can have "equal rights" in Church, but how many women are willing to stay single for the rest of your lives or be married to weak men? As a pastor getting on in age, I would rather have less stress in my life and I can honestly say that this is one of those issues that give me stress. I'm not stressed about dealing with the challenges of feminism trying to creep into the Church. I'm stressed by single women desperate to find a husband and married women frustrated with their characterless spouses. I'm stressed at women in their thirties, who hear their biological clocks ringing loudly, demanding that I find a husband for them.

I want to save myself a lot of aggravation by creating a culture in the Church where men can be men and women can be women. Ideally, if I can create a culture where it would be attractive for men to join and that these men can be trained to be men of character, then I will save myself much headache. It is said that the role of a coach is to get athletes to do what they hate to create what they love. No prizefighter wants to get up at 4am in the morning and run five miles in cold weather, but they want to be champion of the world and have the fame, money, and spoils to go with it.

At the risk of sounding sexist and male chauvinistic, I have to do what the modern woman hates to give her what she wants. While women are more than willing to be involved in church activities, I have to challenge men to rise up. Maybe she can do it better, maybe she is more faithful, maybe she has greater passion, but in the long term it isn't going to be good for anyone. Too many churches sacrifice the future for the needs of today.

So, we have to challenge men to rise up. They may be reluctant, but it is our job as men of God to get them to step up to the plate. We have to challenge them to get a job even if they may get more on subsidies. We have to challenge them to move out of their mother's house and be independent even if it means leaving three square meals a day and a nice comfy bed. We have to challenge them to be on time and be dependable and faithful.

This isn't easy and it can be very frustrating. We are increasingly dealing with men who have never had a positive male role model in their lives and as such find it very hard to take correction. They will sulk and fall into depression and you may not see them in Church for weeks. They may block you on their phones or complain to others in the Church about what you have said. But I have seen deep down the witness in their spirit that what I have done is for their own good. It doesn't mean that they like it, but they know I have done what I have done to help them. Some will respond and others will not, but that is the only way we can reach this generation and start to create real men, men of God.

As pastors it is our responsibility to train men to be men, that is, to be men of responsibility. We are to teach them to carry the load, be a covering to their wives and children and a pillar to the Church and community at large. We are to teach them to work and to work hard and be an example. And we do so by putting responsibility upon them. Yes, women perhaps can do some of the things and even better than the men because they are often more willing, but that would be the easy way out. That would be sacrificing tomorrow for convenience today. It is by giving men roles of responsibility, roles of leadership that we get the best out of them and it causes them to rise up and make the Church a place where men want to be.

There is so much more that could be said about men, especially about the development of their character in order to be husbands, fathers, leaders in the Church, community, and business but that would take another book. Hopefully we will see the spiritual issues that the Church is facing today and take the necessary steps to address these issues.

6 DISCIPLESHIP

It is said that discipleship is a sincere desire to help others reach their destiny in Christ. It is a simple but underestimated statement, for, in that statement, there are the words "sincere," "desire," "help," "destiny," and "Christ." These attributes are critical in achieving those goals, and any missing ingredient will result in the mission being incomplete or even distorted.

In a generation where it seems everyone has an angle or agenda, genuine authenticity in a cynical and suspicious world is fundamentally necessary. A passion for the men and women in our churches, many of them broken by sin and riddled with dysfunctional behavior patterns, are essential. The ability to facilitate and to impart what you have learned yourself, as a disciple and through personal experience, is profoundly crucial. The vision to see the endgame of the process, despite the obstacles, is vitally indispensable. Wrapping all that together is the understanding of the mandate to make the character of Christ our pattern, without which reduces discipleship to a perverse and frightful Frankenstein's monster.

Recognizing the solemn charge as given by Christ (Matthew 28:19) and understanding the importance of the task, we must comprehend what discipleship really is. Over the years, I have heard a lot said about discipleship – some good, some bad, and some completely ugly. I have seen well-meaning men do and say things in the name of discipleship that wasn't. I have heard men talk a good deal about discipleship and yet never imparted what they knew into others. I have seen men abuse the doctrine of discipleship for their ends and agendas.

This doesn't mean that I am the oracle of all things discipleship. The Lord knows that I have my deficiencies, and if it were up to me, I'd spend a year or two in Tucson and Prescott just to learn. But being in the ministry for over twenty years, if I never learned a thing about discipleship, I have no business pastoring. In this chapter, I will outline what I have learned. These include my own experiences, both good and bad, what I have read about discipleship, observing the character, and the application of men who have been great at discipleship and, sadly, observing the character and the application of men who have been lousy at discipleship.

Discipleship is the lifeblood of any church, and the long term survival and effectiveness of that church depends on disciples being trained and raised up. Discipleship is the vehicle by means we pass on the truths of God's word from one generation to the next.

Being saved for over a quarter of a century, it is breathtaking just how fast time flies. Before you know it, if you aren't careful, another generation can come and go. If you have not made discipleship a fundamental process, your church could go from hot to cold in a very short time. I know what I am talking about. I have been there. I have seen it with my very eyes. Nobody can tell me otherwise.

It's incredible to think that when my grandfather was born that the standard mode of transport was a horse and carriage or something similar. That mode of transportation hadn't changed much since Sumer. To see how life has so dramatically changed in one hundred years is impressive. It's not that we have had one or two paradigm shifts in recent years, it's like they are happening every other year.

The point I am making is that with the dramatic pace of change between one generation and the next, if we don't have the baton of discipleship ready to be passed down, we can miss the next generation. Once that happens, it is very difficult to pass it to the succeeding one. We can find ourselves so out of touch in such a short time that the ability to communicate discipleship in a language the next generation understands will be difficult.

This is why churches that were once on fire are now relics, having been disconnected from the community they functioned in for decades. Once again, I know what I am talking about. I have seen it with my own eyes. Discipleship ensures that the gospel is passed down to the next generation, as there is still common ground between one generation and the next, who would then, in turn, pass it to the next generation. It is easier to pass a legacy from grandfather to father to son than it is from grandfather to grandson. It doesn't mean that it is impossible, as we have seen what Pastor Mitchell did to reach the spaced-out youth of the late 60s and early 70s, but it is difficult.

The Need for Coaches

The buzzwords in the secular world today are "life coach," "mentor," and "personal trainer." There are all kinds of organizations and businesses created in recent times to facilitate people's desire to learn, grow, and develop. It is getting to be a huge industry and rightly so, as people are seeking to be more productive in life. The secular world understands that for individuals to get the most out of themselves, they need a coach of some sort. It is not enough for them to read a book or watch a program, although these are very helpful. They also need someone to know their strengths and weaknesses and draw the best out of them.

Oscar de la Hoya, the 1992 Olympic gold medalist, and six-division world boxing champion, said in his autobiography, "Managers guide you, promoters hype you, publicists protect you, family and friends support you, and the media portrays you to the public, for better or worse. But nobody is as essential to a fighter as his trainer. It is the trainer who is with you on some lonely road in the middle of nowhere before the sun has peeked over the mountains, running with you or driving beside you, pushing you beyond exhaustion to exhilaration."

"It is the trainer who analyzes your opponent and designs your strategy. It is the trainer who runs your sparring sessions, determining the number of rounds, the weapons in your arsenal to be tested, and the sparring partners best suited to administer that test. It is the trainer who often works the mitts and wraps your hands. It is the trainer who cooks your meals and monitors your weight, keeps your mind focused and your body tuned."

"And when all the other members of your entourage have exited the ring and the opening bell sounds, it is your trainer alone who will return to work your corner, with help if you need from a cut man, keeping your engine running, your spirits elevated, and your game plan on track, reminding you to throw your jab, launch your hook, and stay alert at all times. It is his voice you hear in the heat of the battle, his advice you heed."

"To a trainer, every opponent is beatable, every round winnable, and every punch thrown by the other guy avoidable. When you win, your trainer is the first guy to hug you. When you lose, he's the last guy to leave you. Over the years I've had all sorts of trainers, young and old, reserved and flamboyant, old school and New Age, each one indispensable at the time and unforgettable to this day."[42]

Here is one of the most gifted and talented boxers of all time eloquently making a case for the need of a coach. Surely if there is anyone who doesn't need a trainer, it is Oscar de la Hoya, but he admits, and not even grudgingly but openly and honestly, the importance of one. It doesn't matter who you are, how brilliant or diligent you are; you need someone to push you on to better things.

Mike Tyson learned the hard way when he fired his long time trainer Kevin Rooney. Mike Tyson was a prodigious student of the fight game, having been taught by the legendary boxing trainer Cus D'Amato. D'Amato, on seeing a thirteen-year-old Mike spar for the first time, predicted he would be the world's heavyweight champion. Mike fulfilled that prediction at the age of twenty in 1986, beating the record set by a twenty-one-year-old Floyd Patterson thirty years before in 1956, another boxer trained by D'Amato.

Unfortunately, Cus died a year before Mike could fulfill his prediction, and the mantle of training passed to Kevin Rooney, D'Amato's longtime assistant. Mike and Cus had spent countless hours watching the old masters like Sugar Ray Robinson, Muhammad Ali, and especially Jack Dempsey and learned from D'Amato a variety of techniques that would help him in the ring. Mike, in his prime, was brutally efficient and practically unbeatable, but when Cus died, things fell apart.

With the fame and fortune overwhelming a young man barely out of his teens having been brought up in abject poverty, Mike went downhill. Using the age-old tactic of divide and conquer, Don King used race-baiting to separate Mike from his Irish-American trainer Kevin Rooney. Mike was now free to do his own thing without any kind of accountability, and while he was initially winning without a decent trainer, this fundamental mistake caught up with him.

In February 1990, an unprepared Mike Tyson went to Japan to defend his undisputed heavyweight title against a 42-1 underdog named James "Buster" Douglas. Tyson spent his preparation period by sleeping with the maids at the hotel and prostitutes in the clubs. He went into the ring to face a highly trained and motivated Douglas who embarrassingly knocked him out in the tenth round. He wasn't just knocked out but looked like a clown as he was down on all fours trying to put his mouthpiece back in.

---

[42] p107, American Son: My Story, Oscar de la Hoya, HarperCollins Publishers, 2008

Although he was utterly unfit to fight, if he had a decent trainer in the ring, he might have been able to use his gifts and power to turn things around. Instead, Don King had hired Tyson's pals, Aaron Snowell and Jay Bright, to train him for peanuts. It only shows you get what you pay for.

On fight night, these two geniuses turned up without standard equipment like ice packs or an endswell (a small piece of metal with a handle kept cold and pressed on the face to reduce swelling). As Tyson's face began to swell due to the frequent blows he received from Douglas, they used a rubber glove filled with ice water. And just as it would seem that the incompetency couldn't get any worse, the chain from Snowell's identification badge around his neck was accidentally dragged across Mike's face, causing him to wince in pain.

Teddy Atlas, the first chief assistant during the D'Amato years, speaking of Bright and Snowell, "It's like wearing plastic thongs under an Armani suit. It's ridiculous – a multi-million-dollar fighter surrounded by a menagerie of frauds." Kevin Rooney, when asked about the training abilities of Jay Bright said, "He's got nothing – unless you count quiche-making as a useful quality in boxing."[43]

Don King, in his infinite wisdom, thought by getting two hangers-on to train Tyson, he would save himself a lot of money. After all, Mike is the best fighter out there, and so it doesn't matter if two dingbats, who haven't got much coaching ability, oversee his training. Even after the Douglas fiasco, Mike was never the same again and primarily because of coaching issues.

What we can learn from Mike Tyson is that talent and gifting isn't everything. One critical factor is the need for a mentor who can bring out all of that talent and bring that individual to achieving their destiny. As great a talent as Muhammad Ali was, he was great in part due to his wise trainer, legendary Angelo Dundee.

In 1963, when Ali got knocked down hard at the end of the fourth round against kayo artist, Henry Cooper, it was Dundee who noticed a small tear on Ali's right glove and ripped it open. He did this, and Ali was given a few extra minutes to recover while they changed the glove. Ali went on to stop Cooper in the next round.

During Ali's first heavyweight championship fight with champion Sonny

---

[43] p303, Dark Trade: Lost in Boxing, Donald McRae, Mainstream Publishing Company (Edinburgh), 2005

Liston, he was partially blinded in his eyes. The common consensus is that the corner of Liston, seeing that their man was getting beat, rubbed liniment over his gloves, and the ointment got into Ali's eyes. Ali got back to his corner at the end of the fourth round and said, "Cut the gloves off. I want to prove to the world there's dirty work afoot." Dundee responded by saying, "C'mon now, this is for the title, this is the big apple. What are you doing? Sit down!" Ali followed Dundee's advice to run from Liston until his eyes cleared, and when they did, he gave Liston such a beating that he quit on his stool at the end of the seventh round.

This is the same Angelo Dundee, when in the corner of another prodigious talent named Sugar Ray Leonard, said at the end of the thirteenth round when Leonard was behind on points in his fight with Thomas Hearns for their undisputed welterweight world title, "You're blowing it now, son." Leonard got off his stool and knocked Hearns out in the fourteenth round.

The Need for Discipleship

There are no such things as self-made men, especially in the church. While we know the importance of talent, character, anointing, and favor, what is also vitally important is the need to be discipled. No one gets saved and immediately understands the dynamics of how to live an effective Christian life and how to reach their God-given destiny in Christ.

There are three main reasons (there may be more) why I believe discipleship is essential.

1. The development of character

Firstly, I have seen first-hand anointed and gifted men who have failed to fulfill their potential in Christ as they were inadequately trained. They may have had some level of success or fruitfulness, but I could always feel that something was missing, as if something was undercooked. This is while taking into consideration people's flaws and idiosyncrasies. It was like seeing a bodybuilder with an underdeveloped arm or a top of the line sports car with a temporary donut spare wheel. It just looks a little bit weird and out of place. These undercooked areas can be passed to the next generation of men and women, inspired by their gifts and success. I am under no illusion that we can be less than we should be due to who we were discipled by. In theory, discipleship should be like a copy of a computer file. Sadly, it is more like a photocopy from an old school Xerox machine, in that every successive copy is a more corrupted version of the previous. In the end, if we are not careful, we can have a copy that looks nothing like the Original, who is Christ.

While discipleship is never something that we grow out of, it is of fundamental importance at the beginning of salvation. It is very difficult to teach an old dog new tricks and especially an old dog who has never been discipled before. The older people get, the more they get set in their ways. While this is not always the case, I have discovered if people embrace discipleship early, they can retain teachable-ness later on in life.

2. Establishing accountability

Secondly, the church world is filled with super-talented and gifted people. Their gifts and abilities have made room for them, but there is a danger that is not only overlooked but also their downfall. Gifted and anointed people are automatically viewed as special. They are seen as individuals who, because of their success, are in a class all to themselves. They have elevated themselves over the need for accountability and discipleship. This is something that they and others around them have deceivingly believed.

It is not uncommon in today's church world, or should I say, more than common, to see such gifted individuals crash and burn. They are like the light of a firework sparkle stick that burns bright but burns away just as quickly. How many gifted preachers and worship leaders have fallen into some type of sin or the other in recent years? These are individuals who are a law unto themselves, and such is the nature of having your way, receiving the praises of men, and the resources that accompany success. These are not counterbalanced with the voice of wisdom from those who know you, accountability, and the humility needed to listen to those voices. As a result of pride, Satan makes short work of these men because pride is one of the arenas in which the devil makes his home.

In a generation with more wealth, opportunity, and access to fame and publicity like never before, we must create checks and balances to help us navigate through what is potentially a spiritually life-threatening minefield and make it to the other side safely. While sins and temptations of every generation have always been the same, the amplification has increased somewhat in recent times.

3. Making reflections of Jesus

Thirdly, discipleship is all about making copies of Christ in the world. Unless someone has experienced a vision or a miracle, most people will never see Jesus except through His followers. In John 8:12, Jesus said, "I am the light of the world." But in Matthew 5:14, He also said, "You are the light of the world." Clearly, we are to be a reflection of Him into this world.

Discipleship is vital because none of us are like Christ at the beginning of our salvation. The righteousness of Christ may have been imputed in us by faith when we got saved, but the character of Christ was not. This has to be formed in us through various means, but one of those means is discipleship. We need to be like Jesus, and this is why discipleship is a process that cannot end on this side of eternity, but it is something we strive for.

Discipleship is an art, and it is an art you have to give yourself to get better at it. Many things are crying out for our attention in life; in all honesty, being a disciple-maker will take the back seat if you are not careful. There are many essential hats we all juggle as men – employee, employer, student, father, husband, Christian, pastor. Being a disciple-maker is an integral part of your life, and it is something you have to give your attention to because the next generation of men desperately needs it.

The Framework of Discipleship

The Ability to Inspire

One of the most critical keys to being able to disciple men is the ability to inspire them. This is easier said than done, but working with men without this crucial ingredient is going to be like pulling teeth. We know men need to be discipled, but they will have to want it rather than you forcing it down their throats. We know we are to disciple men, but we can allow desperation to get hold of us and cause us to do dumb things in the name of discipleship.

I remember once as a still relatively new convert but inspired to preach one day, going to a pioneer church service across town in London. We had a building issue at the time and only had Sunday morning services, so I spent my Sunday evenings visiting other fellowship churches. That particular Sunday, I had visited a church that was opened for about a year or so. He had a handful of people there, and as he was preaching, one male visitor got up and began to walk out.

This pioneer pastor leaped off the stage right in the middle of his sermon and went to speak to the man begging him to stay. I'm not trying to judge my brother because maybe there was more going on that I didn't know of, but my impression then, even as a new convert, is that it smacked of desperation.

I know he was desperate to make things happen, and it showed, in a sense, humility that he was willing to do that, but at the same time, it just didn't settle well in my spirit. I have been in the ministry for over twenty years, and I have never felt the need to do that (Who knows? Maybe in the future I could, as there are things I said I would never do that I ended up doing.)

You can't beg people to serve God, and you can't run after men to be disciples. They are going to have to want it. Consider the discipleship of Elisha under Elijah. In 1 Kings 19:19-20, we read, "So he departed from there and found Elisha the son of Shaphat, who was plowing with twelve yoke of oxen before him, and he was with the twelfth. Then Elijah passed by him and threw his mantle on him. And he left the oxen and ran after Elijah, and said, "Please let me kiss my father and my mother, and then I will follow you." And he said to him, "Go back again, for what have I done to you?""

While Elijah called Elisha to discipleship, he never ran after him because he knew Elisha had to want it, even though he also knew God had called Elisha (1 Kings 19:16). Sometimes we can see men in our church that we can sense the hand of God is upon, and while we are to do whatever we can to help them, they have got to want it. When they desire to have it, they make discipleship easier because they can receive it.

The question then is, "How do we get them to want it?" Well, that's the million-dollar question. This is especially true when you are pioneering. How do you inspire men when externally there is nothing genuinely inspirational? There you are in a new city where you know no one, you have hired a hall in a community center or a hotel, and there is hardly anybody in your church. Maybe you have a few older ladies or a few single mothers with little kids but nothing more. How do you inspire men to follow you?

This revelation dawned on me the minute we started our first church. When the thought crossed my mind, it felt like a vast cavern opened up on the inside, and I felt this colossal emptiness manifest internally. I was in a strange city where I was unknown and inexperienced, and I will admit hopelessness engulfed me.

I remember working with a young Christian of similar age who had moved from Belfast to Manchester and trying my best with him, but he resented a man of the same age trying to disciple him. I could see the hand of God on his life, but I just couldn't help him. The sad thing is that I met him years later, totally disillusioned with his time in Manchester, and was moving back to Belfast.

So, what do you do? The ability to inspire is not a one-directional approach. It will require things like having something to impart, creating relationships and ministering in love, things I speak about in-depth later, but another thing I will put in this section on inspiration is the ability to communicate vision.

When you are pioneering and have nothing except Christ, the only other weapon in your arsenal is vision. You have got to be able to make men see beyond what is not there right now. Let me tell you, over the years, I have realized that vision is more important than having the best building with the best equipment. I learned that lesson in Manchester, having seen churches around me who had better buildings, even better numbers, and finances, but never had what we had – men and women sold out for Jesus believing we could take the land.

But getting them to see vision wasn't easy, especially in the beginning days. It took prayer, preaching on vision, and if I'm honest, keeping people in church long enough to take them to a revival in the mother church or to a Conference. Bringing them to the home church and letting them meet people and see what is happening is such a great way to create vision. They will know that you aren't some Lone Ranger doing your own thing; they will see that you have a connection with other people and learn that church was once as small as their church and what happened there can also happen for them.

Bringing them to a Conference where they can hear sermons on discipleship, listen to reports, see people performing, and hanging out with disciples from other churches does wonders in communicating vision. I have seen men change before me because they went to a conference and when they went back home, they looked at me with different eyes.

Being inspired changes things. It's the difference between being someone who drags their feet to church and always comes in late to someone who is there well before service, ready to pray and help set up. When someone is inspired, you can get the very best out of them.

Another critical ingredient in inspiring men is passion. I remember being a "B" Math student in Junior High, and I had a few competent teachers, but even though I liked Math, I couldn't be motivated to do better. That was until Bevill DeBruin, a.k.a. "Mr. Dibs" became my Math teacher, and things changed. He was a Math genius from Sri Lanka of Dutch-Sri Lankan heritage who looked like Albert Einstein. White shirt, black trousers, a pen in the pocket – all day, every day.

And I wasn't the only one. He was a legend in our school, and when I got into his class, I understood why. To cut a long story short, he got this "B" student to become an "A" student and not just that, I got an "A" in my final exams without studying (because he was giving me one-on-one classes in university Math at this point).

The other teachers were competent, but Mr. Dibs was inspirational. It wasn't by accident. He knew how to inspire people. I thought about it for years, as to why he was able to do what others could not. The reason I can figure out is that teaching wasn't a profession; it was his passion. Looking back, I can see that some teachers were there because of the paycheck, others were there because it was what they were good at, but for Mr. DeBruin, it was his life. He had opportunities to be the Principal, not only of my school but any other top school if he wanted, but he preferred to teach.

I learned from Mr. DeBruin that passion is more than motivational speaking. It is a way of life. It is easy to give pep talks now and again, but your life will communicate if you have passion or not. Passion is when people can't help but see that you love what you do. And passion is infectious, and people will buy into it because you can't fake passion.

I have always been an avid reader except for a time when I was a new convert in the church, and the guys told me that I read too much, and I would backslide. But when Marty Carnegie became our pastor, that passion for reading was reignited. Here was a man who made a trip every Thursday to Book Aid to buy old second-hand books. He would invite young men to go with him, and as he is looking at the books, he would grab me and say, "Look at this, Jay. My goodness! Look at what he just said. Powerful!"

But not just reading, he was passionate about preaching as well, and that made us, in turn, passionate about preaching and sermon writing. When I first got sent out, I used to scratch my head how guys in other churches would prefer to do anything else but preach and write sermons. It seemed as if preaching and sermon writing was like a visit to the dentist. For us, it was the T-bone steak amid the veggies and potatoes; It was the filling in the donut.

To this day, preaching and sermon writing is what I look forward to the most when it comes to pastoring. I don't do it because I have to; I do it because I want to. Passion does that to you.

Something to Impart

Secondly, a disciple-maker needs to have something to impart. You have to have something men want. There needs to be something in you that may not be observable to the naked eye, but it is something that stirs something in the primal instincts of men. John 1:35-37 says, "Again, the next day, John stood with two of his disciples. And looking at Jesus as He walked, he said, "Behold the Lamb of God!" The two disciples heard him speak, and they followed Jesus."

No doubt John and Andrew must have heard the repeated statements of John the Baptist about Jesus, and as a result, seeing Him added with John's testimony, they decided to follow Jesus. Note that this was before Jesus did anything of note. His first miracle of turning water into wine would occur in the next chapter. Now we know that we can never replicate who Christ is to men, but there must be something in us that will cause men to gravitate to us.

One thing I have noticed over the years is how you can have good, righteous men in church, and yet they cannot influence other men for Jesus. They are not necessarily repulsive, carnal, or unspiritual, but they have the aura of a wet dishcloth. When young men get saved, they instinctively aim for other men in the church who have something in them. It's incredible to me how you can have Friday night home groups, and some groups are so packed that it is almost a health hazard, and others can look like a barren wasteland. All that is missing is the tumbleweeds.

You have the other problem of these same good men being sent out to pioneer, or to take over an existing work. I'm all for people developing themselves on the field where one needs to swim or else you will sink, but at the same time, I have seen men who have the personality of boiled rice, unsalted. Good men, men who love their wives and children, who work jobs and are faithful to Jesus and their church, but lack that "special" something.

I'm not trying to sound mean, but let's be realistic. Some guys haven't got what it takes to inspire men. I'm not saying most men are like this, and maybe there are just a few, but there are definitely some, men that are trying their best and not making a dent. They have women in their churches but no men, and even if there are men, they don't seem to be making any progress toward discipleship.

I don't mean to infer that all is lost because disciple-makers, not just disciples, are made and not born. This is an issue that must be addressed by the pastor and disciple-makers in the church. Many times, we are so caught up with other things that we dismiss these issues by saying that he will catch up later on. That may be true, but I believe that many are left the way they are and end up being set in their ways. These are men who need extra work and investment to help them develop.

To a degree, it is that principle Jesus taught playing itself out in Matthew 13:12, "For whoever has, to him more will be given, and he will have abundance; but whoever does not have, even what he has will be taken away from him." We tend to spend more time with the men who are more fruitful and, in so doing, make them even more fruitful. Simultaneously we spend less time with the men who are less fruitful and in so doing make them even less fruitful.

There are men I have seen on the field who have been struggling for years, who really could do with coming back in and being invested in so that they could become fruitful a second time around. As it stands, they are out on the field year after year and have made zero impact. They could have gone back home and sent out again in that space of time and bearing fruit! Such a one could have been back in the body, using his experience out in the field as a catalyst, as he now has something in him he learned out there that he could impart. That, along with being discipled by his pastor, will ignite something in him that can be later on used on the field.

The Need for Relationships

There can be no real discipleship without relationships. There is no such thing as discipleship via a proxy. You may call it discipleship, but it is nothing like the real thing. The apostle John continues in John 1:38-39, "Then Jesus turned, and seeing them following, said to them, "What do you seek?" They said to Him, "Rabbi" (which is to say, when translated, Teacher), "where are You staying?" He said to them, "Come and see." They came and saw where He was staying, and remained with Him that day (now it was about the tenth hour).''

Right at the very beginning, when they sought to follow Jesus, He opened the door to relationship. There was no aloofness, no barrier or walls, no distance or obstacle. There was simply an open door to come in and get to know Him. Mark 3:13-14 says, "And He went up on the mountain and called to Him those He Himself wanted. And they came to Him. Then He appointed twelve, that they might be with Him…" If this was Jesus' methodology, how can we outdo the Master?

I know as a church, we need programs and plans, but sometimes they drive me nuts. Some guys live for programs. I understand a growing church needs these things to keep the church moving forward, to keep disciples active, and for the church to have some expression in the communities, towns, and cities, we minister in. I get it. But sometimes church can become so clinically organized, it feels like too much focus is placed on the package and not much on what's inside.

We are the Christian Fellowship Ministries, not the Christian Program Ministries. Fellowship and relationships are the absolute bedrock of a healthy and growing church, not to mention discipleship. We need men's discipleship classes; we need to instruct men over the pulpit and get them to address issues. Still, at the same time, much discipleship happens in the general interactions of disciple-maker and disciple.

It was in relationship that Jesus was able to see the disciples arguing about preeminence and correcting them on the proper ways of leadership. It was in relationship that Jesus was able to see their fears on the stormy sea and address their lack of faith. It was in relationship that Jesus was able to test them with the feeding of the five thousand. It was in relationship that Jesus was able to challenge them as to their opinion of Him. It was in relationship that Jesus was able to see their faulty thinking and mistakes and correct them into being better men.

In relationship, you can speak into people's lives. No one I know appreciates being corrected by a total stranger. But when you know someone, and you know that person has your best interest at heart, even if it hurts, you know it is for your good. Jesus may have been the Messiah and God overall, but He still instructed these men in the realm of relationship and not as we see in the Old Testament. God in the Old Testament was seen as distant (although He was ever-present). In the New Testament, in Christ, God was with us. John 1:14 says, "And the Word became flesh and dwelt among us..."

You can't get better than Jesus, and if Jesus chose to be around His men, who are we to disagree? I remember years ago hearing one televangelist preach, and while I can't recall what the subject matter was, I do recall him saying that the reason he doesn't invite anyone from his church to dinner is that they have a very high expectation of him and if they saw him in private it may disappoint them. Talk about putting one's failures on another.

Nevertheless, there is something right in that statement. Having real relationships forces us to up our game. I'm not talking about being hypocritical, where we are one thing to our disciples and something else at home. I am saying that in relationships, there is something about having to be an example to others who are in a position to learn. Where there is no contending for discipleship and relationships, there is also a tendency to be slack, and after a while, our slackness develops into habitual flaws. It means we become set in our ways, and while those flaws are not necessarily sinful, they aren't helpful.

The Importance of Being an Example

"Do as I say but not as I do," isn't going to create disciples. Over the years, it has been my privilege to preach revivals in various churches. And while I am in my forties, I still feel I have the capacity to learn. I haven't arrived, and I have seen guys much younger than me still showing me a thing or two. I am not the sharpest knife in the drawer, but I know a good idea when I see it, and if I can, I will make it my own.

But I have also seen things not to do. I have seen things like pastors being so busy getting the services organized that they never pray before service. If I was only doing a Sunday morning shot or something like that, I might not pay it much thought. It may have been just a one-off, and I just happened to be there that service. But if it is an entire revival and he hasn't been in the prayer room once, then I know something is up.

If the pastor doesn't take prayer seriously, neither will the disciples. One-offs can be forgiven, but a habitual pattern of prayerlessness before service is dangerous. I would hope he is praying at home, as he should because praying at church doesn't mean one has a relationship with Jesus. But not praying will reinforce in the minds of the disciples and the church that prayer isn't essential. What is important is getting the equipment ready. What is important is the quality of the sound. What is important is that the praise and worship team has got their songs in order. When the external is more important than the internal, the only thing we get is "disciples" who are shallow men. I have seen that with my own eyes.

I knew of a case where the pastor announced that if you are a member of the praise and worship team, you don't have to go to outreach. Was it a coincidence that he was on the praise and worship team? Was it also a coincidence that even years after he left, the men on the praise and worship team had a hard time going on outreach?

The apostle Paul said to his disciple Timothy, "Let no one despise your youth, but be an example to the believers in word, in conduct, in love, in spirit, in faith, in purity." (1 Timothy 4:12) That still rings true today. As a young pastor, people will despise your youth if you let them, but if you give yourself to being an example and make the passion for the kingdom flow through you, it will cause them to overlook your inexperience. Being an example goes a long way in establishing credibility.

Jamaicans are a cynical lot when it comes to pastors. In all honesty, I do understand why. There are so many wolves in sheep clothing preying on women and money. There is also much skepticism when it comes to overseas missions, as there is a habit of starting, only for that ministry to close down a few years later. When we first went Mandeville, there was a lot of suspicion as to who I was. To some, I was this "older white guy" trying to pick up young black men or trying to pick up young black women, or only to get money out of gullible people. It was crazy.

But as they saw me, my family and I go to church, outreaching on the street and working with people, their opinions changed. It took around two years, but it did change because they saw the consistency of conduct. It was amazing that in a city center so busy, people knew who I was and the church that I pastored. They were watching, and as opinions changed, we were able to gain ground in the city.

It was tough work at the beginning outreaching on the hot streets of Mandeville. Sometimes I looked like I was a broiled lobster. But I found a great tool in witnessing. If I found a remotely interested guy, I would invite him to lunch. To buy lunch at a local fast-food restaurant would cost about $2 and so I would invite him out and ask him to bring his friends. At times I could have a captive audience of about five young men with me, and as they ate lunch, I shared the gospel.

As with the law of unintended consequences, it initially got me the reputation of being gay. As I said, an "older white guy" (I am tri-racial) with all these black youth is very suspicious to the local Jamaican. (Until then it had never crossed my mind.) Even the young men had that impression, but they also thought, "Hey, it's a free lunch, and if he tries anything funny, I'll just knock him out." But over time, they saw through my example that I was the real deal. I wasn't a homosexual, I wasn't after their sisters, and there was nothing I wanted from them except for them to be saved. A number of those young men became disciples and are still in the church today.

Human beings are a funny lot, and when it comes to discipleship, if you leave people to themselves, they will follow the path of least resistance. It is imperative you keep up your standard of being an example and not give anyone a reason to become slack.

Much of discipleship comes by example anyway. How will people know how to pray if they don't hear you pray? Most people who get saved in our church have a minimal church background, and even if they did, their only understanding of prayer is to bow their heads and stay silent. In the pioneer setting, you are their only reference mark for prayer. It annoys me to see pastors find a corner somewhere in the building and mutter words under their breath. I don't doubt for one moment that God hears them, and ultimately we are not praying to please men, but the bigger picture is discipleship.

In Luke 11:1 we read, "Now it came to pass, as He was praying in a certain place, when He ceased, that one of His disciples said to Him, "Lord, teach us to pray, as John also taught his disciples.""' Now we know that Jesus would often disappear to a deserted place to pray by Himself, but there were times He prayed in the hearing of His disciples. This was one of those occasions, and there was something so moving that they asked Him how to pray. Think about it! These are Jewish men asking Jesus how to pray. Prayer is a part of their culture, yet there was something about His prayer that revealed a lack.

This is not limited to just prayer but anything else that another will have to learn. It could be one-on-one evangelism or street preaching; it could be leading songs or running a Bible study. The list goes on, but whatever it is, we cannot underestimate the importance of being an example.

Confronting the Issues

As I said before, in relationships, you have access to the hearts and lives of men. Discipleship without relationship does more harm than good. I have seen men who feel empowered by their title and position to challenge and correct men as if they had access to their hearts. Even if what they have said was right, noble, and true, many times, what has been said hasn't been received. Even if the disciple has a good heart and seeks to submit to what has been said, you can't remove his humanity and what inadvertently happens is that a good man has to battle against having a bad heart. This is an added temptation that godly men shouldn't have to fight along with the other temptations he has to face.

Some men can come across as being abrasive and harsh. They may be able to take tough correction, but it is wrong to think everyone else can. You have to know the men around you. There are some men you can rebuke with both barrels, and they take it, and then there are those who can't. This doesn't mean that you have to rebuke the disciple who can take it with both barrels, but I'm just pointing out that it is only in relationships you will figure out the best strategy to confront men.

While I rather not have to confront men, I do it knowing that if I don't, something worse may happen. I don't fear it in the slightest, but I would prefer to live life with as little confrontation as possible. However, you have some men who hate confrontation. What do you do when there is an issue with a man in the church, and it must be addressed, but you hate confrontation?

What some men do is preach on the issue. They write an entire sermon for that one brother and preach it over the pulpit. The problem with that is that the person rarely ever thinks it is them. In the scattershot approach, the target is rarely ever hit. And if perchance that person figures out that the message is for them, it is even rarer that he thinks it was a message from heaven. More than likely, he will think you aimed a sermon directly at him! Instead of getting repentance, what you will end up getting is an outrage.

What others do if they have a bit of charm is they will use their relationships to manipulate men. For example, when he sees a disciple frequently late for church, instead of addressing the issue, they will dance and skirt around the problem in the hope of solving the problem without addressing it. The hope is that his charm will somehow rectify the issue.

The trouble is that while it may seem that the issue has been dealt with, the character of the individual is still the same. He may be early for church for this pastor, but what happens when a new pastor comes? He reverts to the old person. Why? It is because the new pastor doesn't mean much to him. You can use your charm to bend people to your will, but it doesn't mean you have a disciple.

Christ's disciples never doubted that He loved them, but He wasn't afraid to confront them when the need arose. The church's fate rested upon these men receiving as much instruction as they could get in those vital three years. The spiritual health of the local church, not to mention church planting, depends on disciple-makers being able to disciple men correctly.

What still others do is overcompensate. I have known pastors who dread confrontation but know it needs to be done. They know it is a weakness on their part to overlook things that must be dealt with and go overboard. Perhaps this is down to personal insecurity, but he hammers the poor guy way beyond what is helpful. It's as if the need to validate himself is more important than the man he is confronting.

Let me also mention another factor in why men are overlooked and not confronted. I have seen gifted, fruitful, and charismatic men who have been able to get away with murder because they can either pull the wool over their pastor's eyes or use their charm in such a way as to manipulate. Some guys are so charming that they can get away with anything.

This is not in the same category, but it illustrates my point. My younger brother has the gift of charm. I remember once as kids, we, along with our parents, were at the Hartsfield–Jackson International Airport in Atlanta, waiting for our connection to New Orleans when we lost sight of him. He was around nine years old at the time, and when we did find him, he was surrounded by about ten or so air stewardesses entertaining them. I can still remember them laughing and saying, "Isn't he cute?" Needless to say, he never got into trouble.

I said that just to let you know how charming he is. A couple of years ago, I was speaking to my dad about one of my uncles, and I called my uncle by his first name. (My uncle doesn't care about titles.) My dad said, "It is 'Uncle' to you." I looked at him with amazement. For years my brother has been calling our parents by their first names. I could never dream of calling my dad by his first name. I said, "My brother calls you and mom, 'Veron' and 'Phil' and you have never said anything to him, but I call my uncle by his first name, and you tell me off?" It was hilarious because I finally got to silence my dad, but that's how charming people can get away with stuff.
My brother is not nefarious by any stretch of the imagination, but in the kingdom of God, charm can become a lethal weapon if not kept in check, and some men get away with a lot of stuff that others could not because they have charm. What makes it worse is that these men think they are invincible, and we know they are not. It eventually catches up with them. A good disciple-maker can see through the charm and deal with the issues.

Looking for Teachable Men

Another main factor in discipleship is having teachable men. The word 'disciple' comes from the Greek word 'mathetes', meaning 'learner' or 'pupil'. In other words, a disciple must be an individual who can be taught because you can't disciple an unteachable man.

That may seem to be self-explanatory, but it hasn't stopped some pastors from trying. Due to ignorance or a lack of self-esteem, you have men who will stop at nothing to disciple a man who has no intention to be discipled. While I would advocate much prayer and fasting for such individuals, at the same time, some will not change.

Trying to disciple such men is like pulling a cat by the tail. You can try and do it, but you are going to get scratched, and in the end, you will have to let go. All that effort and all you have to show for it are cuts and bruises. One key factor in discipleship is finding men who are willing to learn. Save time and endless amounts of frustration by focusing your energies on the ones who want to be disciples.

It's interesting to note that at the very beginning of Jesus' ministry, as He initially selected His disciples, He chose John and James. Matthew 4:21-22 states, "Going on from there, He saw two other brothers, James the son of Zebedee, and John his brother, in the boat with Zebedee their father, mending their nets. He called them, and immediately they left the boat and their father, and followed Him." Now we know from John 1 he had already met them previously, but now, as He has passed the acquaintance stage of their relationship, He calls them, along with Andrew and Peter to Himself.

Notice that they were with their father and not only with their father but functioning in the fishing trade with their father. As the custom was in those days, boys learned their trades from their fathers, and right here, we see the root of discipleship, which is fathers training their sons. No doubt, as Zebedee spent time with his sons, he imparted his wisdom and knowledge to them and they, being in a relationship with him, as sons to their father, received and applied that knowledge.

Jesus had piggybacked on an existing framework and used that as a springboard to discipleship. John and James were teachable because they were in a relationship with someone they loved and respected and who had taught them how to receive. That is precisely how discipleship works because you can't correctly receive from someone you have little respect for, and you can't receive if you are too stubborn to learn.

Like I said before, I'm not the sharpest knife in the drawer I have to admit. It took me a couple of years in Jamaica to figure out why I just couldn't seem to raise proper disciples. Oh, yes. I had men and women who came to church and got involved in ministry, but when it came to fundamental decisions, almost everyone failed to take heed.

Kicking people out of church became the norm, young ladies in the church getting pregnant from deadbeats after being warned; young men, ending up in the local jail. It came to the point where I repeatedly preached that I don't buy diapers and don't pay bail. It wasn't as if people were actively in rebellion. It wasn't like they said, "Pastor, get lost. I want to do my own thing, and I couldn't care less about what you have to say." And it wasn't only with me. No one else could speak into their lives, and it seemed that people had to learn the hard way.

It then dawned on me one day what was going on. Without exception, every single young man in the church had a problem with his father. Some have never met their fathers, some have seen them once or twice, and others had real hostile issues with their fathers. All of them had to grow up navigating through life on their own.

While there was a primal need to be validated by an older man, there was also the engrained habit of doing things their way. They were so used to doing things on their own they found it very difficult to listen to instruction. Some would act like they were listening and then do the opposite, and others would sulk or lash out, but the result was the same, an inability to learn. Many of them struggled through high school, as well. These were men who liked to be around me but were unable to receive wisdom at the same time.

The silver lining is that after they had their fingers burnt, they started to listen, but every single one of them had to go through that process before they could receive. I went to Jamaica with the motto "Prevention is better than cure," and I have to admit that I had to do more curing than preventing.

In the times that we live in, this fundamental infrastructure is missing, and more and more, pastors and disciple-makers have to become fathers AND instructors. That in itself shouldn't be a problem, as the apostle Paul said in 1 Corinthians 4:15, "For though you might have ten thousand instructors in Christ, yet you do not have many fathers; for in Christ Jesus I have begotten you through the gospel." But more and more, we have to lay the groundwork that should have been done before.

The Motive of Love

I am glad the apostle Paul gave such words. Discipleship is simply an extension of the father-son relationship. In Philippians 2:19-22, he says, "But I trust in the Lord Jesus to send Timothy to you shortly, that I also may be encouraged when I know your state. For I have no one like-minded, who will sincerely care for your state. For all seek their own, not the things which are of Christ Jesus. But you know his proven character, that as a son with his father he served with me in the gospel."

Paul alludes to the ancient tradition of a father working together with his son in a trade and transferring what he knows to the next generation. The character traits of a good father are the same as a disciple-maker. A good father has a relationship with his son. A good father wants the very best for his son. A good father seeks to instruct his son with everything he has learned. A good father wants his son to do better than he did. A good father is committed to seeing his son develop to the best of his ability. Ultimately, a good father loves his son as himself.

If we have no love for the men and women in our church, we have no business being in the ministry. This is the people business, and anything less than love is unacceptable. I have seen men who are phenomenal preachers with revelation and anointing but have no heart for the people in their church. I have seen pastors who are rude, obnoxious, and condescending, and yet preach some of the best material I have heard. It is simply the grace of God that the people come back every week. Even so, I can't help but feel that with a little more kindness, the building would have been fuller with that kind of preaching.

Men may not always receive correction graciously because of character defects, but I have seen that they do recover in time if they know that the one who corrected them loved them. Loving them doesn't mean holding their hands when they are sulking or giving them money on their birthdays. It means that you are willing to serve them and work with them in patience over the long haul. After all their moping, you are still there for them, ready to wipe the slate clean and work with them all over again.

Listen, many jacked-up men know that they are jacked-up. The fact that someone is willing to work with them despite that isn't lost on them. Over the months and years, they will come to appreciate that.

While we understand that numbers are a great gauge of one's ministry, don't let the temptation of numbers be the focus. I have seen men out on the field whose primary focus is to have numbers to report at a conference rather than invest in the spiritual progress of those in his church. These are the same ones fixated with the numbers in their Bible study groups.

These are the ones who marry couples who have no business being with each other just so that he can send a good report back to the mother church or plant couples out who aren't even ready to lead a Bible study just to make it look like he is someone important. The danger we face with some pastors is that people can become pawns on a spiritual checkboard – shuffling people and playing games with people's lives, destinies, and even in some cases, salvation. People are not ornaments to be used to dazzle others. They are not vehicles to springboard us into better things. They are precious souls who belong to Jesus Christ.

Cus D'Amato had been living for many years as a recluse in the Catskill Mountains of New York state when juvenile detention center counselor, Bobby Stewart, brought Mike Tyson to him. D'Amato had removed himself from mainstream boxing for many-a-year, but when he saw Mike for the first time, he knew that he had the potential world heavyweight champion standing before him. It then dawned on him that Mike was his last shot at the big times and, therefore, the means by which he could get payback against the corrupt boxing world that drove him into exile in the first place.

D'Amato had rules he laid down for his fighters, but very soon, it became evident to Teddy Atlas, D'Amato's chief assistant, that the rules were bent for Mike. When Mike got kicked out of high school for bad behavior, D'Amato got private lessons for him. Whenever Mike did anything wrong in town, D'Amato would pay hush money to cover his misdemeanors. Whenever Teddy tried to discipline Mike, D'Amato would override him.

The final straw for Atlas was when a seventeen-year-old Tyson made sexual advances to his sister-in-law. Atlas, a natural-born hot-head, put a gun to Mike's head and threatened to kill him if he ever tried to mess with her again. D'Amato got wind of this and fired Atlas. D'Amato was an old man now and knew he would never have another opportunity to find a fighter as unique as Mike. D'Amato loved Mike, but what he loved, even more, was the fact that Mike validated his existence, and he was the means by which he could gain back the respect he lost.

In short, Mike was a pawn in D'Amato's plans, and we see later on in life, once D'Amato died, how quickly Mike self-destructed. In an interview years later, Tyson said, "My trainer, Cus D'Amato, made me believe that being heavyweight champion of the world, all my problems would go away. And I had a lot of problems."[44] If D'Amato had simply put Mike the human being first instead of Tyson the boxer and corrected him as much with his character as with his boxing skills, maybe he would have turned out differently.

The moral of the story is not to use people as a tool to elevate your ministry.

---

[44] https://www.hollywoodreporter.com/news/mike-tyson-facing-his-dark-749009

They are to be loved and ministered to, and there is a good chance that if you do that, indirectly, your ministry will be elevated. But elevation should be the by-product of one's ministry and not the end goal. If there are issues in the lives of your disciples, deal with them, but don't sugar coat it with ministry and other stuff to make you look good and pretend that those issues will all work themselves out later.

Making Disciples who can Disciple Men

The apostle Paul gave us a great insight into discipleship when he said in 2 Timothy 2:2, "And the things that you have heard from me among many witnesses, commit these to faithful men who will be able to teach others also." Here we see four generations of men in one sentence – Paul, Timothy, faithful men, and others. Timothy isn't only to pass on what he has learned to faithful men, but to faithful men who can impart what they have been taught to another generation.

I have seen men over the years that can disciple men, but those men, in turn, have zero ability to disciple others. It means that all the fire of the early days will eventually turn into coldness and drudgery. In the early days of a church, a young pioneer pastor only has to take care of those who are what we would call the first generation. It is effortless, relatively speaking, to impart in these men as you have the time and energy to do so. But what happens when the church grows? What happens when now you have marriages, which in turn produces families? What happens when you now plant churches and have responsibilities, not only to your local congregation but baby churches? What happens when you now have to preach revivals or go out of town to help these churches?

You need men in your church who can do what you did in the early days because it is impossible for you to be all things to all men. Sure, we are still in the process of discipleship, and we always seek to work with men, but you can only be in one place at a time. This is why it is so crucial that you not only disciple men in the early days (and continue to do so) but disciple them in such a way that when new people come in, they can disciple them as well. In this way, there is continuity from one generation to the next.

We know that from Genesis 1:11 that, "Then God said, "Let the earth bring forth grass, the herb that yields seed, and the fruit tree that yields fruit according to its kind, whose seed is in itself, on the earth"; and it was so." This is an excellent picture of discipleship, where each seed has in itself the DNA to reproduce another seed with the same DNA to reproduce.

Although companies like Monsanto deny they are involved, there are plants out there that are genetically modified to go against the creation mandate of Genesis 1:11. It is called "the terminator gene," although its scientific name is "Genetic Use Restriction Technology" or "GURT" for short.

The idea behind genetic modification is to enhance the qualities of the plant. The enhancement could be anything such as increasing the yield amount or making the plant more resistant to pests and reducing the need for pesticides. But these companies aren't doing that out of love but out of a desire to make a profit.

But if a seed can reproduce, it would make all that effort in creating the seed go to waste. There would be no need for the farmer to go back to the manufacturer. All he had to do is collect a few seeds and reuse them the next time around. As a result, manufacturers also modified the seed to shut off its reproductive capability, making the seed sterile. In this way, you have to keep going back to the manufacturers for seeds.

When my family and I were in Jamaica, we had a good brother who attended our church named Sanjay. Sanjay was a farmer in St. Elizabeth, and he shared with me a hilarious story. Sanjay had cleared a large piece of land to plant tomatoes when a friend came by and gave him some free tomato seeds. His friend had previously bought a can of high-quality seeds and reaped a crop. The seeds given were the ones found in the harvested tomatoes. Sanjay was well pleased because it would save him approximately US$50, which was the amount needed for a can full.

He planted them, and within weeks he had a field full of beautiful tomato plants. He said they were tall, green and bushy and excited because if the plants looked so good, imagine how beautiful the fruit would be? And he waited, and waited, and waited some more, and one day it dawned on him that there would never be any fruit. All that hard work was wasted because he had sown seeds that were unable to bring forth fruit.

Sanjay found the funny side to it, but there is a lesson to be learned. It is possible to disciple men who have the terminator gene in them. They look great with their designer suits and flashy ties, carrying that expensive leather Bible but they cannot be fruitful in discipling other men. We get excited at the external appearance of what seems to be a disciple, but what we really need is to get excited about those who can disciple others.

Therefore, in our work to disciple men, we must make sure that we are not missing this key ingredient. You're not necessarily making a disciple if you instruct a man on breaking down the equipment and setting it up again. You make a disciple if you can impart in such a way that he will do that in the life of another man. If you can inspire men, you must train your men to be able to inspire other men. If you can teach men to preach, you must train men who can teach other men how to preach. If you can attract men to yourself, you must disciple men to be able to attract men. Don't just train men that they can function as disciples. Equip men so that they will be able to equip others also.

It means you have got to keep your eyes on your men and their interaction with other men and not just on the regular stuff of setting up equipment, ministering in a concert or at church, or leading a Bible study. Some men are natural at working with other men and inspiring other men, but others need you to come to their side and help them to get to that next level in discipleship. While we know running a church is a multifaceted task, don't be so caught up in other stuff that you take your eyes off your men.

Challenging Men to Discipleship

Men respond to challenges. That's how they are wired. As our nations grow increasingly secular, it gets tougher to get men into church. In an attempt to keep men, the automatic approach is to make church easy. What many in the church world don't realize is that it is the very thing that will drive men out. Men respond to challenges, so when we don't, we reduce their Christian lives to boredom. That is hardly the abundant life Christ promised.

Playing it safe won't keep men in the church. It is just delaying the inevitable. I remember once in the early days pioneering in Manchester; we had Pastor Peter Ajala pass through doing a revival. In those days, he was the human hurricane. He still is, but he was a Category 5 in terms of youth, and he belted out a sermon challenging the men in the church. We had a young man in the service that had recently joined from another church, but most of the guys were unchurched coming from a lifestyle of drugs, alcohol, criminality, and gangs.

As he preached on men getting rid of their baggy jeans, cornrow hairstyle and earrings and coming to church looking sharp, the church brother got disturbed. He couldn't believe he would challenge these young men. The fact that they were in church was a miracle, and he shouldn't be rocking the boat, challenging them to fix up their appearance. When one of the guys ran out of the service during the altar call, he felt his opinion was confirmed. He was precisely the type Pastor Ajala talked about – to the tee.

He was so upset at that, but he said nothing, because otherwise he liked the preaching. The next service he came back and lo and behold, the young man who had run out was there, but now he was in a suit with his haircut and the earrings removed. A few years later, that former cornrowed, baggy jeans wearing drug dealer owned his own business and got sent out. The church brother was stunned again but in a different way and realized just how being challenged transforms an individual.

Jesus never made it easy on His men. When He realized His followers were getting comfortable with all the freebies, He began to say things to them that were a challenge to their ears. In John 6:60 we read, "Therefore many of His disciples, when they heard this, said, "This is a hard saying; who can understand it?"" I like how the Message version translates it – "Many among his disciples heard this and said, "This is tough teaching, too tough to swallow." At this point, Jesus didn't retract as some modern preachers would. Instead, He went even further, and at the end of that, in John 6:66, we read, "From that time many of His disciples went back and walked with Him no more."

It said, "many of His disciples went back." I'll be honest, if many of my disciples left, I would be crushed. After all that work only to lose so many men? Devastating! And yet, it didn't bother Jesus one bit. Seeing the Twelve left makes perfect sense to try and keep them happy, but He doesn't. In John 6:67 it continues, "Then Jesus said to the twelve, "Do you also want to go away?"" There is no begging or pleading but a sobering challenge to those who were left.

Jesus was secure enough in His ministry to be able to do that. We often don't do what we should because we are afraid and lack faith in God's ability to give us men, so we do our best to keep them by being soft on them, and what we end up doing is perverting discipleship.

This wasn't the first time Jesus did that to those who said they wanted to follow Him. In Luke 9:57-62, it says, "Now it happened as they journeyed on the road, that someone said to Him, "Lord, I will follow You wherever You go." And Jesus said to him, "Foxes have holes and birds of the air have nests, but the Son of Man has nowhere to lay His head." Then He said to another, "Follow Me." But he said, "Lord, let me first go and bury my father." Jesus said to him, "Let the dead bury their own dead, but you go and preach the kingdom of God." And another also said, "Lord, I will follow You, but let me first go and bid them farewell who are at my house." But Jesus said to him, "No one, having put his hand to the plow, and looking back, is fit for the kingdom of God.""

There are no concessions for any of them. Demands are made, and anything less is not good enough for Jesus. I'm not talking about being overly hard on men, but at the same time, the men in our church need to know that discipleship comes at a price. On another occasion, when confronting the multitude of followers, in Luke 14:25-27, it reads, "Now great multitudes went with Him. And He turned and said to them, "If anyone comes to Me and does not hate his father and mother, wife and children, brothers and sisters, yes, and his own life also, he cannot be My disciple. And whoever does not bear his cross and come after Me cannot be My disciple.""

"Cannot" is a powerful word that is entirely unambiguous. There is no confusion in the word "cannot," and yet somehow, we feel we can make men into disciples if they are not willing to pay the price.

You must remember that there is something far more important than just having a church full of guys wearing nice clothes. We are talking about the fate of the world. This is why Jesus had to challenge His men because these were the ones He would rely on in reaching the world. They had to be made of sterner stuff.

We read the continuing verses in Luke 14 as if it was Jesus telling people to consider the price of discipleship. While it is very true that there is a price to consider, it wasn't the meaning of Luke 14:28-32. In those verses Jesus said, "For which of you, intending to build a tower, does not sit down first and count the cost, whether he has enough to finish it—lest, after he has laid the foundation, and is not able to finish, all who see it begin to mock him, saying, 'This man began to build and was not able to finish'? Or what king, going to make war against another king, does not sit down first and consider whether he is able with ten thousand to meet him who comes against him with twenty thousand? Or else, while the other is still a great way off, he sends a delegation and asks conditions of peace."

He says that a builder has to make sure he has enough material to see if he can finish his task of building a tower. He says that a king has to consider if he has enough men to defeat a rival army. He has to see if his men have enough quality in them to defeat a much larger army. For that to happen, he must have outstanding men.

What am I getting at? Jesus isn't saying that they must consider the price to pay, although that has been implied previously. Jesus is saying that because HE is in the business of BUILDING and BATTLING, HE has to be very careful in making sure that HE has enough quality in HIS disciples to finish what he started. If Jesus is going to build His church and battle the gates of hell, it is only because He has the disciples to do it. He can only do it with disciples who are willing to pay the price. He can only do it with men who have risen to the challenge.

It is better to have twelve men who can take the world than to have a multitude that would stop just outside the gates of Jerusalem when the going got tough.

Like I said, what we are seeking to accomplish is more than just having men in suits running around setting up chairs. We are seeking to build the kingdom of God, and to battle the forces of darkness, soft men just won't cut it. You can have the best-looking building with state of the art equipment and have a church full of guys who couldn't fast till lunchtime or get out of bed to attend morning prayer.

When Sir Ernest Shackleton went about finding a crew for his ship "Endurance" to go on a mission to Antarctica, he put an ad out in an English newspaper that read, "Notice: Men wanted for hazardous journey. Small wages. Bitter cold. Long months of complete darkness. Constant danger. Safe return doubtful. Honor and recognition in case of success." Now in this day and age of motivational speaking and positive confession, that is a definite no-no.

But amazingly enough, around five thousand men applied for a position that could only be filled by twenty-eight men. Once again, it just goes to show what lies in many men's hearts is the desire to rise to a challenge. But even then, Shackleton didn't just choose any Tom, Dick, or Harry. It was going to be an arduous mission. Going to the Antarctic isn't the same as a trip to the Bahamas. In the Antarctic, it could be dark for months on end in addition to seriously low sub-zero temperatures.

In describing his ideal crew, Shackleton's said, "The men selected must be qualified for the work, and they must also have the special qualifications required to meet polar conditions. They must be able to live together in harmony for a long period of time without outside communication, and it must be remembered that the men whose desire lead them to the untrodden paths of the world have generally marked individuality. It was no easy matter for me to select the staff."

For the sake of time, I'll cut a long story short and say that the "Endurance" ended up being stuck in ice, causing the men to become stranded. It took another ten months for the ice to crush the ship completely, but through teamwork, all twenty-eight men made it out alive in what was a horrifying experience. It was almost impossible, but it only confirmed that what

Shackleton needed wasn't just twenty-eight men but men who could build and battle.

Letting Men Fail

Another critical factor in discipleship is learning to let men fail. This is something that gets overlooked very easily. In an attempt to make sure everything is running like clockwork, the pastor can get into the bad habit of micromanaging everything. If the microphones sound distorted, there he is running over to the mixing board to sort it. If the chairs aren't aligned properly, he is there in a flash with his tape measure to make sure every chair is directly an inch away from the other. What's this? Is it a young disciple waffling away during the altar call of a concert? Get up, take the mike while he is in mid-flow and show him how it's done – again and again.

Very rarely does someone get it right the first time. It's unnatural. People fail because human beings are fallen creatures. Not just that, but people fail if they have never done something before. They don't have the experience to fall back on. And yet, failure is an essential part of learning. In failure, you get to learn what went wrong in order not to repeat it. In failure, you learn why things are done a certain way, which reinforces convictions about things.

I have failed so many times it's not funny. I have learned to be an adequate preacher through many failings. I cringe every time I look back on my earliest sermon notes. There is hardly anything in them, and yet for some bizarre reason, God still moved. I preached horribly, so much so I remember once getting a letter from an older lady in church who said God didn't call me to preach. I remember once reading three pages out of a book during a sermon. We had two visitors that day. We never saw them again. I learned that day that it is not a good idea to read a book during a sermon.

I remember the exact date when I preached my worse sermon ever. It was Wednesday, the first of March 2000. I preached a sermon on faithfulness entitled "Semper Fidelis." When Paul said that the letter kills, he wasn't joking. It was unadulterated poison. It was pure letter and zero Spirit. It dropped like a lead balloon, and I felt like gum under the bottom of a shoe. If I could teleport myself to another part of the universe, I would have. As soon as the altar call was over, I chit-chatted a little, but my mind was far away, and as soon as I could, I went home, got into the bedroom, and cried in my pillow.

But hey, the next Sunday, I was back in the pulpit determined never to repeat that. Amazingly, that was the turning point for my preaching, and it got progressively better after that.

Much of what I have learned has been through trial and error. And men must learn by making mistakes. I have purposely put my men in positions where I would do absolutely nothing to help and leave them to figure it out. It is only human nature for people to leave much of their thinking to their leaders. This happens all the time in church. When the pastor is always leading the outreach, concert, or whatever, disciples will switch their minds off.

They may not realize it, and they may say that they know what to do if you aren't around, but that's not usually true. So from time to time, especially in the early days when you have a group of guys you are working with, I would just leave everything to them. Get one of them to organize the outreach one week, the concert scene, the movie night, or some kind of evangelic event you usually do. See how their minds race into overdrive as they try to remember what was done the last time. See how flustered they get as things fall apart. And don't do a thing to help if you don't have to.

Then, when the event has passed, you ask them what they think went wrong, what you know went wrong, and what needs to be done to make it more effective the next time around. I remember in the early days in Wolverhampton when we had an impact team from my old church in Manchester, leaving everything into the hands of the disciples and not lifting a finger to help. The pastor of the Manchester church, a disciple of mine, wanted to help them, but they needed to make the mistakes to learn.

Sometimes you have just to let everything go, knowing that if someone doesn't do something, everything will fall apart. You have to know when to do that, and I have to admit I can't recall ever having to step in to rescue the operation. Usually, someone will see what's about to happen and step up. But you have to do that otherwise your men will always be expecting you to do it.

I see some men get so caught up in creating a happening scene that they and their wives are running around doing everything. Let things go. Let the plates go crashing from time to time if it isn't going to kill the church. Don't be so caught up in trying to be the trendiest church in the city that you lose sight of raising up disciples. Let your men fail and show grace to them. As you do this, your men will grow, and you will have time to do other more important things.

We, as disciple-makers, need to expand our thinking if we are going to disciple men. We all want our churches to grow, and yet we are limited in our thinking. We want to have a church that can have a real impact, and yet we operate with a small church model. There is only so much one man can do. A good, dynamic pastor can have a decent crowd on his own, but that's as far as it goes. After that, no matter how much he does – concerts, revivals, special events, etc. – the church stays around the same size. This is even if people are praying to receive Christ at the altar. Yet, with additional disciples, he can expand that crowd.

If a pastor can train the men under him effectively, they can do what he does to a large extent, which releases him to do more important things. It doesn't matter how talented that pastor is, if he has no disciples, he will reach a cap because the important and urgent are always fighting for his attention. Not everything urgent is important, and not everything important is urgent.

We see this played out in the book of Acts. Acts 6:1-7 states, "Now in those days, when the number of the disciples was multiplying, there arose a complaint against the Hebrews by the Hellenists, because their widows were neglected in the daily distribution. Then the twelve summoned the multitude of the disciples and said, "It is not desirable that we should leave the word of God and serve tables. Therefore, brethren, seek out from among you seven men of good reputation, full of the Holy Spirit and wisdom, whom we may appoint over this business; but we will give ourselves continually to prayer and to the ministry of the word." And the saying pleased the whole multitude. And they chose Stephen, a man full of faith and the Holy Spirit, and Philip, Prochorus, Nicanor, Timon, Parmenas, and Nicolas, a proselyte from Antioch, whom they set before the apostles; and when they had prayed, they laid hands on them. Then the word of God spread, and the number of the disciples multiplied greatly in Jerusalem, and a great many of the priests were obedient to the faith."

I don't think the Twelve had a problem personally ministering to widows and providing for them. They weren't aloof men. After all, they were trained by the Lord Jesus Himself. It was an urgent issue, no doubt, but the growth of the church was their priority. They, as the Lord's apostles, couldn't be bogged down in things that would hinder the ministry's growth. They had to prioritize, and they recognized that there were individuals who could take care of this urgent need while they took care of other important matters.

As Stephen and company responded to the need, the apostles were now free to do what they were sent by Jesus to do, and as a result, the word of God spread, and discipleship flourished and not just a little either. At times pastors can get bogged down in minor details and leave the major issues unattended.

Discipleship is how everything gets done.

Training your replacement

I have heard discipleship sermons on Elijah and Elisha for over a quarter of a century, but I have never really heard it preached on why Elisha was being discipled. Elisha was being discipled to replace Elijah. It's that simple. 1 Kings 19:16 says, "Also you shall anoint Jehu the son of Nimshi as king over Israel. And Elisha the son of Shaphat of Abel Meholah you shall anoint as prophet in your place." Notice the words "in your place"?

We can learn many principles from Elijah's training of Elisha, but what we need to remember is that Elijah did that knowing Elisha was going to take his place as prophet. We can see that his training was first-rate, and in the end, Elisha had a double portion of his spirit, and what that shows us is that he wasn't resentful or jealous of Elisha. He never tried to sabotage his discipleship or lead him down the wrong path like the old prophet from Bethel (1 Kings 13:11).

Old prophets are very much alive today in the church world. These are the men who are secretly resentful of the younger men around them being used of God and would very much like to undermine their ministry. Rather than take these young men under their wing and teach them what they know, they secretly plan and scheme to keep the young men down. They purposely hold them back, put obstacles in their way, discourage them, or mess with their convictions.

In the church world, older pastors can be very intimidated by up-and-coming young men in the congregation. As they feel increasingly out of touch with today's world, they think their relevance is questioned. Insecurities creep in, and they develop a Saul complex believing that the church feels the younger David is far more effective against the enemy than he is. And maybe they are right, but it doesn't mean that God is finished with them.

My old church landlord in Manchester told me that when he was a young man, zealous for Jesus, the pastor undermined him and other young men in the church. As a result, he left, and he has never been the same. There are two sides to every story, but that is not uncommon in the church world. Good older pastors can end up becoming like an old dictator, and what dictators do is drive out the clear-thinking men who can help move the country forward.

The other danger is that when that pastor dies, the church collapses. It has been on more than one occasion throughout my Christian life, hearing of churches closing completely when the pastor died. There was no one groomed to succeed him, and when he died, so did the church. There was no legacy because his fear of a younger man taking over his position was greater than his fear of dying. Old pastors aren't stupid. The older we get, the more we are aware of our mortality. Old pastors know this, but some are not willing to train up an Elisha to take their place.

Just like the old prophet from 1 Kings 13, after a while, ministry ceases to be about God's kingdom and more about man's kingdom. Discipleship is seeing the bigger picture that the work is ultimately more important than the man. Please don't misunderstand what I am saying. I am not saying that we treat the men on the field as pawns on a chessboard. The issue here isn't our view of the man but the man's view of himself.

The apostle Paul said in 2 Corinthians 2:15, "And I will very gladly spend and be spent for your souls…" He also said in Philippians 1:23-25, "For I am hard-pressed between the two, having a desire to depart and be with Christ, which is far better. Nevertheless, to remain in the flesh is more needful for you. And being confident of this, I know that I shall remain and continue with you all for your progress and joy of faith…" Paul understands that to be the minister Christ had called him to be, he has to put the church before himself.

When we become more important than the work, we have disqualified ourselves and don't even know it. We now operate in the flesh, which is why it is easy to undermine men under us.

In all honesty, I have not seen this in our Fellowship. I haven't been around in every church to guarantee that statement, but I would say with our ethos of discipleship, the conditions to create such a church aren't there. (But I think there is a possibility of a nut or two going around, doing his own thing.)

What I have seen, however, are men who, the thought of training their replacement never crossed their minds. One never knows what may happen in the future. You could be called upon to take over a church in another city. The Holy Spirit could impress on your heart to go overseas. You may fall sick and have to be redirected. Worst case scenario, you could have a failure of some kind and have to be removed.

Think about it. Would you like a church you have invested years in, be taken over by a klutz? Now I'm not saying everyone who takes over is a klutz. I have taken over several churches in my time on the field. I don't think I'm a clown, but I have had heard horror stories in my time. I've had guys ring me vexed out of their minds, venting at what some other guy is doing at their previous church.

Now, let me qualify that again. There can be times when it is critical someone outside takes over a church. You may be pastoring a decent-sized church, and your best guy out there with thirty people isn't the best replacement for such a situation. There may be a violation in the church so deep that a novice has no business trying to rectify. But it makes perfect sense to train up men who could take your place.

When I left Manchester to assist Pastor Carnegie in London, one of the brothers in the church took over. When I left Wolverhampton to go to Jamaica, it was as good a transition as it could be for pastoral changes. Pastor Peter Ajala and I had spoken about going to Jamaica two years before we were launched, so we decided to send my best guy out that year with the hope he would get his brains bashed in on the field to prepare him for the takeover. And it worked. Leon Etten and his wife Lulu are doing an excellent job there.

Jesus spent three and a half years training up His replacement. He knew He wouldn't be in the world for too long, and He needed to find the right men. We would do well to follow Jesus' advice.

Of course, there is much more to be said about discipleship that I haven't covered, but I hope that would be helpful, a brick, if you will, in the building of the house.

7 THE ALTAR CALL

In the book, "Beyond the Cross and the Switchblade", author David Wilkerson gave the reason why he founded the Para-Church ministry called Teen Challenge. As he was walking down a hazardous street in Brooklyn, he met a gang of about six young men who were mainlining heroin right in front of him. What they were doing and the conditions they were in, so moved him that right then and there, he turned to God in prayer. He committed that with the help of God, he would reach these young down and outs.

He said that was a reference point in his life, and from that decision, God used him to reach many drug addicts and see them turn to Christ. The organization got so immense that from time to time, he got distracted from what God had called him to do. So whenever he found himself in a situation where he was distracted from his primary call, no matter where he was in the world, he would find his way back to this ghetto in Brooklyn. At that spot, he says, God never failed to meet with him there again and remind him of the calling he had received.

He said, *"Over the years I have developed a habit of visiting…special rendezvous points where in the past I have met the Lord and where I return in time of need, confident that I will find Him there again. There is a strange power in place. This must be one of the main reasons the Bible gives such an important role to altars…For by instinct, we are drawn back to the place where we once met God, trusting that there again we can meet."*

David Wilkerson was at the time a pastor with the Assemblies of God, which is the largest Pentecostal church organization in the world. It is no coincidence that this Pentecostal pastor was familiar with the altar, and one practice synonymous with Pentecostalism has been the altar call. To separate the altar call from the Pentecostal church is like separating the egg white from the yolk. The altar call is intrinsically a fundamental part of Pentecostalism. Yet, it is a practice that has come under heavy scrutiny in recent times, with many churches rejecting its tradition as being unbiblical, manipulative, and counterproductive to true evangelism.

As we gain greater traction into the 21st century and as evangelical Christianity continues to wane in western society, the practice of the altar call will be called into further questioning, not just by the unsaved world, but also by many Christians and Christian denominations. Therefore, understanding the practice of the altar call and why we must continue to make it a fundamental part of our church service is of absolute importance.

One danger we face is that we take this practice so much for granted that we can't even explain to others why we do it. We just assume that it is something everyone should do, and as a result of that little thought is given as to why we do it. Doing the right thing without understanding why it is done can potentially bring harm. This is true with the altar call because there is more to it that just getting someone to the front of the church. There are nuances to the altar call that must be understood to get it right. This will be discussed further on down the chapter.

Objections to the Altar Call

Before we get to understand why we do altar calls, we must look at the objections to them. It is vital we do because there are valid objections to the practice of altar calls that just can't be dismissed as irrelevant. This is for two reasons. (1) Dismissing these objections would be counterproductive as it will foster ignorance as to why we do altar calls. Objections many times cause us to investigate and look into things on a deeper level to get a greater understanding. (2) Dismissing these objections, especially if raised by a young Christian looking for greater clarity, will only make you look like you don't know what you are talking about. It means you will lose credibility.

One thing made crystal clear to me in the six years I functioned as a missionary in Jamaica was the ignorance of spiritual truths, not only by the average Christian but many ministers and pastors as well. I have encountered many Christians with valid questions regarding their faith and who were reluctant to voice those questions to me because they thought they would be met with the usual *"Don't question God!"* or *"You have a bad spirit!"* Many meekly kept quiet due to respect for spiritual headship, but quite a few of the highly intelligent ones realized that their pastor didn't have a clue as to how to answer those questions. The sad thing for me was these smart young men and women who have no confidence in their church leadership and thus lie on the fringe of church involvement.

As Christians and pastors, we must have answers, perhaps not to everything, but at least to why we do what we do. The usual clichéd answers of *"We have always done it like this!"* or *"Are you questioning our ancient landmarks?"* may shut people up, but it doesn't edify. It also doesn't stop the questions in the hearts of the people, which potentially can lead to disillusionment or getting the wrong answer to a good question.

This chapter is as much in defense of the practice of the altar call as it is helping people to understand why we do it. As a matter of fact, in defending the practice, I hope that you may understand why we do what we do regarding the altar call. The criticism of the altar call is what I will use to springboard us into understanding its purpose and its continued relevance today.

Over the years, I have heard many reasons why the altar call is a practice that should be abandoned by the church. The reasons are:

1. There is no mention anywhere in the New Testament about the practice of altar calls and, as a result, is a product of man's wisdom and not God's.
2. The altar call is a recent phenomenon starting with Charles Finney in the 1800s, who, as a result of false doctrine, came up with the idea.
3. In some circles, the altar call is seen as the most critical aspect of the church service. It, therefore, undermines other parts of the service, such as prayer, worship, and preaching, but especially the communion.
4. It can create a mindset in Christians that salvation is something only done during the church service and so people will have to wait until Sunday to get saved.
5. It can deceive people by giving them a false assurance of salvation, thinking that just by answering an altar call, they are now saved regardless of how they live their lives after that experience.
6. Since the altar call involves getting up from your seat and going to the front to accept Christ as Lord and Savior, it, therefore,

means the primary public confession of faith is the altar call and not water baptism.
7. It is manipulative, a means of controlling people's minds to make them get up and go to the front of the church to pray.
8. It denies justification through faith and emphasizes works (getting up and going to the front) as the means of salvation.

The Attack on Finney

According to the detractors of the altar call, it was created by revivalist Charles Finney, also known as "the father of modern revivalism", back in the 1800s as a part of the "New Measures". These "New Measures" included using informal instead of reverential language in the church service. It allowed women to pray alongside men in a public setting. It had an "anxious seat", also known as "the mourner's bench" (the precursor of the altar call) at the front row of the church for those who were genuinely concerned about their salvation, having services daily instead of just weekly, among other things.

In truth, Finney brought razzmatazz into the modern church service. His view was that the world was getting people's attention through theatres, bars, and all other kinds of amusements while the church was dry and dull with preachers preaching "sanctimonious starch". His philosophy was to get and keep the attention of the sinner through excitement, entertainment, and emotionalism. These tactics were a means to an end, that is, to keep the soul fixated on the message preached and ultimately making a decision for Christ.

Later on, famous evangelists such as Dwight Moody and Billy Sunday incorporated the altar call as an essential part of their ministry. Moody further developed the altar call by adding music to his preaching and having church members function as counselors. William Booth, the founder of the Salvation Army, also used the altar call, although in his case, instead of calling it 'the anxious seat', he called it 'the mercy seat'. But perhaps the most famous preacher using the altar call is Billy Graham. We have probably all seen clips of Rev. Graham pull an altar call in a large stadium with many people streaming down the aisles to the front to receive Christ as Lord and Savior.

While many current detractors throw barbs at Graham and Moody, much vitriol is directed at Charles Finney, seen as the originator of the altar call. So, as in the time-honored fashion, if you want to destroy a man's message, you first destroy his character. Finney is portrayed, usually by Calvinists, as a man who denied fundamental doctrines and therefore is a heretic and his preaching a sham.

In this short chapter, we don't have time to discuss the theological leanings of Finney. Regardless of what Finney believed, he did not invent the altar call or any of the "New Measures". Much of those "New Measures" were around years before Finney came on the scene, primarily in Methodist circles, but Finney made them popular. Thus Finney's theology had nothing to do with the creation of the altar call.

Critics of the Altar Call

Much criticism of the altar call comes from two primary sources. The first is the followers of Reformed theology (Calvinists). Perhaps of all the false beliefs in the Christian world, this doctrine is the most damaging. Calvinists believe that some are destined for salvation, and others are doomed to destruction. It, therefore, means that those destined to get saved will get saved regardless. There is no need for an altar call (or evangelism for that matter) because God will save the soul elected for redemption.

This reminds me of a book I read regarding William Carey, who is called "the father of modern missions". In the late 1700s, when he expressed a desire to go to India and preach the gospel to the unsaved, he was rebuked by an older Baptist minister who said, *"Young man! Sit down! You are an enthusiast! When God pleases to convert the heathen, He will do it without consulting you or me!"* I guess to the reformist mind, God will save the sinner if destined for salvation and so He doesn't need an altar call to do it.

The second is perhaps more justified in their criticism. Today there is much easy-believism in the Christian world where if you say a "little prayer" and receive Jesus in your heart, then you are saved. If anyone watches Christian television long enough, you will see a televangelist with pearly-white teeth and a cheesy grin look directly in the camera and ask you to invite Jesus you're your heart. Because of this generation's insistence on cheap grace, the altar call of yesteryear has been perverted in some circles to become the be-all and end-all of Christianity. So in some circles, if you answered an altar call, it doesn't matter how you live your life; you are a Christian because you gave your life to Jesus at the altar.

Therefore, I can understand the criticism of altar calls in such cases, but perversion to an excellent method of evangelism doesn't mean that the method should be done away with. The truth is, however, that what has started as a good thing has, to a degree, been compromised. It is a paradoxical situation where something that is so commonly seen is, at the same time, so widely misunderstood. Some long-standing saints have seen hundreds of altar calls, and yet their understanding of why is shallow. As a result of that, it is no wonder altar calls in the church world have been abused.

I have heard people say stuff like, *"My friend is coming to church on Wednesday to get saved."* Well, why can't you lead him to Christ before he comes to church? A few years ago, someone shared with me a conversation they had with a backslider who fell into long term fornication. She had told her friend, *"You can come to church on Sunday and rededicate your life to Jesus."* If the person is backslidden, why can't you lead him or her to Christ right then and there? Why wait until Sunday?

Then there is the classic example of someone who answered the altar call but left church weeks later and has gone back to a life of sin. A well-meaning Christian brother or sister would say, *"But you got saved at the altar two months ago."* Really? If he or she was saved, why are they back in a life of sin? Does everyone who answers an altar call get saved? If they go back to a life of sin as soon as they leave the church, it shows that they don't.

But perhaps the one that gets to me and I hear it at church conferences all the time and the guilty culprits are pastors. *"We had a concert, and we pulled an altar call, and eighty people got saved. Over the summer between June and August, we had three hundred and fifty people give their lives to Jesus. Hallelujah!"* Wow! Three hundred and fifty! That's impressive. How many are still in church, I suppose? What? Only ten? Where are the other three hundred and forty? In other churches? No? They are back on the streets, you say? But I thought they gave their lives to Jesus?

Saving Faith

While altar calls are essential, let me point out that altar calls are not the be-all and end-all of salvation. One doesn't have to answer an altar call to get saved. And just because someone answers an altar call, it doesn't mean that he or she is saved either. Someone could get saved during the church service as the Holy Spirit moves upon him or her without getting up to either go to the altar or seek a counselor after service.

In Acts 10, the Bible records that as Peter speaks to Cornelius and his Gentile associates that the Holy Spirit fell upon them, and they all spoke with tongues. Acts 10:44-47 says, *"While Peter was still speaking these words, the Holy*

Spirit fell upon all those who heard the word. And those of the circumcision who believed were astonished, as many as came with Peter, because the gift of the Holy Spirit had been poured out on the Gentiles also. For they heard them speak with tongues and magnify God. Then Peter answered, "Can anyone forbid water, that these should not be baptized who have received the Holy Spirit just as we have?"'

These individuals did not answer an altar call, and neither did they seek out a counselor, but right where they sat, they got saved, and as a result of getting saved, they were filled with the Holy Spirit. Acts 10:44 says, *"...the Holy Spirit fell upon all those who heard the word."*

Now we know that we are saved by faith. The apostle Paul wrote in Ephesians 2:8, *"For by grace you have been saved through faith..."* He also wrote in Romans 10:17, *"...faith comes by hearing, and hearing by the word of God."* As Cornelius and the Gentile unbelievers heard the word of God preached by Peter, it created faith in their hearts, which lead to their salvation, and as they got saved, they were then filled with the Holy Spirit. Regardless of the dynamics involved, we can see that they didn't need an altar call to get saved.

As balanced Christians, we know that to be true. Any mature Christian involved in evangelism has prayed with sinners on the street, in the home, at school, or the office, for them to receive Christ. We didn't tell them to wait until Sunday and answer the altar call to get saved but led them to Christ right then and there with a sinner's prayer.

Yet even then, some people have a problem with that. (These are usually Calvinists but not exclusively so.) *"Where is the sinner's prayer in the Bible?"* Sigh! Okay, okay. The sinner's prayer isn't in the Bible, but all a sinner's prayer is, is a biblical framework outlining what is needed for salvation. Romans 10:17-18 says, *"...if you confess with your mouth the Lord Jesus and believe in your heart that God has raised Him from the dead, you will be saved. For with the heart one believes unto righteousness, and with the mouth confession is made unto salvation."* All we are doing with a sinner's prayer is to get people to confess with their mouth what they believe in their hearts. It's as simple as that.]

The Need for the Altar Call

Anyway, back to the altar call. Yes, the altar call in its present form was not seen in the Bible, but it doesn't mean it isn't a valid method in evangelism. I never read where Peter, Paul, or John handed out Bible tracks or church flyers, but that won't stop me from giving them out. James never had a Facebook page of his church in Jerusalem, and Apollos never put his sermons on YouTube either. Andrew never had a Christian radio program reaching distant shores, but these have been instrumental in reaching people who otherwise could not be ministered to.

I find it funny that many of the detractors, who have a problem with the altar call due to its lack of scriptural references, have no problem dating before marriage. The truth is that there are no scriptural references to dating either. Marriage, in the Bible, was usually an arranged affair between families. As the altar call, dating is a modern-day construct. But we justify dating in our culture by using the biblical principles of personal holiness, accountability, self-control, and so on.

Creating a biblical framework to safeguard modern-day courtship is something that has been universally embraced by Western Christianity. While I have heard of matchmaking leading to immediate marriage with Christian families in India, I have never heard of such Christian matchmaking in the West. Does that mean Indian Christians have a monopoly on spirituality in relationships?

Now I would never say that the altar call is the exclusive means of reaching people for Christ, but it would seem that way if you listen to those who are against it. Nevertheless, I believe in this day and age, it is a critical factor in reaching people for Christ.

I have been to church services where the minister has preached a powerful convicting message, and in the end, they sing a song and dismiss the service. In my mind, I am screaming! I feel like rushing up that stage and grabbing the microphone. In such a service, there has got to be someone who felt convicted enough to get saved. Maybe only one person would have the courage to respond, but the opportunity must be given for that one to make a decision. Why not? To some, it would do more harm than good.

How is that possible? Some argue, *"It will make people believe the altar call is the only way to get saved." "It will cause that person to make the altar call his place of public confession rather than baptism." "It is possible that he was manipulated."* So, because of possible faulty assumptions made as a result of the church not letting its members be clear on the uses of the altar call, we must stop the possibility of a soul getting saved? Preposterous!

I read a story years ago of a young man throwing back starfishes into the ocean after a storm. They had washed up on shore due to the severity of the waves. The young man, out of sympathy, was throwing them back in. There was a passerby, who, as he slowly walked along, saw him return them to the sea one at a time. Looking at the hundreds of starfish that were stranded and the amount of work needed to get them back into the ocean, he turned to the young man and said, "There are too many of them to return, and you are on your own. You are only able to help a handful, so why bother?" The young man, with a starfish in hand, turned to the passerby and said, "It matters to this one." And with that, he threw him into the ocean.

Yes, people may come to the altar for all the wrong reasons, but it is also possible that someone genuinely could get saved, and for the sake of that one, we should do an altar call. I believe that because I was that one, but for a time, I was one of the hundreds that lay dying on the shore, desperate for someone to throw me back in.

Back in 1986, my high school did something very unusual; for about an hour or so they canceled regular classes and had the school gather for a special devotion. There were a few black American preachers in the country doing an all-country tour, and somehow they were able to get in to do a mini-service. I have to admit that it was electrifying and convicting. In the end, they didn't do an altar call, but they had the students whose hearts were open pray a sinner's prayer.

I prayed that prayer, and I can honestly say that right then, and there I felt changed. I felt lighter, and there was a joy on the inside I just couldn't explain. I thought I could run and jump all day long. After the assembly, we went back to our classrooms, but I was on my own. I had been raised Catholic all my life, but I never experienced anything like this. Who do I talk to?

Somehow I found out about the ISCF (Inter-School Christian Fellowship), and after school, one day that week, I went there, and as a Catholic kid, I felt like a fish out of water. No one introduced themselves to me or made me feel welcome, and after about five minutes, I left. I knew that what I had I couldn't find in the Catholic Church, but I didn't know anyone who was a genuine Christian who could take me to their church. (My aunt was a Pentecostal, but it was one of those churches where people ran around throwing chairs. I went once when I was about ten and vowed never to return because I was so scared.)

I still had that joy a week later, and that was when I decided to tell one of my closest friends at the time who was also a Catholic. When I told him what happened at the devotion, he frowned (and he was one of the nicest kids you could ever meet) and said coldly and dismissively, *"We're Catholic, Jay. We don't get involved with those kinds of people."*

It was the first time that my friend had offended me, and I resented him for it. Those words had the force of a mule kick. For the next week or so, I avoided him, but his words kept ringing in my ears and slowly, but surely the joy in me began to fade, and I went back to being 'normal'. I made up with my friend, and we were back to being friends again as if that week in my life never happened.

The next time I truly heard the gospel was three years later in 1989 when during chemistry class, a classmate told me about Jesus. My response to him was, *"Yeah! Maybe when I'm thirty, and I travel the world and meet a few girls, I'll consider giving my life to Jesus."* The door to my heart was closed, fortunately not for good, but at that moment, I had no interest in Christ, and it can be rooted in the fact that I was left on my own spiritually.

Had there been an organized altar call, I would have prayed directly with someone who would then be able to help me in the new faith that I had. I would have been given some instruction and linked to a particular person to speak to in regards to attending church. At the very least, with me going up to the front, perhaps a kid like my classmate would have seen me and spoke to me after the devotion and encouraged me as a new convert.

But without the altar call, no one knew anything because no one knew what happened in my soul, and I was left trying to figure out something I had no understanding of. I wonder how many have gone to church and felt something but left not speaking to anyone and ended up having what was in their heart taken away?

It is for this purpose the altar call was created. Back in the late 1700s and early 1800s, the "anxious seat" got its name from the front pew, which would be cleared if sinners who were convicted wanted to pray. This quickly caught on, especially in Methodist circles. Methodist preacher, Henry Boehm, in the year 1800, saw this and was impressed. He recalled, *"It was a great advantage because the seekers scattered all through the congregation, it was difficult to give them suitable attention. By bringing them together they were accessible to those who desired to instruct and encourage them. In the early part of the revival I saw twelve men kneel at the mourner's bench, and they were all quickly converted."*[45]

Here we can see the plain motive behind the altar call and that was to give people who were genuinely open to the gospel a chance to get saved. In a revival service where there are people everywhere, it is challenging to minister to those who are open to the gospel effectively. Inviting those genuinely

---

[45] p469, Centennial History of American Methodism, John Atkinson (1884)

interested in coming to the front allowed the revival service (or any other service for that matter) to accomplish its goal – the salvation of the lost. What's the point of having a compelling and convicting revival service and yet allow genuinely open people to slip through the nets? People like me.

Perhaps if you are a Calvinist, you can believe that God will save whom He wills regardless of a revival service or not. But to us who understand that Satan is actively at work seeking to snatch the seed of the word from people's hearts, we mustn't waste the opportunity. The object is not to manipulate or force people to a false conversion, hoping that if they pray the sinner's prayer, something miraculous will happen, but that we give those who are genuinely open an opportunity to get their hearts right with God.

This is where spiritual sensitivity is necessary, and where a mindless auto-pilot approach to the altar call can be dangerous. In an atmosphere of revival where the Holy Spirit is moving and touching lives, the altar call is simply a natural step in gathering the convicted to lead them to Christ. But in an atmosphere where nothing is happening, a prolonged altar call is like trying to beat a dead horse. That being said, there have been times when it looked like nothing was happening, but in fact, there were people deeply convicted, and the altar call moved them to follow the conviction and seek help in coming to Christ. It, therefore, shows that doing a great altar call is a spiritual skill that requires both sensitivity to the Holy Spirit and experience.

There is another essential reason why doing an altar call is necessary. While those who believe in Reformed theology think the chosen will be saved regardless, we believe that since no one knows when they will die, it is imperative to be saved as soon as possible. 2 Corinthians 6:2 reminds us, *"...now is the accepted time; behold, now is the day of salvation."* Hebrews 4:7 states, *"Today, if you will hear His voice, do not harden your hearts."*

An altar call is given with the understanding that we may not see, and if one hears the gospel today, then today is the opportunity given to get saved. I believe no preacher who genuinely cares for the soul of man will let a sinner walk out of his service without being allowed to get saved. Yes, there is a good chance he may not get saved, but there is a good chance he might.

I can't see the big deal in all the criticisms people make regarding the altar call. *"You may create false Christians." "You are promoting easy-believism." "What if they walk away from the altar and continue their old lives?"* So I should just let a sinner who just heard the gospel walk out the door without allowing him or her to get to know Jesus simply because of a possible misunderstanding or that person not following that decision through?

Ultimately, what an individual does with the gospel once it has been presented is up to him. I have a responsibility to let him hear and give him a chance to accept Christ then and there if he wants to, knowing that tomorrow isn't guaranteed.

I remember years ago, after a Sunday morning church service, a member of the congregation introduced me to his younger brother, who was a backslider. He was a very good-looking young guy who backslid for the usual reason young good-looking Christian men backslide – girls. I spoke to him for a while, and I encouraged him to rededicate his life back to Christ. He refused because, in his words, he was not ready.

The next day I got a tearful phone call from his older brother. After church that Sunday, he went to the house of an acquaintance to collect some money he was owed. Instead of raising that money, he was beaten and killed, and his body found in someone's backyard that Monday morning. Less than twenty-four hours after our conversation, he was in eternity.

Living in Jamaica as a missionary for six years has opened my eyes to the fragility of life. There have been a few who have passed through the church over those years who have since passed away and, in some cases, very brutally. I'm reminded again, and again that time is promised to none.

Back in July 2015, I received a phone call from a lady in her early twenties who used to attend our church in Mandeville, Jamaica. Her mother was sick, and so I promised her that I would visit her and her mother the following Saturday at 11 am with my wife. On that very Saturday, at about 9 am, I received a phone call from the young lady, and she was distraught. Her mother had just died, two hours from the time I was supposed to visit. The mother was only 41, and it was shocking to see a woman who was still relatively young and who had previously been to church, lying on the floor and covered by a sheet. Death comes to all, and many times it happens unexpectedly.

I say that, but every time an event like that happens, it disturbs me, and it is like I always forget that people die suddenly and many times without notice. What I am saying is that it is so easy to forget that the people you meet today may not be around tomorrow. I have to remind myself that I am not guaranteed the next breath.

This is why having an altar call is so vital because even open people can die suddenly and unexpectedly. I'm not saying that we push the gospel down people's throats. Many times that is counterproductive. Perhaps in having a neighbor, a work colleague, or a schoolmate, one can take their time in reaching them with the gospel. Still, there is something about a gospel message preached that gives an immediate allowance to a call for salvation.

Dwight L Moody, more than any other, understood the urgency of the altar call. On Sunday evening, the 8th of October 1871, Moody preached to the largest crowd he ever had in the city of Chicago. He was preaching from Matthew 27:22, "What shall I do then with Jesus, which is called Christ?" At the end of the sermon, he said, "I wish you would take this text home with you and turn it over in your minds during the week, and next Sabbath we will come to Calvary and the cross, and we will decide what to do with Jesus of Nazareth."

Years later, Moody would say that was the worst decision he ever made. The great singer Ira Sankey closed with the hymn: "Today the Savior calls; for refuge fly; the storm of justice falls, and death is nigh…" But Sankey was unable to finish the hymn as the Great Fire of Chicago had started, and the fire trucks began to blare all around the building, drowning his voice.

Over a thousand people lost their lives that night, including people who attended that service. Twenty-two years later, on the anniversary of that tragic night, Moody said these words, "I have never dared to give an audience a week to think of their salvation since. If they were lost, they might rise up in judgment against me…I have never seen that congregation since. I have hard work to keep back the tears today. I have looked over this audience, and not a single one is here that I preached to that night. I have a great many old friends and am pretty well acquainted in Chicago, but twenty-two years have passed away, and I have not seen that congregation since, and I never will meet those people again until I meet them in another world. But I want to tell you of one lesson I learned that night, which I have never forgotten, and that is, when I preach, to press Christ upon the people then and there, and try to bring them to a decision on the spot. I would rather have that right hand cut off than to give an audience now a week to decide what to do with Jesus."[46]

Does that sound like a man who is a manipulator? Does he look like someone who needs his ego massaged by seeing many respond to an altar call? Or does he sound like a man heartbroken at the lives not allowed to respond to the gospel? Now to the Calvinist, it doesn't matter one way or the other because if they were destined for salvation, God would have saved them from the fire, and if they were doomed to destruction, it was their day to die. But to

---

[46] p145, The Life of Dwight L Moody, William R Moody, 1900

men like Moody, who feels the responsibility of reaching lost sinners for Christ, to them, it is *"Woe is me if I do not preach the gospel."* (1 Corinthians 9:6)

Any preacher worth their salt, who recognizes their responsibility to the souls of men, understands the urgency of the hour and that the altar call is one means by which men can be reached. Yes, it can be manipulated by egomaniacs and abused by the lukewarm bunch promoting easy-believism, but handled correctly, it can be a great tool in reaching the lost.

The Altar Call and the Believer

There is a third reason for having an altar call, but not one for sinners, but the believers. Conviction of sin leading to repentance isn't the only purpose of the altar call, as genuinely born again, believers can have an encounter with God outside of salvation. Experiencing the Holy Spirit in service is an opportunity for the Christian to allow the Spirit right of way in his or her life right then and there.

Perhaps this is the reason why the "anxious seat" or the "mourner's bench" later on became known as the "altar". While the terms "anxious seat" and "mourner's bench" were frequently used during the 1800s, the term "altar call" was never used until the 1900s. It was first used by Holiness churches and later on by Pentecostals (which came out of the Holiness movement).

It is around the 1910s or thereabouts, just over a hundred years, that the altar call came to its fully evolved state, that is, from the "mourner's bench" of the Methodists in the early 1800s to the "altar call" of the Pentecostal-Holiness in the 1900s. Pentecostal history is filled with stories of believers waiting on the Lord at the altar, "tarrying" for the Holy Spirit baptism and to receive healing, deliverance, or "entire sanctification".

As a result, the altar call is synonymous to the Pentecostal church as speaking in tongues or praying for the sick. What is very interesting, and I saw it frequently in Jamaica, and I'm sure in the United States, is what is called a return to the "good ol' fashioned gospel service" where believers flock to the altar and seek an encounter with the Holy Spirit.

All that is good, and we need an encounter with the Spirit in our church services instead of dry, dead, and dull religion. But in all honesty, there is nothing old fashioned about it, as what we have in regard to the ministry at the altar is little more than one hundred years in its full evolution. Because most of us are under one hundred years old and have grown up with the altar call being synonymous with a gospel service, we incorrectly assume that the altar call has been around forever.

A Careful Balance

Before I get to the good points of why an altar call is beneficial for the believer and the church service, I want to keep a balanced perspective of the altar call. I have a fear that some people may think I am trying to downplay its importance because of the issues I will highlight, but these issues in no way diminish the significance of the altar call but instead seek to put it in its right context. While the altar call has a significant role in the Pentecostal church, the danger is that we can elevate it above its place to justify its importance.

What I mean to say is this, and for lack of better words, I would suggest that the altar call is an IMPORTANT IDEA, but it is not intended to be a FUNDAMENTAL DOCTRINE. The altar call expresses the idea of God meeting with man and man, having an encounter with God, seeks to work through that right then and there. We see this many times in the book of Genesis, something we will get to later on. But that is as far as we should go, to make it a fundamental doctrine is to create a framework that does not exist in the New Testament.

Let me give an example of what I mean. Anyone who has read anything on Protestant church history in the 1700s and 1800s will see that Sundays were often called the Sabbath. (It is fascinating that we see an example of this on a previous page with Dwight Moody.) Now, it is one thing to call Sunday the Sabbath as a loose thing, simply conveying the IDEA of the congregation getting together to worship God. As long as that is the idea portrayed, then all is well.

But it is another thing trying to make it into a fundamental DOCTRINE where all the rules of the Old Testament now apply, that is, no working, no cooking, no playing, etc. because there is nowhere in the New Testament that suggests such. There aren't any frameworks in the New Testament to hold on to or justify that. But over the years, the Protestant church reached back into the Old Testament to create a framework to justify the use of calling Sunday worship the Sabbath, and with that came the rules and regulations of the Law. One can research on the Internet and read the many sermons written hundreds of years ago where preachers used the Old Testament law and imposed it on New Testament believers regarding the Sabbath.

No wonder the Seventh Day Adventists (SDA) appeared and said, "The Sabbath is Saturday and not Sunday, and so, therefore, we got the day all wrong. We need to go back to worshipping on Saturday and not Sunday." I believe the SDA would not exist today if the right idea of Sunday worship were preached instead of the doctrine of the Sabbath.

It was the idea that Christ is our rest and not the seventh day. It was the idea that we enter into the Sabbath rest through faith (Hebrews 4). It was the idea that the reason why we go to church on Sunday isn't that it is the new Sabbath, but firstly, believers must gather together to strengthen and encourage one another. And secondly, it was the fact that Christ resurrected on Sunday and the Day of Pentecost, the day the church started was on Sunday, and so we go to church on that day to honor those facts.

But Sunday is not the new Sabbath, and Christians can legitimately gather and worship God on any day of the week. Some born again Christians, who immigrated to Middle Eastern countries like Saudi Arabia or Qatar, do by meeting in homes on a Friday to worship.

In the same way, using the idea of an altar call to convey the idea of God meeting with His people and we processing what God is speaking to us about is one thing. Creating a doctrine where the rules of the Old Testament now apply is another.

I say this because, in some charismatic circles, there is a teaching that the altar call is the essential part of the service. It is that the entire service of prayer, worship, and preaching is a means to an end, that is, the altar call. If that is preached, notice that the framework for the sermon can never be found in the New Testament, but rather one must reach back into the law of the Old Testament to find some form of justification just like the doctrine of the Sabbath. We can discover frameworks for prayer, worship, and preaching in the New Testament but not the altar call, and so to say that the altar call is **THE** essential part of the service can be dangerous if one doesn't consider how far that thinking goes.

As long as the idea of the altar call conveys a spiritual truth rather than Old Testament legalism, I believe it has merit and a place in our services. We must remember that there are only two sacraments in the Pentecostal/Protestant churches, and that is baptism and communion, and both these are clearly defined in New Testament scripture. The altar call is not the third, and as crucial as it is, the altar call must know its place in the scheme of things.

It is interesting to note that what we now know as the communion was once called the 'love feast' by the early church, and it was a common meal shared by the saints. Gradually, over the next two hundred years, there was a distinction made between the communion and the love feast. Eventually, the love feast faded out altogether and what we now know as the communion was firmly established.

This was the tradition of the Roman Catholic and Orthodox churches for centuries. In that time, the idea of the communion changed from a spiritual association with Christ and the brethren by the eating of a symbolic meal, as seen in 1 Corinthians 10, to that of a sacrifice. The communion was no longer symbolic but literal. This is the doctrine of transubstantiation where the bread and the wine are literally turned into the body and blood of Jesus Christ.

Thus, this act of sacrifice means that those who perform the ritual are now priests (as it is the role of priests to offer sacrifices) and the place where the sacrifices are done is the altar. This all started towards the end of the second century A.D. Over the years, the altar became central, not just in the church service but also in the church architecture. The altar was found right in the middle, at the front of the church, while the pulpit was put to the side. [Once again, we see the elevation of Old Testament principles.]

With the Reformation of the sixteenth century, the central altar was rejected, and the pulpit purposely placed at the center, signifying that the preaching of the Word of God was central to the Protestant church. For the Catholic Church, the altar is pre-eminent. For the Protestant Church, it is the pulpit that is pre-eminent.

This is a fundamental truth that cannot be compromised. Those who believe that the altar is the most important part of the church service must recognize that it takes the preaching of the word of God to give power to the altar call, as without the preaching of the gospel, there is no repentance. The Spirit of God uses the Word of God to bring conviction, which in turn brings people to the altar. It would be a backward step for the Church of God to once again put the altar at the center of the church service, instead of the preaching of the Word of God.

The Danger of Mindless Ritual

Then there is the issue of abuses. Detractors of the altar call will use these as reasons why we should not have an altar call, but you can always find a reason not to use something beneficial in so many different ways. For example, texting is a good thing as we can connect to people, giving them essential information without having to get into meaningless chit-chat, as we are busy doing other things. But walking while texting is not a good thing as you could fall into an open manhole cover, you could get run over by a car or walk into a lamppost.

Does that mean we should get rid of texting altogether? Of course not! It just means we have got to text more carefully. It is the same with an altar call. Yes, some things can be misused, but it doesn't make it irrelevant.

For example, some people will mindlessly go to the altar every single service. I'm sorry, but I don't believe that there always a valid reason to go every single altar call. To do so means that we are either not growing spiritually or we have no supernatural dominion in our lives to go ahead and do what we promised at the altar. For example, if a sermon is preached on pornography every three months and so for four times in the year you answer the altar call on the same issue, then there is a problem. Why aren't you free? What safeguards have you failed to include in your life? Where is the supernatural power over sin?

I remember preaching a sermon one Sunday, and at a revival the week later, the guest preacher preached on the same topic and made almost identical points, and what happened? The same people answered the altar call. I was stunned. Wait? If I preached on the need to evangelize one Sunday and the next week someone else preaches on the same issue and you answer the altar call again, what happened during that week? Did you change your mind on evangelism on Monday?

Now I can understand certain issues take time to work through, but others aren't psychological strongholds. Being concerned about new converts doesn't require so much praying and fasting that you have to sit through two consecutive altar calls to be involved. Giving to world evangelism doesn't require agonizing intercession. As a result, one can only conclude that some people come to the altar like mindless zombies, just like some people worship with their minds on KFC or the weather.

And not only is the danger, mindless zombies, at the altar, by taking something created to process an encounter of God with the believer, it now becomes a ritual and loses its importance in the minds of those believers. It is more than likely for some people that an altar call ceases to be a meeting with Jesus but a robotic religious exercise every service. I am trying to be balanced here. I am not trying to diminish the altar call. I am equally disturbed with those who answer the altar call for any and everything, and those who never do.

The Biblical Framework for the Altar Call

Now it may seem like a contradiction because right now, I am going to the Old Testament to create a framework for why I believe the altar call is essential today. Genesis may be a part of the Old Testament, but it isn't Old Testament in regard to the giving of the Law. Genesis comes to an end with the death of Joseph. Between the death of Joseph and the giving of the Law, there were at least 330 years. Genesis has nothing to do with the Old Testament law, and as a matter of fact, many of the great New Testament doctrines that we embrace were first seen in the Old Testament.

For example, justification through faith was first revealed by Abraham. In Genesis 15:6, we read, "And he [Abraham] believed in the LORD, and He accounted it to him for righteousness."

Another example is the priesthood outside the Law to which Jesus belonged. Genesis 14:18 says, "Then Melchizedek king of Salem brought out bread and wine; he was the priest of God Most High." Here was Abraham, the great-grandfather of Levi, being blessed by a priest who was not related to Aaron. Psalms 110:4 picks up on this and says, "The LORD has sworn and will not relent, "You are a priest forever according to the order of Melchizedek.""

Right after this is another excellent example, and it is that of the tithe, as we see in Genesis 14:20 that, "And he [Abraham] gave him [Melchizedek] a tithe of all." Tithing predates the law just as justification through faith and the priesthood, according to the order of Melchizedek.

Thus, ignoring the dispensation of the Law, overlooking Exodus through to Deuteronomy, we can look at the altar in Genesis and see how it was used.

For one, the altar was a place of commitment and surrender. In Genesis 26:24-25 we read of Isaac's encounter with the living God, and it reads, "…the LORD appeared to him [Isaac] that same night and said, "I am the God of your father Abraham; do not fear, for I am with you. I will bless you and multiply your descendants for My servant Abraham's sake." So he [Isaac] built an altar there and called on the name of the LORD…"

The term "called on the name of the LORD" is seen before in the book of Genesis. In Genesis 4:26, it reads, "…then men began to call upon the name of the LORD." It suggests that at this time, people began to take the worship of God seriously. As we read these same words about Isaac, it is interesting to note that he had encounters with God before. One has to simply read the first few verses of Genesis 26 and way back in time in Genesis 22 when Isaac was on the altar to be sacrificed when the Angel of the LORD intervened.

But in Genesis 26:25, we see that after this encounter with God, Isaac began to call *"on the name of the LORD,"* showing something different, and that is he was now committed to serving God by his own volition. He was now devoted to God as was his father Abraham, and the proof of that was like his father, he would build an altar to demonstrate that commitment. Isaac was a man no longer doing his own thing but had now surrendered to the will and purposes of God for his life.

I have heard over the years, testimony after testimony of men and women moved by the Holy Spirit during a church service, and during the altar call, they found a place at the altar where they could surrender themselves to the will of God. They left the altar in a different frame of mind from how they came to church, having made the conscious decision to take God seriously.

Secondly, and very close to commitment and surrender is the fact that the altar is a place of sacrifice. It was a place where things were given up in obedience to the will of God. Genesis 22:9 speaks of the sacrifice of Isaac and says, *"Then they* [Abraham and Isaac] *came to the place of which God had told them. And Abraham built an altar there and placed the wood in order; and he bound Isaac his son and laid him on the altar, upon the wood."*

Abraham was about to sacrifice what he loved more than anything except his God, and that was his son Isaac. Thankfully, God isn't into human sacrifice and stopped the event, but it shows just how willing Abraham was willing to give up what he loved the most.

When I first got saved, it wasn't long before I felt this inner desire to preach the gospel. I had no idea where that compulsion came from, but I wasn't really into it. All my life, I wanted to be a professor of physics, and so preaching was never a part of the equation (pun intended). I wasn't sure what to do with that feeling, and I remember once being asked by a friend if I would preach, and I remember saying that I would speak now and again in church if I have to, but that was about it.

(I mentioned this before in the chapter on world evangelism, but it is worth repeating.) Things came to a head when, during a time of prayer, God spoke to me clearly about preaching in Jamaica. I remember instantly getting up on my feet as I had just woken up from a horrific nightmare. I hated Jamaica. Though born in Britain, I grew up there (just like my kids who became missionary kids), and I wanted out, and so when I reached 18, I left like I was running from the plague. It was so bad that when I had dreams about

Jamaica, it was like a nightmare, and I would get up terrified.

So, when God spoke to me about going back to Jamaica to preach the gospel, I instantly rejected it. I remember saying, *"I would rather preach to the Ayatollah in Iran than go to Jamaica!"* And that was that. But over the next few months, I felt the Holy Spirit say, *"Jonah!"* That was it. But I didn't care.

In late October 1993, however, at the London Conference, on Thursday morning, Alvin Smith began to preach on world evangelism and said, *"Some of you need to go back to where you came from."* I remember thinking to myself, *"I wasn't even born there."* And right then and there, Pastor Smith shot back, *"I don't care if you weren't born there. You need to go back!"* That disturbed me, but I was still unconvinced. It could have been a coincidence.

I then prayed, *"Lord, if Pastor Warner preaches tonight on this issue, then I will believe it is You."* That night Pastor Warner said, *"Open your Bibles to the book of Jonah..."* And that was that, and at the altar call, I went up, and I gave up my dream of being a university professor and embraced, not only the call to preach, but also to go to Jamaica. Instantly, at the altar, my attitude towards Jamaica changed. It took years for the call to manifest, but when the opportunity arose to come to Jamaica, I seized it with both hands.

I initially began to write this chapter from my bedroom in Mandeville, Jamaica. It was exactly six weeks and one day before I left the country, and I can honestly say that leaving Jamaica was one of the most heartbreaking things I ever did. We were in Jamaica for exactly six years and eight weeks. We had done more than the five-year basic requirement, and to be honest, I was hoping to find some way to stay longer. The point I am trying to make is that at the altar, as I surrendered my will and sacrificed my dreams, God supernaturally changed my heart.

Thirdly, the altar call is a place of deliverance and empowerment. I can honestly say that I had had real encounters with the Holy Spirit during the church service. Rather than go home to work things through (and there could be a million and one distractions Satan could bring before I got to do that), I went to the altar and did "business with God" as the old cliché goes.

I can remember one particular stronghold that I found impossible to break as a new convert, no matter how hard I tried. But answering a Joe Campbell altar call at a crusade in Walthamstow, London, August 1993, I was set free in an instant, and I knew when I left the altar I was delivered. It has been twenty-seven years, and I am still free today. I didn't go home to think about the message, I didn't sit in my seat contemplating the profound spiritual truths, but I answered an altar call, a prayer made, and I was set free.

One can argue that deliverance could come another way, but the fact remains that it came with an altar call, and it pleased God to bring deliverance there.

One Final Thought

In closing, I would just like to say that we can't put God in a box, and He can move in ways that can blow our minds. God can save by ways and means that we may never even contemplate. I am amazed at the number of testimonies coming out of the Middle East where men and women have been supernaturally saved through dreams and visions. Rarely do we hear of such conversions in the West, but that doesn't mean it isn't of God.

Thus, the altar call isn't the only means by which people come to Christ. Nevertheless, it is a valuable way to do so. Any method that can genuinely get people converted to Christ should be welcomed rather than rejected, and in our time and generation, the altar call is a proven method in the conversion of souls. Let's not throw the baby out with the bathwater or make mountains out of molehills.

ABOUT THE AUTHOR

Jay Nembhard has been pastoring for twenty-three years in the Christian Fellowship Ministries. Originally from the Potter's House Church in South London, he has pioneered churches in Manchester and Wolverhampton, and pastored in Bristol, England. He was also a missionary in Mandeville, Jamaica and is currently assisting Pastor Fred Rubi in his mother church in South London. He is married to Cheryl and the father of two boys and a girl.

Printed in Great Britain
by Amazon